The Top Nine Reasons Family Businesses Fail And The Eight Building Blocks For Creating A SUSTAINABLE Closely Held Company

Wayne Rivers

Published by The Family Business Institute, Inc.
4700 Homewood Court, Suite 340
Raleigh, North Carolina 27609
(877) 326-2493

www.familybusinessinstitute.com

Although the authors and publishers have made very effort to ensure the accuracy and completeness of information contained in this book, we assume no responsibility for errors, inaccuracies, omissions, or inconsistencies herein. Any perceived slights of people, places, or organization is unintentional. Readers should use their own judgment and consult reputable advisors for specific applications to their individual problems. None of the comments in this book are to be construed as individual advice.

ISBN 0-9653193-3-4

Table of Contents

Acknowledgments

I first and foremost wish to acknowledge the supremely talented Family Business Institute team – past, present, and future – which includes Tom Campbell, Ken Maxwell, Dennis Engelbrecht, Bill Provett, Dr. Mike Lyons, Julian Bossong, Mike Halpern, Rick Jefcoat, James Moade, Karen McKee, Jody Watson, David Lively, Lisa Rivers, Jack Ford, Carol Ann Nash, Andrea Weale, and others. I also want to recognize the hundreds of family and closely held businesses around the world who have taught us just as much – if not more – than we've taught them.

Introduction

"The significant problems we face cannot be solved by the same level of thinking which created them."
– Albert Einstein

Everyone knows the dismal success statistics for family businesses; they have been bandied about for years as evidence that family businesses fail the tests of sustainability and transition over time. According to the Family Firm Institute, 30% of family businesses survive the second generation, only 12% survive the third generation, and a measly 3% survive the fourth generation!

As big a problem - if not bigger - in the minds of the professionals at The Family Business Institute is the fact that most closely held businesses are failing to reach their potential. A closely held company could be counted a success if it's doing $2 million or $20 million or $200 million in sales, but what if its real potential is to do $4 million or $40 million or $400 million? It's our estimate that most closely held companies are operating at about 50% of their actual success capacity. If family businesses account for about 60% of the U.S. GDP, why couldn't they just as easily account for 75% or 95%? We subscribe to the same philosophy about which Jim Collins wrote in *Good To Great*:

> "I believe that it is no harder to build something great than to build something good. It might be statistically more rare to reach greatness, but it does not require more suffering than perpetuating mediocrity. Indeed, if some of the comparison companies in our study are any indication, it involves *less* suffering, and perhaps even less work."

Collins maintains it is not harder to build a great company, it's just different, and we agree in spades. He continues:

"The point of this entire book is not that we should 'add' these findings to what we are already doing and make ourselves even more overworked. No, the point is to realize that much of what we're doing is at best a waste of energy. If we organize the majority of our work time around applying these principles, and pretty much ignore or stop doing everything else, our lives would be simpler and our results vastly improved."

Collins hit the nail on the head. One of the primary reasons that most entrepreneurs find themselves overworked, overstressed, frustrated, and on the verge of burnout is because they attempt to do too many things and create business lives of such complexity that no human being could be expected to survive and thrive in such an environment. The only solution during the times when entrepreneurs bump into what Dan Sullivan calls the "ceiling of complexity" is a radical simplification of their lives. This book is a testament to the philosophy of having a great business and a great life, and a how-to manual for building a sustainable closely held family business so that entrepreneurs can preserve their success, maximize their potential, and retain their sanity.

Why is it important for family and closely held companies to maximize their potential? In the Book of Matthew, the Bible relates a story of a master who entrusted his property to his servants while he went on a long journey.

To one he gave five talents of money, to another two talents, and to another one talent, each according to his ability. Then he went on his journey. The man who had received the five talents went at once and put his money to work and gained five more. So also, the one with the two talents gained two more. But the man who had received the one talent went off, dug a hole in the ground, and hid his master's money. After a long time the master of those servants returned and settled accounts with them. The man who'd received the five talents brought the other five. "Master," he said, "You entrusted me with five talents; see, I've gained five more." His master replied, "Well done, good and faithful servant! You've been faithful with a few things; I will put you in charge of many things. Come and share your master's happiness!"

The man with the two talents also came. "Master," he said, "You entrusted me with two talents; see, I have gained two more." His master replied, "Well done, good and faithful servant! You've been faithful with a few things; I will put you in charge of many things. Come and share your master's happiness!" Then the man who had received one talent came. "Master," he said, "I knew that you are a hard man, harvesting where you have not sown and gathering where you have not scattered seed. So I was afraid and went out and hid your talent in the ground. See, here's what belongs to you." His master replied, "You wicked, lazy servant! So you knew that I harvest where I have not sown and gather where I have not scattered seed? Well then, you should have put my money on deposit with the bankers so that when I returned I would have received it back with interest. Take the talent from him and give it to the one who has ten talents. For every one who has will be given more. And he will have an abundance. Whoever does not have, even what he has will be taken from him. And throw that worthless servant outside, into the darkness, where there will be weeping and gnashing of teeth." [Matthew 25:15-30 NIV]

What does this parable teach us? The master gave the money in different proportions to each servant. This was an equitable arrangement reflecting the capabilities and ambitions of the individuals. Besides being an admonition to have faith, Jesus was talking about people reaching their capacities, their potentials for employing the gifts bestowed upon them. The third servant whom the master so harshly described as "wicked and lazy" didn't steal the money, didn't misuse the money, and didn't misrepresent what he'd been given, he simply made no use of it at all. He wasted the potential that his master saw in him. Wickedness, then, is not just doing an act against someone or something, wickedness can be defined as simply doing nothing with the gifts one has been given.

Bobby Knight, the famous coach, said that in the game of basketball, teams don't play against their opponents; they compete against their own potential. Likewise, family businesses don't necessarily compete against their competition, but they work to maximize their own potentials. Unfortunately, at some point in the evolutionary life cycle of most family businesses, they artificially restrict themselves or shut themselves down and fail to continue to stretch.

In the aggregate, family business is big business. There are about 24 million family and closely held businesses in America. The breakdown is as follows (due to rounding, the total is not exactly 100%):

Table One

Less than $1 million revenue	$1 to $5 million revenue	$5 to $20 million revenue	Greater than $20 million revenue	Total
7,661,000	7,941,000	8,347,000	51,000	24,000,000
32%	33%	35%	0.2%	100%

Because closely held companies receive so little publicity compared to their public brethren, most people are unaware of how big an impact closely held companies have on the American economy. In *No Man's Land*, Doug Tatum writes about a paper presented at the 2006 meeting of the American Economic Association:

> "Despite being overlooked or explicitly written out of our economic drama, it turns out that entrepreneurs are resilient in ways never appreciated. Indeed, we are now coming to understand they have an evergreen role to play. They appear to be the sustaining force of democratic capitalism. Thus, in addition to being a species that is apparently hard to see and difficult to exterminate, they play a central role in the undisputed objective of our managed economy, namely, growth."

Only now are policy makers and the media coming to realize how important family businesses are to sustaining the vitality of the American economy and the American way of life. Helping family businesses realize and attain their potential is not only good for the individual businesses in question, it is good for America! *INC.* magazine reports that closely held companies created, "practically as many jobs (10.7 million) as the entire US economy (11.1 million)" from 1995 to 1999. Tatum notes that the National Commission on Entrepreneurship says that growth firms create "two-thirds of all new jobs, more than two-thirds of the innovation in the economy, and two-thirds of the differences in economic growth rates among industrialized nations."

Family and closely held businesses account for about 89% of the business tax returns filed in the United States. 82 million people, or 62% of the workforce, are employed by family enterprises. According to the Small Business Administration, small companies (those with 500 or fewer employees) create approximately three-quarters of the net new jobs and generate 64% of the annual Gross Domestic Product in the United States. Family and closely held companies represent the silent, virtually invisible majority of the North American free enterprise system. When we're talking about family businesses reaching their potential and becoming sustainable over the generations, we're talking about nothing less than perpetuating the life blood of the American economy.

As *Table One* shows, it can't be said that the businesses and the people who run them aren't successful; they are. But as Collins writes:

> "Good is the enemy of great. And that is one of the key reasons why we have so little that becomes great. Few people attain great lives, in large part because it is just so easy to settle for a good life. The vast majority of companies never become great, precisely because the vast majority become quite good – and that is their main problem."

Family and closely held companies fail to reach their potential; good is simply an easier target to hit than great.

What do the academic researchers and surveys tell us about the state of families in business together today? Here's a quick compilation of facts from 4 of the most recent surveys (Mass Mutual and the Raymond Institute, 2007, The Canadian Federation of Independent Business, 2005, Laird Norton, 2007 and 2008, and KPMG Australia, 2006):

- 40% of family businesses expect the leadership of their companies to change hands within the next 5 years
- Well over half expect a leadership change within 10 years
- More than 4 out of 5 businesses are still controlled by their founders
- About a third of the companies have a chief executive who's older than 60
- The average chief executive age is 54
- With respect to exit planning:
  o 26% intend to transfer their businesses to family members
  o 26% have created no plans at all
- Only one-fourth of exiting senior generation leaders say they will have no attachment to their companies after transition. 3 out of 4 will be senior executives, special advisors, consultants, or simply don't know what their role will be after transition
- The reasons why business owners don't have succession plans include:
  o Too early to plan for succession

- o Can't find adequate advice/tools to start
- o Too complex
- o Don't want to think about leaving
- o Conflict with family or employees
- Of CEOs 61 or older who expected to retire within 5 years, 55% have not yet chosen a successor
- Only one-third of owners have a plan to sell, transfer, or hand down their businesses in the future. Even those with a plan, moreover, say it's likely to be unwritten and informal as opposed to formal
- Only 16% of closely held company owners are seeking the input of their successors in developing plans
- There is a huge communication gulf between the generations:
  - o 74% of senior generation leaders report there is a clearly-communicated succession plan; however, 78% of their successors report there isn't!

So why do entrepreneurs and families working together in businesses decide – and it is a choice, make no mistake about it – to stay small and elect a no-growth or slow-growth future? The answer lies in what growth and business success does to the typical entrepreneur (irrespective of generation). Tatum writes about a study of rapidly growing companies. Even among companies that went public, those who reached "escape velocity" and grew to at least $1 billion in size, they experienced exponential growth ONLY after transitioning through an inflection point that occurred on average around $50 million in sales (and with some as early as $10 million). At that inflection point, management transformed the companies – in their thinking at least – from small to large. Many of the companies in this study reached the point of inflection and found themselves unable to cope with their growth. Another group reached the inflection point and made a conscious decision to stay small. Among the leading reasons identified was the fact that, as Tatum writes: "The conditions of success are often not what their owners bargained for." To many closely held business leaders, the entrepreneurial freedom they so desired becomes, over a period of time, more like enslavement. For more on this subject, please read the article *Entrepreneurial Freedom = ENSLAVEMENT* at www.familybusinessinstitute. com/8blocks/.

In *What Got You Here Won't Get You There*, Marshall Goldsmith writes that the trouble with success is that our previous success often prevents us from achieving more of it. Entrepreneurs can begin to stagnate mentally, and that famous adage "if it ain't broke, don't fix it" comes into play. They think, "Why change if everything's working so well?" Michael Gerber, creator of the *E-Myth* series of books, says that entrepreneurs are actually "technicians suffering from an entrepreneurial seizure." These technicians "make the same, fatal assumption; that because they understand how to do the technical work of their business – building a house, cutting hair, practicing law, cooking food – they understand how to build a business that does that work." That's the E-Myth, and it is patently false. Knowing how to do the work of a business has little to do with building a business that works.

> "The technician builds a business that depends upon him, around his skills, his talents, his interests, and his predispositions. He devotes his time, energy, and his life working for a living albeit self-employed. In the end there's little equity to show for the investment of his time. The entrepreneur, on the other hand, builds an enterprise that liberates her, creates endless amounts of energy, and increases her financial, emotional, and mental capital exponentially. In the end, there's significant equity to show for her investment. The enterprise runs itself in the hands of professional management."

Most entrepreneurs DO NOT, in fact, have *businesses,* they have *jobs.* It may even be said that they have some of the worst jobs imaginable. They are responsible for almost every aspect of their company's operations, finances, administration, HR, and everything else. They are subject to incredible stress and unrelenting pressure, and they have little if any of the commodity that contributes most to a balanced and satisfying life – time. If your son was graduating from college, and he applied for a job similar to the real life, unvarnished reality of the job most entrepreneurs have, no one in his right mind would advise him to take it!

In addition to the backbreaking, overwhelming jobs most entrepreneurs have, they're also faced, at some point in the life cycle of the company, with trying to deal with the most challenging management trick of all, that is, managing the transition process from generation current to generation future. Senior Family Business Institute consultant Dr. Mike Lyons wrote in his book *The Knowledge Based Organization* the "transition leader is often saddled with running today's business while trying to build tomorrow's. The leader is so caught up in the old business that he or she never gets around to doing the hard work needed to create 'the new organization'." Lyons states the best way to deal with the transition of the business from one group of leaders to the next is to create a special transition project supported by adequate time, people, and resources. Treating the transition as a special project has several advantages. First, the project has a set beginning and a set end; it creates clarity in a time of confusion. Next, the project is made up of a number of interrelated tasks that can't be done by any one individual, so the group must form a team to manage the discrete project steps. Third, since a project, by definition, is unmanageable, project management really implies that the best the group can do is guide the project to the desired conclusion through smart planning by smart people. They must think through contingencies and implementation steps. Fourth, although the project may be unmanageable in technical terms, it is up to the project managers to accomplish the objectives. To do this, they need a sound and thorough project plan.

Eventually, the success of a closely held company will lead to Tatum's inflection point or what we call the "keep or sell" decision. At that point, the entrepreneur or the ownership family has to make one of the 4 – and only 4 – business choices available:

1. Close the doors and walk away from the business
2. Give the business away to family or others
3. Sell the company to insiders
4. Sell the company to outsiders

Of course, a fifth solution might be to use elements of each of the 4 items. For example, a company could elect to shut down a division, retain some assets in the family through gifts to future generations, sell part of the business to an ESOP or a management team, and finally to spin off or sell chunks of the business to interested outsiders. The point is that the keep or sell decision arises only about once per generation, but it generally becomes the most complex, frustrating, nerve-wracking, and dangerous point in the life cycle of the company.

What we'll explore in this book is a radical concept – and the 8 building blocks supporting the concept – which can create a sustainable closely held company. The concept is as follows: *Build your family or closely held business as if you're going to sell it to outsiders for top dollar.* This is an absolutely no-lose proposition: either you're going to sell it to outsiders, create wealth in your family which could last for generations and open many new doors of opportunity, or you're going to keep it in your family (or at least in your business family among your closely held company employees) as a wonderful, profit-making investment which doesn't depend on any one or small group of people for its continued success. If your heirs take over a company which has a strong management, a robust infrastructure, and a steady stream of delighted customers, what's the downside for them? On the other hand, turning over to them a company which requires 80 hour work weeks and unrelenting stress and pressure has plenty of downside.

Investment bankers who have looked at dozens of potential family business acquisitions outline a short list of the things that a potential buyer wants when considering a family business purchase. They want to see that:

- Customers and suppliers are loyal to the company, not just the owner(s)
- The company has a unique niche with barriers to entry
- There's relatively little competition, and giants can't easily squash the company
- The management team can run the company without the owner being there
- There are assets which might be leveraged (property, receivables, etc.)
- There is a recurring, predictable stream of revenue
- There is motivation for employees to stay rather than leave and compete

The absence of any one of these items dramatically reduces the value of the potential transaction, and the sad fact is that most sellers receive far lower prices than they anticipated. In order to get these 7 attributes in place in your company, you'll need to work ON your business instead of simply working IN your business. If you do achieve these 7 beautiful characteristics, you may find that you simply *can't afford to sell your company*! That's what the "Eight Building Blocks for Creating a SUSTAINABLE Closely Held Company" are all about, and that's the advantage of structuring your company as if you were going to sell it to outsiders for top dollar.

This book is designed to help rectify the business failures the statistics point out so bleakly. Leon Danco wrote the first book tailored to family businesses, *Beyond Survival*, in 1974. The sad fact is that not much has changed in the practices of family and closely held businesses over those 35 years. Business itself has changed, and the Baby Boomers became Generation X which became Generation Y, but the management and ownership succession practices of family and closely held businesses have evolved very little indeed. Marshall Goldsmith writes:

> "Imagine that you're 95 years old and ready to die. Before taking your last breath, you're given a great gift: the ability to travel back in time – the ability to talk to the person that's reading this page, the ability to help this person be a better professional and lead a better life. The 95 year-old you understands what was really important and what wasn't, what mattered and what didn't. What advice would this wise 'old you' have for the you who is reading this page?"

This exercise is unbelievably powerful. It helps to see that when we're on our death beds we won't be surrounded by our coworkers or our customers;

friends and family will be the people who care. The cliché is that no one on his death bed says he wished he had spent more time at the office. While it might be trite, it also happens to be absolutely true. This book is designed to help the family or closely held business owner who marches courageously into the arena every day to pursue her entrepreneurial dreams. Following the path of the Eight Building Blocks is a way to achieve balance in work and life.

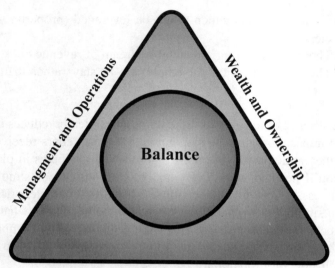

Family and Interpersonal

In the family business balance triangle, there must be equal attention devoted to not only the management and operations of your closely held company, but also to the wealth, money, and power you create and – most importantly – to the family and interpersonal relations which give quality and meaning to life. That's why family is always at the base of the family business balance triangle.

This model is a practical and common sense image for thinking about and working with your family and your business. Only by engaging in big picture, balanced use of the self, the family, and the business, can family and closely held leaders find the entrepreneurial gold mine they so desperately seek. To paraphrase Stephen Covey, balance is more than simply a matter of running between the bases fast enough to touch them all. Balance implies healthy relationships, healthy body, healthy mind, healthy business, healthy spirit, and healthy self-image. It is possible to build both a great business and a great life, and *The Top Nine Reasons Family Businesses Fail – and the Eight Building Blocks for Creating a SUSTAINABLE Closely Held Company* is designed to help business leaders get there.

Chapter One
The Top Nine Reasons Family Businesses Fail

Many readers will note that it's an oversimplification to list simply 9 reasons why family businesses fail and, just as notably, fail to reach their potential. In preparing for this book, we were able to quickly come up with over 50 reasons significant enough to merit serious consideration for inclusion. Once we decided that 50 reasons were simply too many and would be off-putting and depressing to many readers, we settled on the 9 we thought had the highest impact in the most closely held companies over our 200 years of combined experience. As you read on, you'll probably see something of yourself and your closely held company in each of the 9 reasons. It's also quite logical to assume that the reason some companies fail to reach their potential is not just one but a combination of the top 9 reasons. We'll begin with a brief discussion of each of the reasons and conclude each with the chapters most relevant to resolving that particular issue.

Reason #1 - Lack of a Common Vision

Lack of a common vision may seem to be a curious choice for the number one reason why family businesses fail to reach their potential. Vision, as it relates to the future plans for a closely held company, is one of those terms that are awfully hard to define. It's like pornography; very difficult to define, but the kind of thing you know when you see it. For our purposes, we define vision as the *formal, distilled articulation of your dreams and desires for the future. It's what energizes and motivates you (and ultimately those around you).*

Here's an example of why having a common vision is so important. We were once approached by 3 brothers in a manufacturing business. We'll call them for purposes of this example Scott, Richard, and Doug. Dad had started the company many years prior, had enjoyed modest success, and the 3 boys had joined the business. During their tenure they more than quadrupled the sales of the company. They had reached a point, however, where, in spite of the fact that their offices were side by side, their communication had broken down to where they rarely spoke to each other and communicated almost entirely through email. When we first met with them, they assumed positions around the conference table as far away from each other as possible, rarely made eye contact, and tended to address each other through the third party meeting facilitator. Our first question was, "What's your vision for the future of this company?" The brothers responded enthusiastically and unanimously, "We want to take this company to the next level." Our follow-up question was, "What does that mean?" Utter silence. They could give us the generic, 99 cent version of what they perceived as an answer to our question. However, when it came time to drill down, they really had no idea what the other brothers were thinking, dreaming, planning, or doing to make a shared vision a reality.

An analogy for the state in which these 3 brothers found themselves is one of the wagon. If you received the assignment of hitching mules to pull a wagon, and you hitched the mules to various points on the wagon without yoking them together, how well would you expect it to move? An experienced teamster would quickly have the mules harnessed and yoked in such a way so as to pull the wagon efficiently in one and only one direction. In this case, however, the mules (Scott, Richard and Doug) were clearly not pulling in one direction, and while the company was successful, its future was in serious doubt as the oldest of the 3 approached age 60 and the next generation of family members was set to come aboard.

While the existence of a common vision is simply assumed in most family and closely held companies and is an item which receives little time, attention, and effort, it is the most important thing you could and should work on. If you want your company (or your wagon) to move ahead efficiently, it's well worth the time to harness and yoke your team in such a way that it will move efficiently and relatively effortlessly. Putting the team together haphazardly without time and training devoted to building the vision virtually guarantees inefficiency and unnecessary difficulty.

What's the result of a lack of a common vision in a closely held company? Lack of vision produces differing agendas, confusion, turf battles, factionalism, conflicting or missing goals, stagnation, and opportunities missed. One way to demonstrate why vision is important is to look at the opposite condition. What happens when vision is absent? If you've ever been involved with a civic or church group which didn't have vision and appeared to be rudderless and leaderless, you can identify with this situation. Putting a bunch of confused people together doesn't create strength or purpose. It doesn't make sense to think that adding more blind people to the mix that clarity would somehow be the result. Conversely, if you've ever been in a group which had a strong common vision coupled with strong leadership, clarity and forward progress are the rules of the day. One person with a strong vision is more powerful than dozens who lack vision.

If having a common vision is so important, what keeps family and closely held companies from having it? The first reason, and an underlying reason for the existence of each of the top 9 reasons family businesses fail, is poor communication. People in entrepreneurial ventures are overwhelmingly doers, not talkers, mentors, or planners. They're high intensity, high action, get it done types of people. Sitting down and talking about things as nebulous as vision appears to them to be a waste of time. Other reasons for why closely held companies don't have a vision are the lack of time to think and plan due to the urgent press of day to day activities and the lack of an all-encompassing strategy for implementing the vision. The fear of discord ("What if Sister Sue or Cousin Connie doesn't agree with my vision for where I want the company to go?"), the assumption that everyone already shares a vision, and the lack of "how-to" knowledge of how to get a vision established and integrated also contribute to the lack.

We'll address the lack of a common vision in Chapter Two.

Reason #2 - Poor Self and Time Management

Over our years of interacting with family business owners at meetings and events, we hear people brag (or perhaps lament) about how many hours they work. It's a badge of honor they proudly wear to show their commitment and dedication to their enterprises. And yet, when we interview the same people privately about what things are most scarce in their business and personal lives, the number one, universal, not even close answer is TIME. Time is the most precious commodity anyone on this earth enjoys, and yet we blithely disregard how we use it. We genuinely don't appreciate the fact that success in business or in life is simply the accumulation of how we use our minutes and hours on a day to day basis. I'm sure there are people who have won the lottery who consider themselves successful, but the reality for 99.9% of people is that success is not a sudden event but rather an aggregation of successful minutes, successful actions, successful thoughts, and successful choices over long periods of time.

Watching leaders in closely held companies, we observe an incredible amount of wasted time, and perhaps more importantly, time which is underutilized or utilized in the wrong way altogether. Many closely held business leaders over commit and try to do too many things, or do things which CEOs have no business doing in the first place. While we have no statistical data to support this, we believe that guilt underpins some of these time management choices. In our estimation, a surprisingly high number of family business owners don't fully believe in themselves or their own success. They see people in their communities, or even in their employ, who aren't as successful as they are, and some slice of their brain tells them that they are somehow unworthy of the success they've enjoyed. Their guilt drives them to undertake jobs to demonstrate they still work as hard as anyone and can understand the plight of the "common man." While the sentiment might be noble, the activities they undertake as a reaction to the guilt are almost always underproductive.

Why is it important for family and closely held business managers to utilize their time wisely? First of all, these people are usually the MVPs of their organizations. They have the most experience, the most know-how, the clearest vision, and the greatest ability to get things done. If MVPs aren't managing themselves and using their time wisely, they're hurting the entire organization. Another reason self and time management are important are to simply get control of one's life. So many family business leaders are despondent – bordering on depressed – because they feel that they are completely out of control. They don't feel their time is their own, they don't think that their entrepreneurial dream of freedom and success are within their grasps, and they just don't see a light at the end of the tunnel. Learning to effectively manage oneself and one's time is powerful medicine for getting off that vicious hamster wheel. A third reason why self and time management are important is that if you can't manage yourself, it makes it extremely hard to manage and develop others. As we will see later, the single greatest determinant of whether or not a closely held company is going to achieve breakthrough success is the quality of the other people on the team. If you have difficulty managing yourself and your own time, you're going to have difficulty attracting and retaining the kinds of people – family or otherwise – who can help catapult you to a new level of success.

What's the result of poor self and time management? Projects take too long, initiatives go unfinished, and bottlenecks appear in production or service delivery. Inefficiency becomes the rule of the day. Not only does much of the entrepreneur's time go wasted, the time of the other managers around him probably gets wasted too because they have to wait for him to show up for meetings or to render decisions. The result is a "rolling snowball" effect of greater and greater ineffectiveness which ultimately has an effect on the overall productivity and morale in the company. Entrepreneurs bemoan the poor quality of people and execution in their organizations. What they often don't realize is that the person who requires the most work is actually the entrepreneur herself! Gaining greater control of self and time can pay tremendous dividends for a closely held company seeking improvement.

If self and time management are so important, what keeps closely held business leaders from having them? Lack of awareness of the fact that time is manageable and controllable is a fundamental reason. Other reasons include not having benchmarks or standards for how leaders *should* spend their time (this led to an interesting discussion with a group of construction company CEOs a few years ago which we will discuss in Chapter Three) and not having a definitive job description for the leaders. Another reason why poor self and time management exists is the simple ego need of the entrepreneur. Why, in a company of 20, 50 or 100 people is one person the "go-to guy" for virtually every decision large and small? While it might be difficult to hear, the reason is ego; it simply feels good to the entrepreneur to feel so needed, so necessary, and so vital to his organization. It's a type of entrepreneurial self-indulgence that virtually every businessman falls victim to at one time or another. While it feels good in the short run, it becomes limiting in the long run. Those entrepreneurs seeking not only to have great businesses but also great lives come to this realization and take steps to positively manage themselves and their time in a way that can be a model for others. We'll deal extensively with self and time management in Chapter Three.

Reason #3 - Poor Next-generation Leadership, Skills Development, and Preparation

The way entrepreneurs train and develop their next-generation leaders (family or non-family) is tried and true; it's on-the-job training, or OJT. OJT was the way Granddad trained Dad who trained his son. OJT means that upon entering the family company, Junior gets the dirtiest jobs there are so he can demonstrate his capacity for hard, uncomplaining work and earn the respect of the people in the organization. Later, Junior gets a bit more responsibility and takes on managing a few tasks, jobs, or people. Dad delegates the things he doesn't like to do to Junior so he can have a bit more freedom and enjoyment. When new things come up that Dad either isn't interested in or doesn't have the capability to handle (such as emerging IT issues), Junior inherits those too. Ultimately Junior finds himself doing important jobs in the organization, working 60 to 80 hours a week, and falling into the same trap Dad created for himself, namely, having zero time to find true balance and happiness in life, and having zero time to get the kind of training, networking, and grooming that will allow him to run the company over the next 10 years. The mantra is simply this: "that's the way I learned the business; that's the way my son or daughter will learn it too."

Why is developing the leadership capabilities of next-generation managers and owners so important? The answer's easy: the very future, survival, and prosperity of the company depend on it. As many entrepreneurs have found when taking companies over from their parents or grandparents, it takes a different set of skills to run a $10 million company today compared to running a $2 million company 15 years ago. If the company expects to grow in the future, it will take an even different set of skills to run a $20 million or $50 million enterprise. Only by dispensing of some of the old things that Dad and Granddad did can new generations of leaders hope to cope with the challenges they face. The default idea of many closely held company leaders is to simply clone themselves (which happens to be a very bad strategy) and put that virtual clone in place as the future leader.

Consider this analogy: a successful closely held company leader has followed his university's football program for years and contributed money, time, and attendance. A new coach has come in with great fanfare. On opening Saturday, the star quarterback goes down in the first period with an injury. There's panic on the sideline. *There's no backup!* The much heralded new coach has focused all of his time on his MVP player. He hasn't taken the time and initiative to groom a successor. The closely held company leader would be horrified; he'd be livid. He would call that coach every name in the book and demand he be fired immediately. He would invest time and effort into channeling his outrage into productive action. Surely that coach would have no place in a big-time football program! But that's exactly what most closely held company leaders are doing right now. They're focusing their time and attention on the urgent needs of their companies, spending 90% of their time in operations, and investing very little time in charting the future by developing themselves and next-generation leaders. Poor next-generation leadership skills development can be a death sentence for a closely held company.

What are the results for poor next generation leadership and skills development? Confusion is the rule of the day. Weak decisions or no decisions at all hamper the company's progress. Good employees decide to leave for other, better opportunities. There's a lack of confidence and trepidation about the future. Battles for control break out as 3 or 4 potential leaders vie for the top spot although they don't know what qualifications or mileposts they need to hit in order to grab the brass ring. Next-generation managers know how to do the technical jobs of the business, but they are not tested in the big picture. They've never actually managed a department to turn a net profit, handled finances or administrative tasks, or met with attorneys, CPAs, and bankers about matters affecting the company. The lack of next generation preparation leads to a limited view of the work of the company and its ultimate potential.

If having strong next generation leadership and skills development is important, what keeps closely held businesses from having it? The press of day to day operations is so great for most entrepreneurs that "nextgen" leadership development is one of those desirable things that they'd like to get around to but never seem to have time for. Some entrepreneurs simply have a disdain for training. Training isn't producing profit for the company today; therefore, it's something that must be eschewed in favor of matters more urgent.

Many entrepreneurs are poor at mentoring; they're doers, not teachers. Most entrepreneurial companies have no history of developing leaders and their skills, and so they just don't know where to begin. Finally, many family business leaders really have no desire to test their children. In other words, choosing Johnny means that Susie and Frank weren't chosen, and that's not a family risk worth taking.

We'll talk more about next generation leadership and skills development in Chapter Three.

Reason #4 - Poor Technology for Getting the Right People On the Bus and the Wrong People Off

When we talk about technology in this case, we're not talking about computer hardware or software; we're talking about a system or a set of processes that closely held business owners can use for building a great team over time. Here's a real life example to illustrate this problem:

> Grant, a second generation family business owner, approached us. He and his brother took the business over from Dad about 20 years ago and had bought him out over time. Grant's brother, a 50% owner, was a very nice guy, but he wasn't really a hungry entrepreneur, and he had no ambition to serve in anything greater than a clerical role. Yet, because he owned 50% of the stock, he could effectively block Grant in any strategic initiatives he took. After years of being frustrated and unable to grow the company as he wanted, Grant wished to buy out his brother in a way that would not jeopardize his future financial security or jeopardize their family relations. He also wanted relief; after over 20 years of serving as the General Manager, Sales Manager, and Financial Manager of the company, Grant was simply burning out. He needed relief, and he needed it soon. He really didn't know where to go next.
>
> The solution to his problem had two avenues: one was to create a win-win buyout for his brother that allowed him to cash out immediately and share in any appreciation if Grant sold the company in the future for a price greater than their initial buyout price. More important to the long run operations of the company and to Grant's mental and physical health, we began shopping for a highly qualified, highly experienced general manager. Part and parcel with that, we began to train Grant on what it was to

7

be an owner and an investor rather than being a line manager with overwhelming day to day responsibilities. The goal was to free Grant up to have time to work ON his business rather than simply working IN his business all the time. To accomplish that, we needed to deliver to him a system for getting the right person on his bus.

Why is having a system for getting the right people on the bus and the wrong people off so important? *Ultimately the people surrounding the entrepreneur will determine the long term fate of the company for good or ill.* Grant's solution wasn't rocket science, but he had never been able to recruit, hire, and retain a good general manager, and his poor experiences in the past led to despair of being able to do so in the future. Once he was able to envision the system for doing that, his optimism brightened considerably.

The system should define not only how to get the right people on the bus but also how and when to get the wrong people off. This is best illustrated by an example in a manufacturing company led by Mike. Mike had the unhappy responsibility for making layoffs in his company for the first time in its long history. For weeks prior to the event, he laid awake at night dreading letting people go and the potential fallout. Because his business was off by about 30%, he no longer felt he had a choice, and the fateful day eventually arrived. A couple of weeks later Mike called and reported the following: "Three things immediately happened. 1) The sun came up the next day, 2) Productivity went up, and 3) Morale went up!" He was thrilled. Not only were his worst fears not realized, the opposite proved to be true. He told us that the people he let go, the least productive people in the organization, had had an unexpected "chilling effect" on the others. Once those bad apples were gone, everyone else was free to be as productive as they could be without being held back. Mike's experience trumpets a powerful lesson.

What's the result of having no system for getting the right people on your bus and the wrong people off? One of the negative consequences of not getting quality people is that the most capable people on your team ultimately get the most jobs which, in the long run, render them less capable! Think about it: those handfuls of people in your organization who can truly handle responsibility get all you can heap on them. Ultimately, they struggle as much as you do because of the lack of time they have to engage in preventive maintenance instead of the mad rush of day to day operations. There's an eventual breakdown of family life, spiritual life, and physical life. People become unable to focus on the big picture because they're continually sucked into the nuts and bolts of little picture tasks everyday. Your company is forced to turn down growth opportunities because you don't have the human resources to execute them.

If having a system for getting the right people on the bus and the wrong people off is important, what keeps closely held companies from having it? There are several reasons: many don't know how to develop the system. Some are not inclined to change it (the old cliché "if it ain't broke, don't fix it"). There's little time to plan and no time for other people on your team to plan either. Thrift is a barrier to getting the right people on your bus; some closely held company leaders are simply not willing to pay market rates for getting great people. They'd rather have mediocre people at lower unit prices and do more work themselves.

We'll talk more about a technology for getting the right people on the bus and the wrong people off in Chapter Four.

Reason #5 – Lack of Clear Roles and Responsibilities with Accountability

Formal job descriptions in closely held companies are pretty rare. Even rarer are companies that actually manage their employees according to their job descriptions or use them as administrative and evaluative tools. The job description – especially for family members in a closely held company – is: "DO WHATEVER IT TAKES!" That, we submit, is not a job description at all, and it is a recipe for confusion and inefficiency.

Why is it important to have clear roles and responsibilities supported by accountability in your company? When we interview non-family managers in closely held companies, we continually hear the lament that they desperately want formal, regular evaluations of their performance. Good performers care about their jobs, and they want to see their employers demonstrate care too by devoting time and attention to designing jobs and actually letting people know how they're performing. Many family business leaders fall back on the old saw, "I'll let you know if you're *not* doing a good job." There are 2 problems with this methodology. First, it relies on the boss to have a perfect recollection and mental balance sheet of all transgressions offset by outstanding performances. The second problem is that this evaluation methodology does not allow for self-correction on the part of the employee. If the employee clearly understands what's expected of him in his role, sees that the results are not up to the standard, and self-corrects, he saves the boss time, energy, and probably money.

Employees want to know they're part of something bigger than themselves. Good performers especially want to know how their contributions relate to the overall success of the company and the bottom line. If you want to know why having clear roles and responsibilities supported by accountability is important, let's simply look at it from the reverse point of view. Who actually wants to avoid clarity and accountability? It's your poor performers!

What happens when there is a lack of clear roles and responsibilities supported by accountability? Confusion, waste, overlap, and redundancy abound. Employees mill about in frustration, never knowing exactly who's supposed to be doing what and when they're supposed to do it. It's easy to say that most experienced employees know what they're supposed to do, and that's probably true 75% of the time. There's waste, confusion, and overlap during that other 25% of the time. The absence of clarity means that the boss must personally intervene, must render decisions on things where decision making could be pushed down farther into the organization, and has to spend time refereeing disputes between employees, departments or, worst of all, customers and employees.

If having clear roles and responsibilities supported by accountability is so important, what keeps family businesses from having it? The first answer is the same for most of the other deficiencies, and that's a simple lack of time. Most family business leaders are overwhelmed by all of the commitments and tasks they must personally undertake during a given day. The task of sitting down and writing job descriptions and then following up by doing formal employee evaluations simply sounds too daunting. Another reason is that many employees push back against the concept because they don't want it; mediocre to poor employees simply don't want accountability. Another reason is that some family business leaders think that having clear roles supported by accountability may cause them to have to evaluate family members and friends in a negative light. If objective evaluations came back negative, the leader may be forced to take corrective action against those close to him, and the thought of that is just too painful to bear.

We will discuss having clear roles and responsibilities with accountability in Chapter Four.

Reason #6 – Poor Operations, Sales, and Financial Skills and Metrics

In some ways, closely held companies are victims of their own success. It's easy for them to ask, "Why do we need operations, sales, and financial metrics, and why do I need to improve my skills in those areas? Dad and Granddad built this company up from nothing without those things, and it never seemed to hurt us. Why do we need them now?" That's a great question, and, while it's easy to answer, it's often hard to dislodge people from their "if it ain't broke, don't fix it" conviction. Why then is it important to have excellent operations, sales, and financial skills and metrics?

The most important job of the entrepreneur who's building a growing enterprise is, in the words of Michael Gerber, to translate the business skills of the entrepreneur to a company which can do what the entrepreneur himself was originally good at. While in the early days the entrepreneur may have done all of the task work during the day and kept the books at night, at some point business demands drove him to hire other people in order to build his company. Having excellent operations, sales, and financial metrics allows him to build out the organization in a way where he can maintain control over the organization's functions while not putting his hands directly on them each and every day. Without good operations, sales, and financial metrics and skills, the company simply cannot grow beyond one human being's span of control. Without them, the company will eventually hit an artificial ceiling imposed on it by the entrepreneur himself. If he chooses not to have these things, he has, by default, chosen a methodology for controlling his company that, because he's a human being, is often erratic, lacks objectivity, has subjective standards, and has personal biases. The old saying is that what gets measured gets improved; if you don't have standards of measure, then you're operating by the seat of your pants, and you artificially limit your opportunities for insight, understanding, and growth.

What's the result of having poor operations, sales, and financial skills and metrics? Poor efficiency and lack of accountability pervade the company. There will be a lack of focus on transferring internal best practices from Manager A to Manager B to Manager C. There will be no "XYZ Company way" for doing things; things will get done in whatever manner an individual employee sees fit to do them. There will be an absence of standard operating procedures. Finally, the lack of metrics puts an additional time demand on the entrepreneur to exert personal control, and, as we've already discussed, time is the scarcest commodity for leaders.

If having poor operations, sales, and financial skills and metrics is so important, what keeps family business leaders from having them? As always, the lack of time is a giant bugaboo. There's often a lack of awareness of the importance of these items; since Dad and Granddad didn't have them, they weren't able to train Generation III on why they're important and helpful. Most entrepreneurs have a lack of access to benchmarks. They don't know what their competitors around the country are doing in certain operations or sales areas. If they did have access to these numbers, they could measure their performance against the norm or the average. Benchmarking is a great way to test yourself against others to see if your belief in what you're doing is reality. For example, many family business leaders talk about the quality of the service or products they deliver. In the absence of objective benchmarking data, how do they really know their quality is as good as they assume? If the scrap rate for a manufacturer is 10%, and the industry standard is only 3%, doesn't that put the lie to the entrepreneur's quality claims? In the absence of having that data, he's basically operating his company blindly. Finally, entrepreneurs don't have good operations, sales, and financial skills and metrics because they often lack interest in them. Doing all this administrative "stuff" isn't what attracted them to becoming entrepreneurs in the first place. They love selling cars, buying and developing real estate, erecting buildings, or working on complex engineering projects; they didn't get into business to be administrators and bookkeepers. We'll talk more about metrics for operations, sales, and administration in Chapters Five, Six, and Seven.

Reason #7 - Unwillingness or Inability to Address Problem Issues Due to Fear of Conflict

The universal, number one family desire is to exist in a state of love and harmony. Most families, whether in business together or not, treat any threats to their harmony as fearful conditions to be avoided or suppressed. Problem issues which require difficult, sometimes painful, evaluation of family members and drawing controversial future situations into the present are avoided like the plague. If a second generation family member comes to Mom and Dad and says, "I want to be president of this company," that conversation is quickly discouraged. What might brother and sister say if they knew that there was a push for this change, and how might they react when they consider how they may be affected? The potential for disagreement over this issue is frightening.

Why is it important for family and closely held businesses to master their fear of conflict? The morbid fear stunts their business and family growth. It hampers their vision for the future of the company and business planning. It crimps healthy communication and causes important issues to be shunted to the back burner repeatedly – even to the point where the family has few viable options remaining. It prevents positive resolution of problem issues so they persist, and morale plummets. Avoiding healthy conflict allows the squeaky wheel family member or manager to get the grease. Issues which need to be discussed in the light of day are avoided or suppressed because "talking about that issue always makes Jane angry," or "you know your mom always gets upset when we discuss controversial issues." The person who exhibits the most vivid, emotional, or loud reaction tends to be the one who controls whether or not difficult issues receive the attention they deserve. Here's an example:

A family in the farming business was led by a strong, successful matriarch. 2 of her children worked in her business, and 2 did not. Under her leadership, the company was quite successful and profitable, and at the end of each year she distributed bonuses of $100,000 to each of her 4 children. This to her was a fantastic solution. She loved her children equally, so why shouldn't they all share equally in the success of the company she built? After several years of this arrangement, Mom began to notice some dissension in the ranks. It seemed that her 2 employee sons, the 2 sons who were responsible for the company's day to day success and profitability, didn't think it was fair for their 2 non-employee brothers to receive the same amount of money at the end of the year. The 2 non-employee siblings didn't really have a problem with the arrangement; after all, who wouldn't want to receive a $100,000 check as a symbol of a parent's love? Mom's reaction to her employee sons raising the issue was to become angry. This discussion threatened the balance of harmony in her family, and she considered her employee sons to be ungrateful. It took a measure of counseling for Mom to understand that her employee sons had a legitimate complaint. They were receiving rewards for excellent *management*. Their brothers were receiving rewards for family *ownership*. The employee brothers simply wanted equality. They wanted management bonuses to be paid out *before* ownership distributions were shared. Then the employee siblings would get appropriate management rewards while all 4 would participate in Mom's generous ownership reward system. Once Mom got over her irrational fear of conflict, she was able to see that while her intentions were noble, her execution left a bit to be desired. Once a new system of distinguishing ownership rewards from management rewards was implemented, a sense of harmony and fairness was restored.

What's the result of conflict avoidance or suppression? Communication breaks down, problems go unsolved, and the company's growth and progress are retarded. If difficult issues or subjects are continually avoided, good people will eventually leave the company – family members included. A sense of fatalism or pessimism can break out. Explosions take place as small issues which could have been resolved rather easily pile up on each other and turn into giant dissatisfactions that can't be contained. Ultimately, a company that avoids conflict to an irrational degree begins to address decisions by simply deciding not to decide.

If developing a willingness and an ability to address conflict in a healthy manner is important, what keeps family and closely held businesses from doing it? The main reason is the human dread of pain and emotional discomfort. Resolving conflict isn't easy, and anyone who actively seeks conflict on a daily basis must have a bit of a screw loose. Most people have never taken any conflict resolution training, and, therefore, the way they have learned over time to resolve conflict is from their family of origin. However Dad learned to resolve conflicts came from his mom and dad; they learned from their moms and dads. Unhealthy cycles of poor conflict resolution get built into families who then bring it into their businesses. You can imagine that a company with 100 employees probably has 100 different conflict resolution techniques all distilled from their families of origin. It's a recipe for disaster. As one Family Business Institute consultant says, "In the absence of weed control, you get weeds." Learning healthy conflict resolution skills is the weed control that can help people in closely held companies put their fears behind them and move into the future with confidence. We'll talk more about conflict resolution in Chapter Eight.

Reason #8 - Ineffective Succession Planning

The last few years have seen an unprecedented amount of research into family businesses. Mass Mutual, KPMG, Laird Norton, and the Canadian Federation of Independent Business have undertaken intensive studies into the nature of private businesses. What the research shouts out is a startling lack of preparedness on the part of closely held companies for transition from one generation of managers and leaders to the next. Even when companies do undertake succession planning, they spend 90% of their time on ownership succession planning (i.e. who gets the stock) versus management succession planning (i.e. who is actually going to do the many and varied tasks necessary to keep the company healthy and profitable in the future?). Transition planning is the cornerstone of the family business consulting industry, and it's the topic of discussion whenever family business consultants get together. In spite of 40 years of presentations, articles, books, and even nagging, however, most closely held businesses are simply not ready to survive beyond the lifetimes of today's owners and managers.

Why is outstanding transition planning so important? In the absence of good planning, the very survival of the closely held company is in jeopardy. Poor transition planning causes family companies to be set back by years in terms of reaching their sales and profit potentials. Poor planning threatens family and business harmony. It jeopardizes the livelihoods of the owners of the closely held companies and all the employees who depend on them for their incomes. Poor transition planning can also threaten the economic viability of a community. In many places, family businesses are among the largest if not the largest employers in town. If a company which happens to be a significant employer goes belly up, what will that do to the local job market?

What's the result of ineffective transition planning? Anger and resentment build. There's confusion and frustration among the family members, key managers, and employees of the business. Groups begin to take sides to support, intentionally or unintentionally, one potential successor over another.

Family and business harmonies erode. Visions for the future become more constricted and negative as they see opportunities and options begin to close down.

If effective transition planning is so vital, what keeps family and closely held companies from having it? There are several factors. Since family companies only have to undertake succession planning about once every generation, there's little if any institutional know how that points them in the right direction. What worked for Granddad back in the 1950s may not work in today's world of different tax laws and business realities. Transition planning is something that's vitally important to most family businesses, but it's something that's rarely urgent. Unless someone's on his death bed, there's always more time to get it right, and there are always more pressing business issues which have to get taken care of today. Transition planning is often accompanied by the fear of having to choose one child over others or the fear of retirement and no longer being the MVP of the family business. Finally, the lack of access to multi-disciplined experts is a significant barrier. The lawyer who does estate planning for local doctors may be technically proficient in avoiding estate taxation, but he might not be very well versed in the dynamics of family businesses. He also may have little to no ability to assist in helping the family craft management succession strategies.

Reason #9 - Failure to Grow

Most family businesses reach a certain size, say $5 million or $50 million of sales, and they plateau. Often the stagnation lasts for years if not decades. The reasons for their failure to grow and prosper are discussed at length in this chapter, but why is their failure to grow an issue in and of itself? A business which is of sufficient size to support one family in a satisfying way may be incapable of supporting 3 second generation families or 10 or more third generation families with any degree of comfort and security at all. If the feeding trough is of a fixed size, at some point it becomes impossible to feed more hogs.

Why is growth important for family and closely held businesses? One has only to reread the story of the talents in the introduction; failure to reach one's potential is almost as great a sin as outright failure. There are also the difficult to measure opportunity costs associated with a failure to grow: family harmony can be threatened, good employees leave to seek greener pastures, or communication becomes heated as people begin to compete for limited or scarce resources. The levels of satisfaction and fulfillment for stakeholders both inside and outside the company decline.

We're not advocating growth simply for the sake of growth; we're simply advocating that family and closely held companies continually seek to get outside their comfort zones and struggle to reach their potentials. It's good for the people involved, it's good for the companies, and it's good for America.

What's the result of a company's failure to grow? There are all the stresses of having too many people simultaneously trying to get their bites from only one apple. There are unhealthy competition, frustration, and stress. Family harmony becomes strained and family gatherings, instead of occasions for anticipation and excitement, become occasions to avoid.

If growth is important to family and closely held businesses, why don't they have more of it? There are many reasons. The lack of a common vision is a primary one. Without common goals, people work at cross or counter-productive purposes. Most closely held companies have inadequate infrastructure to support growth; once they get beyond one individual's or a handful of individuals' control, they lose their appetite for risk. They have poorly defined roles and responsibilities and little accountability. They have poor recruiting and hiring practices to bring fresh talent on board. They don't have marketing strategies to support future growth. Perhaps most importantly, they don't have a plan and a strategy for how to grow responsibly and effectively. We'll talk about how to grow responsibly by design in Chapter Nine.

There are dozens if not hundreds of other reasons an imaginative commentator might dream up for why family businesses fail or at least fail to reach their potential. These 9 reasons taken individually or collectively are the *primary* barriers in today's family and closely held business world to creating sustainable businesses. The following 8 chapters – the 8 building blocks for creating a sustainable closely held company – represent a "how-to" manual for simultaneously generating more money, more time, fewer headaches, and a higher quality of life.

The Top Nine Reasons Family Businesses Fail

Executive Summary

1. Lack of a Common Vision

2. Poor Self and Time Management

3. Poor Next-generation Leadership, Skills Development, and Preparation

4. Poor Technology for Getting the Right People On the Bus and the Wrong People Off

5. Lack of Clear Roles and Responsibilities with Accountability

6. Poor Operations, Sales, and Financial Skills and Metrics

7. Unwillingness or Inability to Address Problem Issues Due to Fear of Conflict

8. Ineffective Succession Planning

9. Failure to Grow

Chapter Two
Building Block #1 - Vision

The lack of a common vision is the top reason family businesses fail or fail to reach their potential. This sounds counter-intuitive, and it may be met with skepticism by closely held business leaders and family business commentators who have spilled tons of ink about the need for family retreats, the importance of estate planning, and strategies for family governance. While all these topics are important, none can match the potential for devastation inherent in family businesses not sharing a powerful and compelling vision for the future.

Think about it:

- How much time, money, and emotional energy does it cost the family and the business due to a lack of clarity?
- How much waste, overlap, and confusion is there due to conflicting agendas or disagreements over priorities?
- How much time does family and key management spend engaging in blaming, pointing fingers, and deciphering garbled communications?
- If these negative conditions didn't exist, how much more successful could the business be? How much happier and harmonious could the family be? How much greater would the overall level of morale and enthusiasm be if everyone shared a common, compelling vision for the future of the family and the business?

The lack of a common vision is problematic in virtually all closely held companies, but it is especially toxic in the situations of sibling partnerships and cousin collaborations. In sibling partnerships, for example, the brothers

19

and sisters have been taught all their lives that they are equals, none has family authority over the others, and the parents love them the same. However, once siblings are grown and are managing their family business, the concept of sibling equality becomes a barrier to clarity. In most organizations and for any combination of reasons, a leader usually can and does emerge; as with the Roman triumvirate, one sibling usually becomes "first among equals." Most sibling partnerships have a tenuously balanced détente: Sister A has her turf, Brother B has his, and Sister C has hers. Each manages his respective department as an individual fiefdom with little accountability or communication between them. The following is an example of a "broken" vision.

Case Study: Broken Vision

Two brothers, Kevin and Earl, had a successful construction company which had grown from its modest beginning to a regional powerhouse renowned for its ingenuity and reliability. Kevin was the visionary, the more aggressive businessman, the promoter, and the builder of employee teams and administrative and financial systems. Earl ran the operations side of the business tirelessly and was a stickler for customer service and quality execution. At the time of our engagement, the business had been growing by approximately 20% per year for the last 5 years. The reason the brothers approached us was that they had reached a critical crossroads. Kevin wanted to continue to build people and systems to maintain their double-digit growth. Earl, on the other hand, had reached the limit of what he could do, and he wanted absolutely no more growth. He also was not willing to mentor and train others to do the work he had done solo up to that point. The company's growth, in essence, was jeopardized by Earl's reluctance to work ON the business rather than simply working IN the business. To him, they had achieved enough success, made enough money as a company and as individuals, and did not need to grow further.

There was no compromise between the brothers. If one brother advocated 20% growth and the other brother advocated none, neither would be satisfied by meeting in the middle with a 10% growth rate. That would involve Earl doing things he was not ready, willing, or able to do, and it wouldn't satisfy Kevin's long-term ambition and drive – at least not for very long. Over a period of months, scattered over approximately 3 years, we first attempted to take the high road by helping the brothers develop a common vision that would represent a win-win for each of them. We even got members of the management team to participate in an effort to begin to institutionalize some of Earl's amazingly broad and deep knowledge. This is an important point: Earl had reached a bit of a personal crossroads as well. Because the geographic footprint of the company had grown so large, he found himself starting early, finishing late, and spending many, many nights on the road overseeing distant projects. The straw that broke the camel's back was when he showed up late for his daughter's high school graduation. In addition, his personal health was beginning to decline; clearly he was beginning to suffer from burnout if not outright exhaustion.

Progress was slow, but the brothers communicated on a high level. They were direct with each other, said what was on their minds, and didn't pull any punches in a misguided effort to avoid conflict. They were interested in resolving their issues, not burying them. Even so, there were no quantum leap breakthroughs. Over time, Earl did begin to relinquish a little daily responsibility and began to delegate and trust others more. However, he still wasn't comfortable not overseeing every aspect of the company's field operations. Kevin, on the other hand, was quite happy. The company was still continuing to grow at a double digit pace, and training of others meant that some of their projects could be handled by non-family managers.

Still, all was not well, and the level of disconnect between the two brothers grew. Eventually they reached what might be considered a startling decision. They concluded they had had a wonderful run of 20 years, both had made plenty of money and gotten plenty of satisfaction out of building a business, but, since they couldn't agree on a common vision, they decided to separate. They hired a valuation expert and developed a financial plan for Kevin to buy out Earl over a period of time. We even built in certain escalators so that in the unlikely event that Kevin sold the company to a third party for a higher price than that at which Earl sold out, Earl would participate in the upside. Both brothers knew that while their visions had been aligned for the first 20 years of the company's history, the inability to reconcile their visions for the next 20 years spelled frustration and disharmony.

21

Since the buy out, Kevin has continued to grow the business, and Earl has been able to pursue his passions of boating and fishing while starting a small business with his own son in which he can control the operations rather easily. Both brothers remain successful, are happier and healthier than they were before, and have eliminated the major source of conflict between them allowing their relationship as brothers to improve.

Let us attempt to further illustrate the importance of aligned vision. You have a choice to purchase one of two companies. They're roughly the same size in sales and profits, they're in the same industry, and each has 10 employees. Company A is a typical entrepreneurial company where the mantra is "busy hands." The entrepreneur has a vision for where he'd like for his company to go, but he hasn't formally communicated it to his employees. The result (*Figure 2.1*) is the employees sort of know what they're supposed to be doing and in what direction they're supposed to be heading, but they're not 100% sure. Company B, on the other hand, has taken time for the entrepreneur to make her vision of the future explicit. Furthermore, she's gotten feedback from her employees for how their visions for where they're going as human beings align with her vision for where she and her company want to go. The 10 employees are aligned in a common direction and take time and make effort periodically to refocus themselves on building an explicitly designed future. If you were a potential buyer, which company would you want? The sadomasochistic reader would probably say Company A, but the lion's share will choose the obvious answer: Company B. How much easier would it be as an owner and manager to get things done in Company B? What's the likelihood that the harmony is higher there and it's a more fun place to work? Having a common, compelling vision for the future of your closely held enterprise is like passing a powerful magnet over scattered iron filings; the magnetic field attracts and aligns all of the filings so they're pointing in one direction.

Figure 2.1

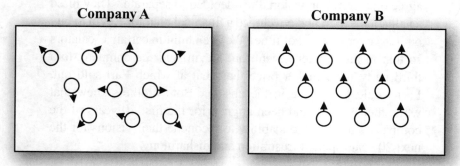

22

What is vision? For the purposes of consulting with family and closely held businesses, we define vision this way: vision is the formal, distilled articulation of your dreams and desires for the future. It's what energizes and motivates you (and those around you).

> **Vision:** *The formal, distilled articulation of your dreams and desires for the future.*

Helen Keller said, "The most pathetic person in the world is someone who has sight but has no vision." In the Book of Proverbs, the Bible says, "Where there is no vision, the people perish." In *What Matters Most*, Hyrum Smith uses the following illustration.

> "Let's say you're going along the highway doing 65 or 70 miles per hour, and in an instant you find yourself in a dense, thick fog. How do you feel the minute you can't see more than, say, 30 feet in front of your car? Your initial response is probably a bit of panic. Most likely, your foot goes immediately to the brake, and you slow the automobile down to a crawl. You move as slowly as you dare so that you won't run into someone up ahead and inflict bodily harm on that person, yourself, or your automobile. Suppose that as you go through the fog it gradually grows thicker and thicker until you can only see 2 or 3 of the dashed white lines in front of you. At this point maybe you even find yourself rolling down the window to try to see the lines near your wheels. Few experiences are more panic producing. You find yourself afraid to stop for fear that someone will plow into you from behind, but you can barely move forward because you really aren't sure if you're going to stay on the road.
>
> Next, think about how it feels as you emerge from the fog. At first, instead of just 2 or 3 of those white lines in front of you, you can see 4, 6, or 8 of them. Then you can see the next turn in the road, and suddenly the fog totally lifts and your headlights illuminate the road 200 yards in front of you. What is your immediate emotional response?"

When you have no vision for yourself or your business, the emotions you might experience are the same as those on the foggy highway; the lack of vision can be physically and emotionally exhausting.

23

At about the turn of the 20ᵗʰ century, the director of the U.S. Patent Office said, "Everything that can be invented, has been invented." When talking pictures first burst onto the scene in the roaring 1920s, the head of Warner Brothers Pictures said, "Who the hell wants to hear actors talk?" In 1975, the founder of Digital Equipment, a Fortune 500 company at the time, predicted, "Nobody is going to want a computer in their house." Clearly, these leaders lacked vision (and they also appear to have lacked optimism and faith in the human capacity for curiosity and invention). Vision enables a leader to peer into the future and see exciting possibilities.

My wife Lisa created a small business of buying old houses in desirable neighborhoods and renovating them. Some of the houses have been, frankly, dogs. One of the reasons she can buy them so cheaply is because she has vision to see not the house as it is, but how it might be. Her vision is powerful and unerring. Another way to describe vision is seeing not how things are in the present but how they might exist in the future.

Why Is Having A Compelling Vision So Important?

Viktor Frankl was an Austrian psychiatrist who, because he was Jewish, was sentenced to the concentration camps of Nazi Germany. Psychological theory at the time said that if everything was taken away from people they would revert back to animalistic behavior. Frankl suffered along with all of the other concentration camp prisoners, but part of him as a psychiatrist was interested in observing his fellow inmates. Some of the biggest, strongest, and toughest inmates broke first, became weak, and died quickly. Others – old, frail, weak prisoners – gave whatever scraps of bread or clothing they had to others to ease their suffering. There didn't appear to be any rhyme or reason to who perished or who survived.

Frankl made a jarring discovery. The reason some people were able to survive wasn't because of health, intelligence, social standing, or political influence. The most important factor was a sense of *future vision*. Those with vision had a reason to live. They were able to focus on that vision and use it as a pathway to survival and a better future.

Covey writes: "Vision is the best manifestation of creative imagination and the primary motivation of human action. It's a deep, sustained energy that comes from a comprehensive, principle-based, need-based, endowment-based seeing. It's fueled by the realization of the unique contribution we have the capacity to make – the legacy we can leave. It clarifies purpose, gives direction, and empowers us to perform beyond our resources."

Expanding your personal vision into your company and among your employees allows you to create a passion of shared vision. Covey writes:

"Shared vision empowers people to transcend the petty, negative interactions that consume so much time and effort and depletes quality of life. The passion of the kind of vision we're talking about has a transforming, transcending impact – probably the greatest impact of any single factor on time and quality of life. Shared vision unleashes and combines the energy, talent, and capacities of all involved." When you develop your vision for yourself and your company, you allow other people to tie their aspirations and energy to your goals and aspirations. It allows for other people to commit to you and your company in a bond not unlike marriage.

Marcus Buckingham writes in *The One Thing You Need To Know* of 5 important characteristics derived from having a strong and compelling vision for the future. Briefly discussed, they are:

1.   Great leaders use their great vision to rally people to a better future. The great leader carries in his head a vivid image of what the future can be, and this image drives him.

2.   His vision, this better future, is what he talks about, thinks about, ruminates upon, designs, and refines.

3.   The chief reason why it's important for the entrepreneur to have a clear and compelling vision is more emotional than rational. Employees are anxious about the future, and to turn that anxiety into confidence, the leader must tell them what the vision is and why they'll be successful in achieving it.

4.   Clarity is the antidote to anxiety. Since clarity is the antidote, having a compelling vision must become the preoccupation of the entrepreneur.

5.   Having a clear and compelling vision will increase employees' engagement. Best Buy, for example, can point to data that demonstrates an increase of employee engagement of 2% resulting in an annual $70 million in profitability.

McKinsey & Company spent years researching 231 large companies to find out what people really want from their employers. What they found was that people (even family members in closely held companies) want a compelling vision for the future. Coupled with 2 other sound management practices, namely clear roles and responsibilities with accountability and an open and trusting culture, those 3 attributes increased organizational effectiveness more than any others. To have these 3 attributes, it's necessary to work ON your business instead of just IN it, and the starting point is to develop your compelling vision for the future.

Of all the human longings, the need for safety, for companionship, for clarity, for authority, and for respect, the need for clarity when met is the most likely to engender confidence, persistence, resilience and creativity. Buckingham writes of a study undertaken by anthropologist Donald Brown describing the universal traits of human nature. He eventually compiled a list of 372 universal human traits! The list of universals paired 5 of the most common fears with 5 common needs (see *Figure 2.2*).

Figure 2.2

Fear of Death	Need for Security
Fear of the Outsider	Need for Community
Fear of the Future	Need for Clarity
Fear of Chaos	Need for Authority
Fear of Insignificance	Need for Respect

One of them, and only one, demands focus from closely held business leaders. The only one that deals explicitly with the future is the third one, fear of the future. The beauty of a compelling vision is that it simplifies a complex world into a single organizing idea around which people can rally and begins to dispel this universal fear.

I'm Convinced! Now Where Do I Begin?

It may sound elementary, but the place to begin is with you. Whether you are a sole proprietor, a member of a sibling partnership team, or the non-family president of a closely held company, the place to start is with you! We once had an assignment working with 2 sisters who owned a real estate development company. They were quite successful, but had become dissatisfied with the direction their non-family managers were taking. The managers, from their point of view, were dissatisfied because they didn't really know what the sisters wanted from them. The place to begin in the assignment, we discovered, was to work with the sisters to update their visions for where they individually and collectively were going with the company. Once they were able to crystallize their visions, they were able to set much clearer objectives for their managers, and the uncertainty and confusion disappeared. If, as writer Laurie Beth Jones says, people's number one deadly fear is "having lived a meaningless life," then developing a compelling vision is certainly a worthwhile pursuit.

With Respect to the Future of My Business, What Are My Choices?

At some point during the life cycle of an entrepreneurial company, the owners and leaders reach a crossroads. They have to make a decision to either stay small or continue to grow. Continued growth means that the company will have to change drastically because it will be too big to function effectively under the control of one or a tiny handful of people. Furthermore, as it continues to grow, it will run into larger competitors. Therefore, it will have to build new systems and competencies as the competition intensifies. Staying small means that all leaders may not have their entrepreneurial needs met. It means continued toil for the leaders. It means limited resources and the threat of lower priced competition from beneath. There are only 3 real choices:

1. Stay small in order that one or a tiny handful of people can control the activities of the organization.
2. Sell the company to insiders or outsiders and move on to other pursuits.
3. Build a company that doesn't depend on one or a tiny handful of people to show up for its continuing success. Build an organization which shares your entrepreneurial vision for the future.

We maintain that far too few family and closely held business leaders elect choice #3. The sad reality is that most entrepreneurs don't have businesses - *they have jobs*. They are high-paying jobs, and the entrepreneur gets to call the shots because he's indisputably the boss, but it's a job nonetheless. A job implies that someone works a minimum of 40 hours a week approximately 50 weeks per year to earn a paycheck. If he shows up and produces, he gets his check. A business, on the other hand, is perpetual. A business doesn't depend on whether one person shows up or not, on whether one person is happy or sad, energetic or exhausted. A business can function in the absence of one of the members of the team, even if the team member is the founder and MVP. A business produces not only paychecks but also equity and opportunity. Until they elect to build businesses instead of just having jobs, most entrepreneurs will fail to reach their potentials.

How Do I Build My Vision?

The following are some questions and exercises you can use to help develop your vision for yourself and your company. While you may not need to undertake every single question or exercise, using a number of them will have the effect of challenging you to think deeply about this subject. Once you've done some initial introspection and talked about your vision for the future with your family or team, put it away for 48 hours to one week, and let the seeds you have planted germinate. Then come back to them for more polishing and refinement. Don't be afraid to dream big!

1. **What is your purpose in life? What are you called to do?**

2. **What is the purpose of your business?** (Don't give the clichéd answer "The purpose of my business is to make a profit." No entrepreneur started a company simply because he was hungry to make a profit. Companies become reality because entrepreneurs see a way to build a better mouse trap. Saying that profit is the purpose of your business is like saying that breathing is the purpose of life. Breathing is necessary to life, but it's certainly not the purpose. Profits are necessary for business success, but they are manifestly not the purpose of the business!)

3. **What do you have too much of in life?**

4. **What do you have too little of?**

5. **What things do you fear the most?**

6. **Who are you (or your company) here to help?**

7. **How would the perfect business look to you in 5 years, 10 years, and 20 years?** What would you need to do differently now in order to hit those ideal targets?

8. **Think about how you'd like to be remembered by family, friends, and the community after you're no longer here. What did you stand for? What were your accomplishments? What will your life have meant for those you've left behind? What kind of a difference did you make?** After you've thought through these questions, write your own eulogy as you would like to have it read to the mourners at your funeral. While this might seem a little morbid, try to have fun with it. Think big: this exercise is designed to be creative and to stimulate your thoughts.

9. **Compile a list of your highest values.** Try to write down at least 40. After you've done that, put the exercise away for 24 hours, come back to

it, and choose your 10 highest values. Finally, write a clarifying sentence or two about what each of your top 10 values means to you. Use the values to help flesh out your vision.

10.   **What frustrates you or angers you the most?** If you can define those things, think about the opposite of your frustration, and you should have the raw material for an aspiration or an improvement.

Conclusion

The research and the wisdom literature indicate that thinking about, working on, and developing your vision for yourself and your enterprise will rally people to your cause, increase the clarity in your life and in the lives of the people around you, and even help you make more money. It's the first building block for creating a sustainable closely held company.

Building Block #1 – Vision

Executive Summary

⇨ Vision is the formal, distilled articulation of your dreams and desires for the future. It's what energizes and motivates you (and those around you)

⇨ Research and the wisdom literature show that having a clear and compelling vision is one of the greatest desires of business family members and employees

⇨ Building a vision begins with self-diagnosis and questioning

---

Chapter Three
Building Block #2 - Self Management and Leadership Development

I can hear a collective groan from readers now. "I've been running this business for 32 years, and on my watch we've grown from $5 million in sales to $50 million. Obviously I'm doing something right. Why is he writing about something I have so obviously mastered?" The blunt fact is that most closely held business leaders have not mastered the concepts of self management or leadership development and, even if they have built their companies 10 times larger than they once were, they still don't have the requisite skills necessary to take the company to an entirely new level.

Companies are simply aggregations of human beings who've come together out of mutual self interest in order to pursue a common cause. Our belief is that organizations emulate their leaders. If the leaders can't or won't exercise discipline and manage themselves, the company's people and results will reflect that. The organization needs to know who it is collectively, what it stands for, and where it's headed. The company gets that information directly from its leader(s). The corporation's identity, loosely defined as its "culture," comes from the people who populate it.

Self Management

Gerber states that if you cannot manage yourself, you cannot manage anything. He is absolutely right. Self management is at the core of a closely held business' success – past, present, and future. Management guru David Maister has research showing that most senior executives spend 40% to 50% of their time doing work that a more junior person could do. Imagine if your local power utility operated at this sort of low efficiency. What if your automobile or your household plumbing operated as such a dismally ineffective level? You'd be outraged! When the most senior people in your organization, yourself included, are spending half their time doing things they shouldn't be doing at all, this represents an incredibly high opportunity cost. This is why self management and leadership development are so important.

Why do family business leaders waste so much of their valuable time? Why are they so dismal at delegation? We believe there are 3 reasons. First, most entrepreneurs run their companies at very low staffing levels. We'll look at this phenomenon more in Chapter Four when we talk about people management, but most entrepreneurs look at hiring administrative and support people as a cost rather than an investment. They rationalize that it's just better to do it themselves than to hire people to do routine or mundane tasks, and they further rationalize that "I don't really spend all that much time doing them anyway." They're dead wrong, and if they truly analyzed the opportunity costs, they'd be shocked and dismayed. Being brutally realistic, ask yourself the following question: if I had 10 extra free hours per business week, what could I do with that time, and what would be the effect on my company? Here's a quick analysis:

> Suppose an executive could free up, by better delegation and smarter hiring practices, 5 hours out of his normal 60 hour work week. Assuming the executive worked 50 weeks per year, that's 250 hours per year now available to undertake any number of high-level tasks and opportunities. For example, an entrepreneur might now be able to call on one new business prospect every other week. That means that he'd see about 25 new business prospects per year. Assuming a hit rate of 25% of the new prospects, that would mean 6 new business relationships developed in a given year which, depending on industry, could mean thousands or even millions of new dollars at the company's top line. Put simply, finding that extra 5 hours per week could mean $50,000, $500,000, or $5,000,000 per year not to mention the psychological benefits of the executive doing executive level work!

If the entrepreneur simply had the discipline to find a way to carve out the 5 hours, use the time productively in finding new business, reengineering his company, communicating with his people better, etc., there's no telling what sort of tremendous benefits he could produce. Unfortunately, because everyone is so wrapped up in being busy on a day-to-day basis, they rarely engage in this sort of opportunity cost analysis; therefore, they don't really know what difficulties they create for themselves.

Another reason for systemic under delegation is guilt. In our experience, most entrepreneurs consider themselves "average Joes." They grew up in middle class backgrounds, attended middle America high schools and colleges, worked their way up through the ranks in their first jobs, and don't consider themselves to be any more or less accomplished than most of the people on their staffs. At some point during their entrepreneurial rise they either consciously or subconsciously begin to ask themselves questions. "Am I really worthy of this success? Why me, and why not the other people here? Am I really this good, or have I just been lucky?" Their success comes so naturally to them as entrepreneurs and business builders that they often question whether or not their accomplishments have been truly earned or simply, as one politician put it, they are "winners of life's lottery." They begin to feel guilt over having more power, more money, more opportunities, and more excitement than the people around them. They question their self-worth, and they don't feel comfortable telling people what to do and holding them accountable. Simple guilt is at the root of some under-delegation.

A third under-delegation factor is rooted in myth. Everyone's heard the old saw, "If you want it done right, you better do it yourself." Or, "By the time I teach someone else how to do it, I could have done it myself just as quickly." Any objective reader will see the self-limitations imposed by these old clichés. There's a kernel of truth in them, but over the long run these are barriers to continued success.

Self management sets the table for future leaders to succeed the entrepreneur. Senior generation family business owners often lament the quality of their potential successors. They're just not sure that the next generation has what it takes to be successful in business. They blame their successors for not having the fire in the belly or the entrepreneurial drive that helped them be successful. Ultimately though, this is a failure of self management. As John Maxwell wrote in *The 21 Irrefutable Laws of Leadership*, "But then it hit me. If I had done a really good job there, it wouldn't matter what kind of leader followed me, good or bad. The fault was really mine. I hadn't set up the organization to succeed after I left." The seeds of a successor's poor performance are usually sown by the senior generation. If they had done a great job of mastering the discipline of self management and leadership development, their successors would have a much easier path to sustaining the enterprise. If the succession pool is poor, and the prospects for building a sustainable company are dim, ultimately the blame must be placed at the feet of senior generation leaders (with some attention given to junior generation executives who failed to press the issue).

In *What Got You Here Won't Get You There*, Marshall Goldsmith writes, "The higher you go, the more your 'issues' are behavioral." He discusses a tool psychologists have developed to help people understand themselves called *Johari's Window* which was named after two real people, Joe and Harry. Johari's

Window is divided into 4 quadrants (*Figure 3.1*). Quadrant I contains blind spots which are things unknown to us but known by others. Quadrant II contains things that we know about ourselves and others also know. Quadrant III contains things that are unknown both to us and to others. Quadrant IV contains private knowledge which is known only to us but not others. Goldsmith says, "The interesting stuff is the information that's known to others but unknown to us. When that information is revealed to us, those are the 'road to Damascus' moments that create dramatic change. They are the moments when we get blindsided by how others really see us, when we discover a truth about ourselves. These blind-side moments are rare and precious gifts."

Figure 3.1

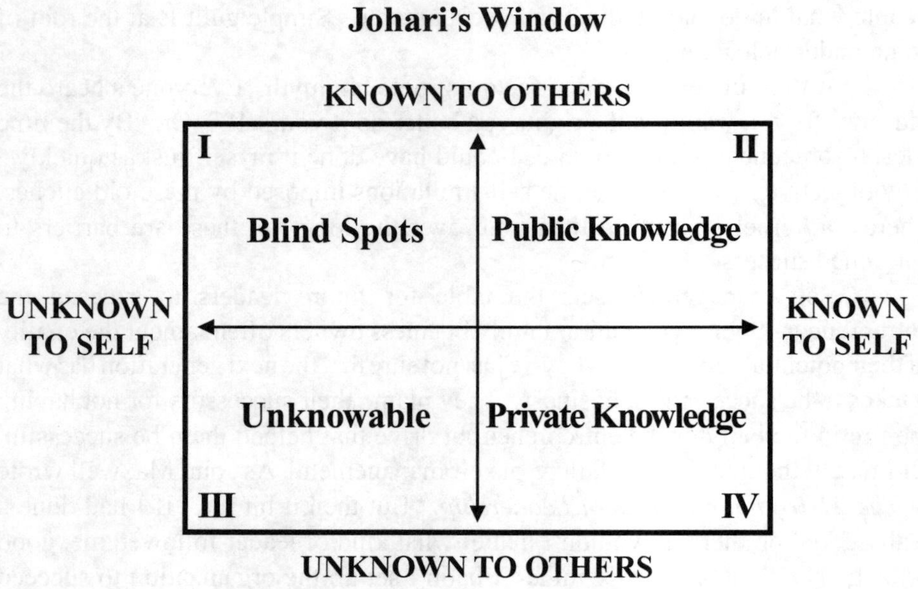

Johari's Window

KNOWN TO OTHERS

UNKNOWN TO OTHERS

For example, a family business leader went to a self awareness workshop. During the course of the workshop, he took several analysis instruments and also worked in small groups. His self image was one of a caring, beneficent leader who kept everyone's best interests at heart at all times. What he found out was that his subordinates found him to make decisions slowly and randomly, he often exhibited erratic behavior, and he filtered all information, business or otherwise, through a lens of "How will this affect me?" Initially, he was wounded and offended by his employees' views of him, and he couldn't reconcile his own self image with the image gathered through this blunt, confidential feedback. The workshop helped reveal his blind spots to him, and he used the information constructively to improve himself and his team. He continued the self awareness and self improvement process, made some drastic changes, and became more successful as time passed.

In addition to an individual Johari's Window, closely held companies eventually pick up a collective Johari's Window. This window is cluttered with legends and myths about why the company has been successful in the past and why it's currently successful. Sometimes the beliefs even conflict with each other, and organizations have a mini-identity crisis while they try to reconcile apparently irreconcilable beliefs. For example, two of the incredibly common collective beliefs on the Johari's Windows of closely held companies are: 1) the entrepreneur needs to review the mail every day, and 2) the entrepreneur needs to review every single check that goes out the door. Some book or some management guru from the distant past must have made hay with these 2 management directives because they are pervasive in the minds of dozens if not hundreds of entrepreneurs we've come in contact with over the years. Both are designed to allow an entrepreneur to "know what's going on" in his company. Both are colossal wastes of an entrepreneur's time and energy, and, with the proper people and management controls in place, can easily be delegated to others on the team.

For a closely held company executive to improve his organization, he first must improve himself. This requires a tremendous mental shift for most. The entrepreneur must see herself as the owner and investor versus the worker doing technical things. She must view her company as an organization which can be sustainable rather than a place which simply provides her with a job and a paycheck. Once the entrepreneur makes that mental leap, the rest of the organization will follow. However, if she doesn't change her mindset, the future growth and sustainability of the enterprise are in jeopardy.

Case Study: Hands On or Hands Off?

A second generation family business owner had built his company to well over 100 employees and over $70 million in sales following his father's exit. He realized early on that he could not grow rapidly by adopting his father's direct, hands-on management style, so he built a 4 person executive team, clarified their roles in the organization carefully, gave them substantial authority, and held them accountable regularly. He was quite happy with the way his organization was running, so why did he need to enlist the services of a family business consultant?

35

His wife had grown up in a family business where her father exhibited a very different management style. He ran a small grocery store where he worked 6 days per week, opening the store in the morning to meet the fresh product deliveries and closing the store in the evening before going home for dinner. On Saturdays when his children were out of school, they all arose together at 4:00 A.M. and began their workdays. She had been shaped by her father's direct, hands-on management style and was alarmed to see her husband moving away from the style which both her father-in-law and father had embraced. She decided that her husband was too removed and aloof from day to day operations and needed eyes and ears on the ground level of his organization, so she appointed herself office manager and went to work. Every day she listened to the conversations of the other employees and watched what they were doing. Every night, she went home to her husband and regaled him with every line of gossip and every malfeasance, real or imagined, on the part of employees always insisting that he "do something about it." This was not the way the entrepreneur wanted to run his company, and the failure of his wife to buy into and subscribe to his vision was becoming both a business and a marriage issue. Once the spouse became more comfortable with her husband's entrepreneurial vision for the future and realistically assessed the impact her employment was having in their marriage, she resolved to change a few things. The result has been continued business success and, more importantly, a dramatic improvement of their relationship. The point of this story is that the decision to change on the part of the entrepreneur, which led to a dramatic change in the culture and operations of his organization, was inconsistent with his wife's belief window; it was that misaligned belief that caused the problem.

An up and coming General Electric executive was recruited by his father-in-law to come into the family business to bring big business concepts and discipline to the growing organization. In his first few days on the job, another company executive cautioned him, "Don't get sucked into the work." He thought that was an interesting comment, but dismissed it. A few months later, having been "sucked into the work," he knew exactly what his coworker's counsel was about. The work of any entrepreneurial organization is seductive and alluring. It's easy for an entrepreneur to forget what it is to be a leader and a CEO because there's just so much to be done, there are so many pressing issues, and there are so many demanding customers. Many entrepreneurs tell us that even if they worked 24 hours a day 7 days a week, they still couldn't do all the things they'd like to get done in their organizations. And yet they still don't see the need to bring better talent on board in order to build their companies!

We've conditioned ourselves as a society and as individuals to work hard. Getting tasks done provides us with a sense of daily accomplishment. Putting our feet up on the desks, sitting back in our executive chairs, and thinking for a day about the future organization leaves most entrepreneurs stone cold. Just as bad, if they saw their senior managers doing the same thing, they'd excoriate them and call into question the executive's need for continued employment. While it may be true in some instances that idle hands are the devil's playground, that rule is not true for entrepreneurs who intend on building sustainable companies.

Dan Sullivan, creator of The Strategic Coach™ program, has developed a concept he calls the "Ceiling of Complexity™." Entrepreneurs use past experiences to solve current problems. Most entrepreneurs have learned to bulldoze through business problems by simply working harder. Because that technique has always been successful (either they work harder or they hire additional people to work harder alongside them), that tends to be the solution of choice for almost any business problem. At some point, however, the entrepreneur bounces into the Ceiling of Complexity™ where that old way of problem solving based on past experience simply doesn't work anymore. He may bump his head on this artificial ceiling one or dozens of times, but it represents an impenetrable barrier that ultimately creates a crisis for the organization or for the entrepreneur himself. Sullivan coaches that the *only way* to break through the Ceiling of Complexity™ is to start over through a period of self-analysis, create a new state of simplicity by focusing only on big picture tasks, and build a team which supports doing those tasks successfully. After observing thousands of entrepreneurs, Sullivan's Ceiling of Complexity™ concept is absolutely spot-on, and his theory of bursting through the ceiling and creating a new state of simplicity is just what the doctor ordered.

The first part of this chapter has been a none to subtle attempt to persuade family business leaders that the second building block for creating a sustainable closely held company is self-management and that a critical step in that process is to undertake a new way of thinking that requires the executive to look at herself not as a doer but as an orchestrator, to shift her thinking from worker to executive and investor, and to disengage from the day to day tasks which consume so much of her time in favor of stepping back to view the big picture and designing a better future. How does one go about that? We'll provide you with 3 concepts and tools which can help you in the transformative process from being the boss to being the leader.

The first tool an executive should use is one which is pervasive in large corporations but is fairly rare in closely held and family owned businesses. It's commonly called "360° feedback." There are any number of informal and formal types of instruments which can help in the 360° process. While some people criticize its use, there really is nothing more effective at helping executives in undertaking a process of self-awareness and self-management. Undertaking a feedback process and listening to the results of a 360° survey can be painful. It can directly challenge a CEO's self-image and even the image he has of his organization. Psychologically, people accept feedback which is consistent with their self image and dismiss that which is inconsistent. Therefore, informal feedback processes are usually ineffective. 360° feedback, which is done formally and – most importantly – *confidentially*, works best.

Feedback is beautiful because it tells us where we stand at the moment. It gives us insight into how we might improve as people and executives. It gives us information which we can use constructively in order to remake and improve ourselves and, by extension, our organizations. Best of all, it's easy to administer and use. There are dozens if not hundreds of organizations, methodologies, and instruments which could help in the 360° feedback process.

The second tool is another Dan Sullivan creation. Sullivan and his organization have produced a book, *Unique Ability™ – Creating The Life You Want*, which defines and provides a process for uncovering an executive's Unique Ability™. Sullivan defines Unique Ability™ as follows:

- It is a superior ability that other people notice and value
- We love doing it and love to do it as much as possible
- It is energizing both for us and for others around us
- We keep getting better at it, never running out of possibilities for future improvement

This discovery allows an entrepreneur to organize himself and his time so that he is utilizing his Unique Ability™ as often as possible. This sounds daunting to some at first blush; however, Sullivan recommends that entrepreneurs engage in highest payoff activities only about 20% to 40% of their time. That leaves 3 to 4 days per week to do things as you've always done them. In other words, he's not recommending a radical reordering of your life, simply more time and attention spent on the things you love to do, the things that drew you to be an entrepreneur creating a business in the first place. Undertaking a Unique Ability™ discovery process, which involves elements of 360° feedback as well as rigorous self-analysis of how you spend your time, can pay tremendous dividends.

The third self management technique is to develop your personal mission. Frankl said that we don't invent our missions; we detect them. Everyone's familiar with the concept of having a corporate mission statement; however, this drills down farther in the area of self management by creating one that's unique to the entrepreneur herself. Laurie Beth Jones has written an excellent how-to book on developing a personal mission called *The Path*. She says there are 3 simple elements to a good mission statement:

1. A mission statement should be no more than a single sentence long
2. It should be easily understood by a 12 year-old
3. It should be able to be recited by memory at gunpoint

She says that all great leaders in history have had missions that were no more than a single sentence long. Abraham Lincoln's mission was to preserve the Union. Franklin Roosevelt's was to end the Depression. Jesus' mission statement was, "I come that you may have life, and have it more abundantly." If these great, visionary leaders could have simple, one line mission statements, you can too!

Again, there are dozens, if not hundreds, of tools and techniques for developing a personal mission statement and plenty of consultants who will offer to help with one. It's not important to choose the "perfect" delivery system; it's more important to undertake a process and refine it going forward than to get it 100% right the first time. For more on this, please read the article *Your Personal Mission* at www.familybusinessinstitute.com/8blocks/.

Successful closely held business management begins with successful self management. The reverse is also true: the failure to engage in the process of assessment and self management on the part of the leader creates an artificial but real barrier to future success and business sustainability.

Time Management

One of – if not the most important – facets of self management is time management. Many closely held business executives will immediately scoff at the concept that they need to be educated in the area of time management. However, the last 20 years of working with business leaders has demonstrated to us beyond a shadow of a doubt that 95% of them would be well served to enroll in a Time Management 101 class.

At a recent meeting of construction company CEOs, we had a bit of fun at the expense of one of the participants. James Braswell, a successful South Carolina builder, made a statement about how he expected his superintendents to behave. Superintendents, as the name implies, are best used on a job site coordinating the flow of work among subcontractors, the movements of equipment, and delivery of materials. They are not meant to have their hands on work directly; theirs is a management and coordination role. James made the comment that if he ever walked onto one of his job sites and saw one of his superintendents "wearing a tool belt," he'd immediately have a heart to heart with that superintendent who clearly didn't understand his highest and best use. I immediately ribbed James about his comment; I had been on my soap box for some time about how CEOs themselves "strap on the tool belt" far too frequently. James smiled at me sheepishly and said, "I know I'm going to regret making that statement."

We had fun with that discussion, but it underscores a serious point. CEOs, the most valuable "superintendents" in their organizations, all too often have their own hands on work, do work inefficiently, and worst of all, spend their valuable time doing the wrong things altogether. Goldsmith writes about a friend who asked for some informal coaching. The friend had a vague feeling that things just weren't clicking. Goldsmith shadowed the executive from the moment he walked into the building in the morning and became a "fly on the wall" observer. Here's what he found:

> "What I saw explained everything. He arrived at the office about 15 minutes before his assistant. The first thing he did was check his emails. Then his cell phone rang, and he answered it. During this conversation his assistant arrived at her desk. She poked her head in to say good morning. He waved while still talking. When he ended the call, he turned to his computer screen and jotted down some notes and answered a few emails. His assistant popped in to say one of his accounts was on the line. Did he want to take that call? He did. 3 other calls came in during this 20 minute conversation. When he hung up, he returned those calls – all the while scanning his computer for incoming emails. This pattern continued all morning. By noon I had seen enough."

This is the reality for most closely held business leaders. They dutifully craft a task list of 2 or 3 important things they plan to do during the day. Then they come into the office only to be besieged by incoming emails and calls, coworkers who need to discuss an issue with them, inquiries from people in the field or other departments, requests for their time by suppliers, vendors, sales people, and community leaders, and on and on. At the end of the workday they look sadly at their carefully crafted list only to find they haven't spent any meaningful time on high impact tasks. The list gets carried over to the next day with similar results. At the end of the month and at the end of the year, the big issues that the CEO knows in his heart he really should be working on attract only a pitiful fraction of his time, and he loses the potential for impact that working on these big picture items would have brought.

As Gerber would say, most closely held company leaders spend their time working IN their businesses rather than working ON their businesses.

Covey asks a simple question: "Why is it that so often our first things aren't first? If you were to pause and think seriously about the 'first things' in your life – the 3 or 4 things that matter most – what would they be? Are these things receiving the care, emphasis, and time you really want to give them?" For most executives, if they're brutally honest with themselves, the answer is an unequivocal no. If a consultant were to review your calendar – the real agenda, not the sketchy mess you've actually committed to paper – what would he find? If it's true that the secret of success is found in your daily agenda, what would the consultant discern from yours? Why is it that when asked the question, "Of what do you have too little in your life?" family business leaders universally give a one word answer: TIME. Why is it that entrepreneurs who, after all, started their companies in an effort to create more freedom and more life for themselves, find their lives so out of control and unfulfilling just at the time when they believed they would be enjoying the greatest fruits of their entrepreneurial success?

Part of the answer can be traced to what Covey calls "urgency addiction." In *First Things First*, Covey has an instructive self test one can use to determine objectively if they are in fact urgency addicted or suffer from what some psychologists call "hurry sickness." Users grade themselves on a 5 point scale replying to such statements as:

- I often blame the rush and press of external things for my failure to spend deep, introspective time with myself
- I'm often frustrated by the slowness of people and things around me
- I hate to wait or stand in line
- I feel guilty when I take time off work
- I frequently find myself pushing people away so that I can finish a project
- I feel anxious when I'm out of touch with the office for more than a few minutes
- I assume people will naturally understand if I have to disappoint them or let things go in order to handle a crisis

When in public appearances we have used a similar evaluative tool to assess the urgency addiction of closely held business leaders, at least 7 out of 10 freely admit that they're addicted to the adrenaline rush of being the shining knight on the white horse who rides to the rescue of every issue brought forth by every employee in the company. Always being the go-to guy is heady stuff, it simply feels wonderful, but in that headiness lay the seeds for the destruction of the entrepreneur's ability to control his own time and manage himself. The fact is that everyone gets to choose how to spend his time. For those who lament that they don't have enough time in their lives to do all the things they want and need to do, they must wake up, smell the coffee, and realize that the time mess they find themselves in is simply a result of the cumulative choices they've made about how they invest their minutes and hours. Just as closely held business leaders carefully decide how to spend their money, they must be just as diligent, if not more so, about how they spend their time.

The time management problems of entrepreneurs can be squeezed into four broad areas:

- Doing things they shouldn't be doing at all
- Doing the right things, but doing them inefficiently or ineffectively
- Time spent which is purely waste
- Possessing no system or technique for mastering the 24 hour day and all the executive requirements that must fit into it

When it's boiled down to its simplest, time management equals life management. Zig Ziglar says the most successful people "run their day by the clock and plan with the calendar." Later in the chapter, we'll deliver some tips and techniques for improving time management skills. Before we do that, however, let's take a look at what our anecdotal observations and empirical research say about how executives actually spend their time. For more on this subject, please read the article *When Is A Vacation Not A Vacation?* at www.familybusinessinstitute. com/8blocks/.

How do executives actually spend their time?

In 1979, Tom Peters wrote in the Harvard Business Review (HBR): "A leader's typical day is marked by too many meetings, constant interruptions, and limited options." The article states that: "The speed of business is the enemy of tidy rationality. Urgent phone calls interrupt long-planned meetings, noisy problems break into time allotted for quiet reflection, and the orderly world of the executive's schedule is in shambles." The fact that an executive's time is fragmented increases the potential for leaders to send mixed, garbled, or inconsistent messages to his followers. This fact makes it more important than ever for leaders to concentrate on a laser-like vision for where they want their companies to go and to communicate that concise vision frequently and clearly to their teams.

The definition of what managers do in a business centers around 4 classic words: plan, organize, coordinate, and control. It's awfully hard to correlate the meanings of those 4 words with what managers actually do on a day to day basis. HBR says: "Study after study has shown that managers work at an unrelenting pace, that their activities are characterized by brevity, variety, and discontinuity, and that they are strongly oriented to action and dislike reflective activities." A few statistics from HBR:

- Of verbal contacts in which chief executives engaged, 93% were arranged on an ad-hoc basis
- Only 1 of 368 verbal contacts was unrelated to a specific issue and could therefore be called general planning
- Managers strongly favor verbal media, telephone calls, and meetings over documents
- Chief executives treat mail processing as a burden to be dispensed with primarily because only about 13% is of specific and immediate use
- Brevity, fragmentation, and verbal communication characterize manager's work; the pressures of a manager's job are becoming worse
- CEOs spend about 40% of their contact time on activities devoted exclusively to the transmission of information. Communication IS their work
- Chief executives supervise as many as 50 projects at the same time

And so on, and so on. The long and short of it is that executives find, as one wife of a textile company executive put it, "Their time is not their own." They are continually sought after by internal and external forces, they are continually putting out fires and resolving disputes, the pace of business today pushes them harder than ever before, and they have precious little time for the big picture projects about which they dream. In public appearances, we ask CEOs, most of whom are 55 and older, whether they're working harder now than they were 5 years ago. About 90% inevitably raise their hands. Just at a time when they as entrepreneurs thought they'd be slowing down, reaping the rewards from their labor, and enjoying life more, they're working harder than ever.

The mythology of what makes a closely held company successful is a part of this growing problem. At a recent speech to a group of highway builders, we talked about what's necessary in the training and development of next generation leaders. One of the audience members, an earnest third generation 40-something family business manager, said, "One of the key ingredients is to work harder and longer than any of your employees. If they don't see you working hard, they won't either, and they won't respect you." This is a powerful and pervasive myth which exists in closely held companies, but the concept is simply folly. The idea that a 100 hour work week is the only way to earn employees' respect is simply ridiculous. Just because Granddad and Dad did it that way and stressed it as a part of their lifestyles doesn't mean it's inviolable business law, nor does it mean it has to be the cornerstone of the next generation's leadership.

A 65 year old second generation leader bought into the long hours concept, worked alongside his men in the field while doing office work at night, and maintained a full calendar of civic duties as well. His 30-something daughter, however, does not share the same philosophy. She worked as a teenager in the office and learned the business in a different way, a different sequence. She's not trained as an engineer, and she rarely had muddy boots and dirty fingernails as part of her early training. Her gifts are in administration, people handling, and marketing (perfect in the sense her dad's gifts lie elsewhere). She also has 2 young children to care for. While her dad often insists on longer working hours and more time spent in the field, she asserts they're not necessary ingredients in the style she plans to employ as she continues to build the business, and she's correct. She has determined that there's a different way to skin the cat, and she's widely respected among the employees for bringing different – but no less valuable – gifts to her family enterprise. Insisting there's only one right way to lead is simply a denial of reality. What worked for Dad doesn't necessarily work for the next generation.

The long hours myth underestimates your employees. Aren't there, conceivably, other ways to gain their respect without working yourself into an early grave? What if you're a gifted marketer or salesman and spend a great deal of time eating out and playing golf with prospects? Can't rank and file employees see the value of lead generation and conversion? What do you think your employees really value in the long run: the time and effort you put in, or the results you produce on behalf of the company?

Working vast numbers of hours is self-limiting. The hours you spend at work doing tasks that others could do at least as well or better crowds out so many other things. When will you spend time with your family? When will you have the time for rest, relaxation, and rejuvenation? When will you have time to plan, dream, meet, and deliberate on the future of the business so you can – once and for all – get ahead of the firefighting curve? As you age, is it realistic to think you can keep up the brutal pace and be at your best and healthiest? In your heart, do you genuinely WANT TO keep up the killer pace? Don't your employees want you to be the best you can be, and aren't they smart enough to know that the CEO working his fingers to the bone isn't necessarily in anyone's long term best interest?

The myth doesn't allow for the evolution of the company's growth. In the early years, the entrepreneur does it all: sales, production, administration, human resources, and finance. As the company grows, the wise entrepreneur surrounds himself with good people who specialize in these functions freeing him to do higher order projects. Those who insist on working extreme hours in order to earn their employees' respect miss opportunities to learn, grow, and lead in other ways. With only 24 hours in a day, an entrepreneur who tries to keep a hand in all areas of a growing firm's operations at all times becomes a bottleneck and artificially limits the growth of his company.

The myth requires that entrepreneurs build traps for themselves. By working extreme hours and being the go-to-guy for every decision, the leader makes the company and its future success depend on his production. He fails to cultivate superstar employees because their growth opportunities are cut off by the man who does it all. He instead cultivates mediocre "yes men" who are content to watch him do the lion's share of the work so they can work at a slow, comfortable pace. The trap springs when the leader desires a little more freedom only to find his most senior employees can't, won't, or are not capable of making sound decisions in his absence. Are inhuman hours spent outworking employees one way to earn their trust and respect? Yes. Is it the only way? Not by a long shot! Don't become enslaved to the long hours myth!

Another time management myth has to do with how to best undertake a process of self improvement. In the 1970s, the New York Yankees had a talented center fielder named Mickey Rivers (no relation). During spring training one year, Rivers and his manager, Billy Martin, almost came to blows over the best tactic for Rivers' continued improvement as a ballplayer. Martin wanted Rivers to focus on his weaknesses to try and improve them. According to a Gallup poll, a majority of Americans, British, Canadian, French, Japanese, and Chinese citizens all believe that this is the best strategy for success. Rivers strenuously disagreed. He said the purpose of spring training and the focus of his improvement should be on maximizing his strengths, not trying to strengthen his weaknesses. Baseball observers debated the question: who was right, Rivers or Martin? Certainly rational arguments can be attributed to both points of view, but it was Rivers who had more right on his side. Focusing on the things he did well and doing them with the maximum amount of frequency made sense for him, and it makes sense for most family business CEOs. If a family business executive carefully examined his agenda for the past 6 months, he'd be aghast at how much time he spent doing things he didn't enjoy doing, attending to details which were forced upon him by other people, and how little time he spent on the big picture items so important to the long term improvement of his company and ultimately his life.

In *The One Thing You Need To Know*, Marcus Buckingham has a startling recommendation for how to build on the Mickey Rivers philosophy of self improvement. Buckingham boldly states, "The one thing we all need to know to sustain our success is *discover what you don't like doing and stop doing it*." He further states:

> "Your strengths…are your natural appetites, and are, in this sense, irrepressible. Your strengths are activities that strengthen you. When using them you feel powerful, authentic, confident, and, in the best sense, challenged. As such, they are self reinforcing. Left to their own devices, they will, they must, be expressed. If your strengths are those activities that strengthen you, your weaknesses are the opposite. They are activities that weaken you. Confusingly, you may experience some achievement when using them, but, they leave you feeling depleted, drained, frustrated or merely bored. To sustain success in life, you must recognize these weaknesses for what they are and ruthlessly eradicate them from your life. Sustained success is caused not by what you add on, but by what you have the discipline to cut away."

This is a radical concept and fits beautifully with the philosophies of Covey and Sullivan. Most family business leaders have horribly undisciplined daily lives. The daily to do lists grow and grow. Executives attempt to do more and more. The results are unsatisfying, and the executives feel their lives are out of control. Collins says in *Good To Great*, "Those who built the good to great companies made as much use of 'stop doing' lists as to do lists. They displayed a remarkable discipline to unplug all sorts of extraneous junk." If more family and closely held leaders would adopt this philosophy, it would unleash a tidal wave of productivity and business success which would have ripple effects in economies around the world. When we claim that most closely held businesses are operating at only 50% effectiveness, the poor utilization of CEO and executive time, energy, and focus is probably the most significant reason. The best advice we can give entrepreneurs is two-part advice. One part is the Mickey Rivers concept of strengthening your strengths, and the other is the radical Marcus Buckingham concept of finding the things in life you don't like and stopping them. For more about this, please read the article *Want More Success In Business? Get In Shape!* at www.familybusinessinstitute.com/8blocks/.

In order to get a handle on how you actually invest your time, we advocate keeping a record of all the things done during a typical day at work and at home, ultimately expanding the inventory to include weekly and monthly activities. We have a free, downloadable time log for tracking your daily and weekly activities available on our website at www.familybusinessinstitute.com/8blocks/. Only by accurately tracking how an executive's time is spent in reality versus in his idealized imagination can one assess how time is actually spent against how time should be spent. The time log is the most fundamental of all time management analysis tools, and it is horribly underutilized. Most entrepreneurs recoil at the very thought of carrying a notebook and jotting down how they spend their time during the course of a typical week. Ed Bowman of W.E. Bowman Construction in Richmond, Virginia, had a radical experience utilizing the time log evaluation system. Here are some of his observations:

> "I kept the time log diligently for 2 weeks. I was amazed by the amount of crap I did. I was letting myself be tossed around like a beach ball. Even though one of my top strategic priorities was getting some good employees on board, in reality I had scheduled *no time* to focus on hiring! As a result, I resolved to push more responsibility back to others and delegate more. There were some things I resolved to stop doing like getting trapped outside the chain of command. Instead of stopping and answering questions from operations people, I directed them back to their supervisors who probably knew the answer better than I did anyway. While I kept the time log, everyone took notice and was very careful with what they came to me about. It definitely had ripple effects. The time I freed up now lets me find higher and better uses for my time like checking in with customers to assess their satisfaction with our work and talking to new potential customers."

Appropriate Executive Roles

One of the best time managers I ever met was an investment manager. I was having lunch, and he was at the table beside me. He was leaving for the day in the early afternoon to pick up his children from school. We had a few minutes to converse, and I asked him whether it was typical that he was the spouse responsible for the duties of child care. It turned out his wife had passed away a couple of years earlier. He knew that – using a pure, undiluted, "first things first" philosophy – he and he alone would be the greatest influence on his children until the time they became adults and moved away. Therefore, he took a radical approach to managing his time at work. He was quite successful in the investment business and intended to stay that way, but he also needed to balance his workday with the needs to get his children off to school in the morning and back home again in the afternoon. Using time logs and other techniques, he analyzed how he spent his time and eliminated absolutely anything that could be done by other people. Delegating so many tasks required that he add staff assistance, but it also had the profound effect of unchaining him from his desk. Having utilized this time management and life management methodology for a number of years, his income had actually grown, his client satisfaction levels were higher than before, and he was a full-time father.

This gentleman's approach to time and self management grew out of necessity due to a personal tragedy. There's no reason for you to require a tragedy to be your wake up call. If it's true that what you focus your attention on in life becomes stronger, then most family business executives need to be reoriented and retrained on what an executive *should do* versus what they currently do.

At a meeting a couple of years ago of 8 successful CEOs, the group was discussing how to get the most out of an industry-standard software package. They all used it, but some got more out of it than others. One CEO asked a question about how to key in data to produce a desired result. At that time, FBI's consultant slammed his hand down upon the table, leaped from his chair, and exclaimed, "You mean to tell me that you, the CEO of a $40 million company, are at the office at 8:30 at night keying in data into a computer program that one of your $20 per hour employees could run when you should be home with your wife and children?" The CEOs were aghast; no one talked to them like that. One of them said, "That's why you're here; we've always run our companies this way, and it's the only way we know. What *should* a CEO be concentrating on in order to build his business?"

Since that eventful meeting, we've spent a great deal of time helping CEOs understand what it is that they should do (and what they shouldn't). The following is a top 10 list of CEO behaviors which produce deep, impactful, and lasting results. The highest payoff roles for CEOs are:

1. **Keeper of the corporate/family vision.** The CEO should be the steward of the corporate and/or family visions. Most businesses don't have explicit, written, mutually understood visions for what they want their companies to be and become. As with undertaking strategic planning in a corporate setting, pursuing a common vision which is exciting to all stakeholders is a fun and rewarding exercise; the main benefit comes from aligning everyone on the team during the process itself.

2. **Identifier, codifier, and protector of the corporate/family values.** The CEO is the policeman of the family business to make sure everyone's day to day activities adhere to the explicit and implicit values of the company. We were recently contacted by a second generation business leader who was distraught that his newly instituted drug policy uncovered that one of their highest performing employees had been using marijuana. He

48

wanted to give the employee another chance and keep the drug results confidential from other company officers until the employee had time to clean up his act. We talked at length about the importance of the drug policy, about how they had adopted it wholeheartedly, enthusiastically, and unanimously as a zero tolerance policy, and what it might mean to the others if this young executive gerrymandered the results to protect an individual employee. He could see clearly after our discussion that protecting the employee – in spite of his perceived value – was inconsistent with the values everyone in the business had agreed upon. While this young executive isn't yet the CEO, he received valuable training as his father continues to groom him to be the next leader of the business.

3. **Grandmaster of the corporate strategy.** CEOs must be the lead strategists in their companies. Developing and nurturing the company strategy is a high leverage, high payoff activity. Abraham Lincoln once said if he had a cord of wood to chop in 6 hours, he'd spend the first 4 hours sharpening his axe. Even the best CEOs can't spend 100% of their time on high value, 30,000 foot strategy; however, it's reasonable to set a goal for a CEO to spend 20% to 40% of his time working on strategy and long term issues. Due to the press of work in closely held companies, many CEOs spend zero time on this critical activity.

4. **Great communicator of the vision, values, and strategy.** After all the work put in to have these things, it's not wise to keep them a secret! Talk about your vision, values, and strategy until you hear others begin to parrot your exact words. Then talk about them some more!

5. **Bird dogger and evaluator of talent.** The CEO must be the steward of his talent pool. He must develop procedures and processes for evaluating the current employees of his company, and he must attempt to figure out where gaps exist for the purpose of placing future talent. For most closely held business owners, there is no strategy or technique for evaluating or attracting new talent. A concise, easily digestible discussion of the subject can be found on our website at www.familybusinessinstitute. com/8blocks/ entitled *Get the Right People on Your Bus – Hiring for Excellence!*

6. **Charismatic and authoritative spokesperson for the company.** The CEO should be the face and the personality of the company. People are intrigued with courageous, fearless,

rugged CEOs who succeed in spite of long odds. The CEO should be the point person on public relations efforts. It's good for overall company morale to see the CEO in public places receiving recognition, it's good for the marketing team, and it's good for the company's business developers. Suppose the CEO is shy and retiring and isn't comfortable being in the public eye? That's okay. Simply find another in the organization (a senior non-family manager, a rising family business executive, etc.) who can ably fill the role, and train him on what you'd like to see conveyed in the marketplace.

7. **Personification of corporate teamwork.** The CEO should be the person who leads by example and gets on board as a team player with everyone else. We recently had a call where a non-family partner was frustrated. Led by the president's initiatives, the management team continually came up with new rules, policies, and procedures which the president summarily ignored. For example, employees were required to adopt new voice and email technology. The president was 100% behind the initiative, and promoted it enthusiastically. He, however, held onto paper telephone messages and refused to use the new system. The appearance was that everyone else in the company should be available and reachable using the new tools; the CEO, however, didn't think the initiative applied to him. This is an area where a CEO should lead by example; poor teamwork by company leaders trickles downhill quickly and undermines team building initiatives.

8. **Advocate for corporate quality and customer service.** The CEO should be the head cheerleader when it comes to providing perfect quality and outstanding customer service.

9. **Custodian of the corporate cash.** The CEO doesn't have to be an expert on accounting or function as an unofficial CFO. However, it is up to the CEO to manage the corporate cash in a responsible way. Cash is king in business, and many profitable companies have found themselves perplexed by a serious lack of it. They ask, "How can our margins be so good, how can we show so much profit at the end of the year, and yet we never seem to have any cash?" The CEO should have systems in place for forecasting cash flow. Simple budgeting is a start in this process, but cash management can be quite complex. It may require bringing in outside help for some tutorials and to help develop systems and procedures.

10.　**Referee and mediator of disputes and dissatisfactions.** Another way of defining this role for the CEO would be the Chief Morale Officer of the company. In the ideal organization there aren't any disputes and dissatisfactions, but the ideal is just that; it's a point which can never be reached. It's up to the CEO to make sure that he has the right people in place and the right chemistry among his employees. In a 100 person organization, 2 or 3 bad, morale-busting employees sprinkled in can be a nightmare. Many CEOs consider themselves to be the stewards of their employees, and they're reluctant to let people, especially long term employees, go; however, it's much better to prune the business family tree and get rid of bad apples quickly. The CEO should keep his finger on the pulse of the organization at all times and be continually looking for potential morale issues. When there are disputes and dissatisfactions, the CEO must be a wise, sage mediator.

Basic Time Management Tools

We've talked about the use of a time log; what are some other basic time management tools which are fairly easy to understand and implement?

- Time-blocking: Some entrepreneurs find it impossible to block off whole days at a time. A baby step toward being able to do that is to block off chunks of time on any given day. For example, depending on one's schedule, an executive could block off from 9 to 11 A.M. on Tuesdays and 2 to 4 P.M. on Fridays for big picture, high impact, and uninterrupted time to focus. Time blocking, like time management itself, requires iron discipline to produce results.
- The "4 Ds" for paper handling: Many executives find themselves buried under mounds of paper (wasn't the computer revolution supposed to eliminate the clutter of paper from our lives?). Here's a simple methodology for handling all of that paper which crosses your desk on a typical day. It's called the 4 Ds, and they are:

  o　**Ditch it**
  o　**Do it**
  o　**Delegate it**
  o　**Delay it**

Ditch it means exactly what it says. If it's not important, don't save it, don't store it, don't put it in a stack on the corner of your desk, get rid of it. Be jealous of the things you spend your time on and eliminate things that waste your time! *Do it* simply means attend to the paper at hand right away. *Delegate it* means jot a note with instructions or use a sticky note to pass the item along to someone else to handle. *Delay it* means this is something which is important enough to demand your attention, but you simply don't have time to deal with it right now. The delay it directive has a component part; if something is important enough to require your attention at a later date, schedule it so you'll have a specific time to attend to it in the future. The goal of the 4 D's is that you touch every piece of paper which crosses your desk (or every email) only *one* time.

- Batching: Do similar things all at the same time for peak efficiency. For example, close your email box when you're working on other tasks. Only reply to emails at certain times of the day, say, first thing in the morning, right before you leave for lunch, and at the close of the workday. Email is on the verge of replacing the telephone as the greatest time waster in an executive's busy schedule. There's no way to ascertain whether or not a telephone call or an email rises to a level high enough to demand your attention. Therefore, since 80% or more of these are mere interruptions, relegate them to specific times of the day which leaves other blocks of time to attend to more important tasks.

- Limit phone calls to 4 minutes in duration. I have found in my years in business that 4 minutes is usually quite sufficient to attend to almost any matter on the telephone. If you know that a telephone call is going to exceed your 4 minute limit, schedule a specific "telephone meeting," and give it the attention it truly deserves.

- Unclutter your desk and your office. Sullivan actually recommends that, to achieve maximum productivity, the executive eliminate his office altogether! He makes a powerful point, but since that's probably too radical for most entrepreneurs, at least make the attempt to – or better yet place your personal assistant in charge of this – eliminate clutter from your immediate surroundings. If you insist on keeping old magazines and stacks of papers and documents, at least put them in a closet or an underutilized space so that the piles and stacks aren't constantly distracting you or producing guilt because you haven't gotten around to them yet.

- Schedule first things first. Plan personal and family activities *first*. Plan your vacations well in advance, and order your business life and schedule around your personal needs rather than the other way around. At the very least, your spouse will appreciate this change in your attitude. Turn off your cell phone and stay away from email during family activities. Psychologists have actually identified what they call "Blackberry addiction" for business people who seem more married to their smart phones than to their families.

- Finish one thing before starting another. If you've identified one or 2 key tasks that you have to get done that day for maximum impact, by all means do them first! Don't make the mistake many people make of saying, "Oh I'll do these reports or answer these emails first. They won't take up much of my time." Those consumers of time lead to other consumers of time which crowd out the high impact things you most need and want to get done. Focus on the important tasks, and do them as fully as possible before moving on to next things.

There are many other time management 101 techniques such as having an agenda and a firm beginning and end time for all meetings, closing your door to plan for 10 minutes at the start of each day, etc. The point is that time management is a critical component of self management. For an executive to have maximum impact on a closely held company, she simply must master herself and her time. Once an executive has leveraged herself as much as she can and focused diligently on her top priorities, she should be working as hard and as smart as she can. Then she can begin to develop the talent and future leaders around her. That's when she'll exponentially increase the impact of her entrepreneurial experience.

> "The best executive is one who has sense enough to pick good men to do what he wants done, and self restraint enough to keep from meddling with them while they do it."
> – *Theodore Roosevelt*

Leadership Development

Leadership development is the hottest of hot topics these days. One writer claims that about 2,000 books *per year* are now being written on the subject of leadership and leadership development. Given the noise and confusion in the marketplace, we're not going to try to reinvent the wheel here. What we'll do in this section of Chapter Three is to peel away some of the fog and confusion, discuss why leadership development is so important, provide a simple definition of leadership (and perhaps just as importantly attempt to define what leadership is *not*), discuss some myths and misperceptions about leadership, and provide some "how to" advice.

Leadership is often a murky and nebulous concept, but it is important. How many times in the sports world have you seen a coach or manager fired and a new leader come in, take his place, and with the same cast of characters produce far different results? Leaders in family and closely held businesses are, as Reggie Jackson of the New York Yankees once described himself, "the straw that stirs the drink." Leadership experts around the world can point to the quantitative impact leaders make. Warren Bennis says, "Leadership accounts for, at the very least, 15% of the success of any organization." Afsaneh Nahavandi says that leadership can account for up to 44% of a firm's profitability. Researchers at the Wharton School of Finance concluded that 15% to 25% of the variation in a corporation's profitability was determined by the character of their chief executives. In a small study, 40% of the variation in the herring catches among fishing boats in the North Sea depended on the leadership of the boat's captain. Even researchers attempting to debunk the power of leadership concluded that it accounts for a minimum of 7% to 14% of a company's performance!

Imagine how western history would be different in the absence of some of our great leaders. What if 300 Spartan hoplites had not stood fast against the Persian hordes at the battle of Thermopylae? What if George Washington had not been able to rally his ragtag, underfed, and underpaid troops through the brutal winter at Valley Forge? What if George Patton hadn't been able to drive the Third Army to disengage from a pitched battle and move hundreds of miles through icy weather to save the day at the Battle of the Bulge? Leaders are difference makers.

Conversely, what does an organization look like in the absence of strong leadership? If you ever worked for a company where the leaders were weak, lacked vision, or were ineffective, you know what the results were in terms of low morale, lack of enthusiasm, and mediocre results. Leaderless organizations are rudderless, and there's no sense of mission or fun in trying to exist in an organization like that.

In family businesses, all too often the leadership mantra of senior executives is to look at what the company did last year, add a few dollars for anticipated growth, and defend the strategies and tactics that it has used in the past to get where it is. That's *not* leadership; that's defending the status-quo, and it's ultimately a recipe for stagnation and failure. Real leaders peer into the future, seek new paths and new ways for doing business, and continually reinvent and reengineer themselves and their companies. In *Mastering The Rockefeller Habits*, Verne Harnish says one of the main barriers to growth common to closely held companies is "the need for the executive team to grow as leaders in their abilities to delegate and predict." He says flatly, "One great person can replace 3 good people." Harnish also says that one of the most important attributes of leaders is their ability to delegate to others. "Getting others to do something as good as or better than yourself is one of the hardest aspects of leadership, but necessary if you're going to grow the business. The success of a firm is determined by the extent to which the senior leadership team can grow the next levels of leadership, and teach them in turn to delegate effectively. Leadership isn't just *doing*, it's also delegating, trusting, mentoring and teaching, and holding people accountable."

The majority of family and closely held company executives struggle with the concept of letting go of day to day tasks and duties. Often, as we'll explore in Chapter Four, they don't think they can delegate effectively because they are surrounded by mediocre talent. While this is certainly true in some cases, it's also used as a crutch for not delegating, for not trusting, and for not pushing decision making and action authority down to lower levels in their organizations. Leadership is vitally important to the sustainability of closely held companies, and all evidence points to this fact. So what *is* leadership?

Leadership is a difficult to define and complex process which has 3 important components. They are: 1) the leader, 2) the followers, and 3) the situation. It's important to note that leadership is a process, not necessarily an event or a person; it's quite a broad concept.

A leader is "any person who influences individuals and groups within an organization, helps them in the establishment of goals, and guides them toward achievement of those goals, thereby allowing them to be effective" according to Nahavandi. She continues: "Leadership is a group phenomenon; it always involves personal influence or persuasion. Leaders use influence to guide others through a certain course of action or toward the achievement of certain goals. Therefore, leadership is goal directed and plays an active role in groups and organizations. In some cases, the leadership hierarchy is formal and well-defined with the leader at the top; in other cases, it is informal and flexible." Maxwell has a wonderful, concise definition of leadership: "Leadership is influence – nothing more, nothing less."

Leaders are effective when their followers can achieve their goals, can function well together, and can adapt to changing demands from external forces. A leader, who takes charge of a group in one context, say in a crisis or emergency, may not be the leader in normal, day to day situations. For example, at the scene of an automobile accident, emergency medical personnel immediately take charge and become leaders of the crisis situation. Put into another setting, say a civic club or a group of church members, the EMTs may exhibit few, if any, leadership characteristics at all.

There are certain characteristics associated with leaders. Some are quite positive: motivational, charismatic, trustworthy, decisive, smart, energetic, and ambitious. There are also negative characteristics commonly associated with leaders: isolated and lonely, authoritarian, pushy, non-conforming, and ruthless. What makes leaders different is how they respond in uncertain and unclear situations. They provide direction and help others see the possibilities of order emerging from chaos.

Warren Blank in his book *The Nine Natural Laws of Leadership* writes: "A leader has willing followers. The traditional view defines leaders by a list of traits, qualities, habits, or behaviors. However, individual qualities and behaviors do *not* clearly differentiate leaders from non-leaders." Leaders become leaders when they gain followers. This is important because it's different from the traditional view of leaders which heaps accolades on them at the expense of the followers. There can't be a leader without followers, and Blank says this "changes our view of followers because it recognizes the collegial, partnering role they play. Followers are allies who represent the necessary opposite side of the leadership coin."

Blank also makes the point that while people view leadership as a continuous, ongoing characteristic belonging to a person, leadership is actually transitory in terms of the relationship between a leader and her followers. He says, "People can lose interest in a leader's particular path." The presidency of George W. Bush is a good example. Spirits were quite high following his reelection; Bush had a historical opportunity to follow through on his campaign pledges to win the war on terror, reform social security, and reduce taxes further thereby lengthening America's unprecedented economic boom. Anticipation was high for a historic second presidential term; however, by the end of the term Bush's public opinion ratings were among the lowest ever recorded for an incumbent president (although still quite a bit higher than the abysmally low approval rating of the U.S. Congress), and what may have been an historic opportunity to build on the values which made America great withered on the vine.

Unlike a manager's authority which is defined by the company's organization chart, leaders inspire followers to follow. Leadership isn't necessarily a position of formal authority; it is more about person to person influence than authority dictated by a box in the organizational hierarchy. How many managers have you known who, in spite of their formal authority, have been unable to produce results for their teams because of their lack of leadership characteristics and qualities? Formal position, titles, or membership in the family-owned company are no substitutes for developing leadership.

Another characteristic of leadership is that not everyone will follow. No matter how strong, charismatic, and visionary a leader is, it's just not possible to get a 100% buy in – especially if a son or daughter is taking over for a parent in a family company or a group of senior managers buys the company from a departing executive. As we'll see in Chapter Four, people management is quite important, and when it comes to leadership it's worth noting that, since "followership" is not a given, it makes sense to give most of your time and attention to those who will support your leadership initiatives. Gathering a few key allies can be instrumental in furthering leadership plans. For those who won't or can't follow, it may be time to prune the family or employment tree in order to secure the faith and commitment of those who will follow.

In *Good To Great*, Collins says, "In over two-thirds of the comparison cases, we noted the presence of a gargantuan personal ego that contributed to the demise or continued mediocrity of the company." The reason that closely held businesses fail or fail to reach their potential is often rooted in the attitudes of its leaders. In case after case, we have seen family businesses clinging to concepts and practices which made the company successful in the 1960s or 1970s but have little relevance to the business world of today. It's important that the company's history and values inform the present; however, a slavish devotion to doing things the way Dad or Granddad did them becomes a barrier to future success, not a guarantor of success. The reason companies so desperately cling to these concepts of the past stems from a lack of vision and leadership on the part of today's managers. Due to ever-changing business conditions, a company simply must reinvent itself periodically in order to maintain its competitive position. Company growth creates even more pressure for reinvention. The systems and infrastructure which adequately supported a $10 million company will not support a $25 million enterprise, and customer and employee satisfaction will dip as a result of the lack of foresight and leadership.

It's often been said that people fear that which they don't know. One of the reasons leaders occupy such an exalted place is that they calm that fear of the unknown by providing vision and direct action which leads to impact. Buckingham writes: "Actions are unambiguous. They are clear. If you, the leader, can highlight a few carefully selected actions, then we, your followers will happily latch on to these actions and use them to calm our fear of the unknown." A leader's bias toward action versus inaction keeps him at the point of the charge.

Collins writes: "Good to great companies were not, by and large, in great industries, and some were in terrible industries. In no case do we have a company that just happened to be sitting on the nose cone of a rocket when it took off." Greatness is not a function of circumstance. Greatness, it turns out, is largely a matter of conscious choice. Leaders choose to bring order and clarity into messy or uncertain environments. They choose to build themselves, their teams, and their organizations to rally around common goals and to form a team interested in each other's mutual successes. They are seers and action takers, but interestingly, they're not necessarily self promoters in the image of Donald Trump or Lee Iacocca. Collins writes: "The good to great leaders seem to have come from Mars. Self effacing, quiet, reserved, even shy – these leaders are a paradoxical blend of personal humility and professional will. They are more like Lincoln and Socrates than Patton or Caesar..." Collins continues:

> "...an effective leader catalyzes commitment to and vigorous pursuit of a clear and compelling vision stimulating higher performance standards." The highest order leader, however, goes beyond that. The exceptional leader "builds enduring greatness through a paradoxical blend of personal humility and professional will. They channel their ego needs away from themselves and into the larger goal of building a great company. It's not that Level Five leaders have no ego or self-interest – indeed they are incredibly ambitious – but their ambition is first and foremost for the institution, not themselves. Level Five leaders want to see the company even more successful in the next generation comfortable with the idea that most people won't even know that the roots of success trace back to their efforts. In contrast, the comparison (less effective) leaders, concerned more with their own reputation for personal greatness, often fail to set the company up for success in the next generation. After all, what better testament to your own personal greatness than that the place falls apart after you leave? In over three-fourths of the comparison companies, we found executives who set their successors up for failure or chose weak successors, or both."

Collins was describing public corporations, but he may have just as well been describing private companies. The greatest tragedy we've observed after 200 collective years of observing closely held companies is that they do not survive through the generations; they don't reach their potentials. It's not only a personal tragedy; this failure is a loss for everyone with a stake in the outcome – employees, suppliers, and the hometown communities of these businesses.

What are some of the characteristics of leaders who fail? The Center for Creative Leadership (CCL) has identified the following as the primary characteristics of leaders who don't succeed:

- An abrasive, intimidating style
- Coldness and arrogance
- Untrustworthiness
- Self-centeredness
- Poor performance
- Inability to delegate

Difficulty managing relationships and/or people skills seem to be front and center on the CCL's list. Writing in the *Harvard Business Review*, Daniel Goleman, the "E.Q." guru, says:

"Most effective leaders are alike in one crucial way: they all have a high degree of what has come to be known as emotional intelligence (E.Q.). It's not that I.Q. and technical skills are irrelevant. They do matter, but mainly its threshold capability; that is, they are the entry level requirements for executive level positions. But emotional intelligence is the *sine qua non* of leadership. Without it, a person can have the best training in the world, an incisive analytical mind, and an endless supply of smart ideas, but he still won't make a great leader. When I calculated the ratio of technical skills, I.Q., and emotional intelligence as ingredients of excellent performance, emotional intelligence proved to be twice as important as the others for jobs at all levels. The higher the rank of a person considered to be a star performer, the more emotional intelligence capabilities showed up as the reason for his or her effectiveness."

This sounds great, but it's awfully touchy-feely. Consider this: when senior managers have a critical mass of emotional intelligence capabilities, their divisions outperformed yearly earnings goals by 20%. Meanwhile, division leaders lacking that critical mass underperformed by almost the same amount. If Gerber is correct and most closely held business owners are not truly entrepreneurs but "technicians suffering from an entrepreneurial seizure," then developing and nurturing emotional intelligence characteristics can be the difference between a company reaching or failing to reach its potential.

Myths and Misperceptions About Leadership

We have spent quite a bit of time talking about why leadership is important and the characteristics of successful leaders. It's also worthwhile to invest attention in "myth-busting" some of the persistent misunderstandings about leadership. Here are some of the most common myths:

59

Anyone can be a leader – this is simply not true. Some people, including some of your most senior family members or managers, simply don't have what it takes. They may not be self-aware, they may not possess empathy for others, or they may not want to be leaders. Some do want to be leaders, but they don't have the technical background, business competence, emotional maturity, or execution ability which would allow them to lead others.

My top people are my leaders – don't be so sure. Some people in leadership positions in your company are in those positions because they've stuck around the longest. If you think about it, some of the most talented and ambitious people you've ever had working for you have gone on to start their own companies. Think about how those entrepreneurial personalities could have had a positive impact on your company had you been able to partner with them and get them to stick around. Some people have risen to positions of responsibility because of their political skills more than anything else. Leaders aren't leaders simply because of their place on the organization chart or because they belong to the same blood line as you.

Leaders are great mentors – this is rarely the case. Superstars like Wilt Chamberlain, Bill Russell, Wayne Gretsky, Frank Robinson, and other top athletes have had mostly unsuccessful coaching careers. Doing and leading out front isn't the same as mentoring and teaching in the back office. It's possible that a great performer could be a great coach, but it's pretty darn rare.

My son (or daughter) is the next logical leader of this company – since it's true that leaders must have followers, wouldn't it be wise to undertake some analysis of the potential followers before jumping to this conclusion? A father in a successful construction company recently named his daughter president and assumes that she will be the next beloved leader of the company. He's in for a rude shock. His daughter is constantly embroiled in personality differences in the organization and acts as the "mother confessor" to the entire group, attends to silly administrative and clerical details that no one with the title of president should ever consider doing, and doesn't have enough self confidence to either delegate internal functions or to do business development work outside the company. Face the fact that as a loving parent it's virtually impossible to be objective about your children. Get some inside and outside perspectives before you leap to this conclusion.

Leadership is the same as management – no it's not. Leaders focus on the future while managers focus on today. Managers work to maintain the status quo while leaders are continually reinventing and creating change. Leaders use personal influence while managers rely on their artificial position on the corporation's organizational chart for their power and authority. Leaders constantly discuss vision and values while managers implement policies and procedures. As a closely held company executive, you can't ignore management, but don't confuse it with true leadership.

We're really successful, and we've never focused on leadership before; therefore, this stuff isn't necessary for us – Maxwell writes about the "Law of the Lid": the lower an individual's inability to lead, the lower the lid on his potential. He cites the example of the McDonald brothers who started what would become the most famous restaurant in the world. Dick and Maurice McDonald revolutionized the restaurant business. They cut all the fat from their operation and ruthlessly re-engineered their delivery of service. By any account, making $100,000 a year in business in the mid 1950s was pretty darn successful. Why is it then, that my 14 year old son asked, "Why is it called McDonald's when the guy who built it was named Ray Kroc?" The McDonald brothers had hit their ceiling. They lacked vision, and they lacked leadership. They were comfortable in their success, and having reached that level spent their time protecting the status quo. Maxwell said, "They were efficient managers. But they were not leaders. Their thinking patterns clamped a lid down on what they could do and become." Ray Kroc, who bought the concept from the McDonald brothers, opened 100 restaurants between 1955 and 1959, and today the company has 21,000 restaurants in over 100 countries. Leadership ability and vision were the things that separated Ray Kroc from Dick and Maurice McDonald.

61

I can't get leaders; we've tried to hire talented people before, and it never works – we'll discuss this at some length in Chapter Four, but let's put it simply: on your first date with your high school sweetheart, did she say yes to all your advances? Of course not! And yet you kept asking her out and taking her on dates until one day she concluded you were Mr. Right and settled down. Even in the face of failure you kept on trying. Just because you haven't found the right kind of leaders in the past doesn't mean that if you keep trying you'll never find them in the future. You will.

Jane Doe is by far the smartest person under this roof. Therefore, she is the next logical leader of this company – don't be too sure. While knowledge does equate to power, the most intelligent folks working for you aren't necessarily your best future leaders. They may not possess the people skills or the vision they need. Haven't you known incredibly smart people in your life that didn't seem to have the common sense to get in out of the rain? Knowledge is a component of leadership, but it doesn't automatically confer leadership in and of itself.

There are probably a dozen other myths about leadership we could discuss. In order to see your way through the myths, simply keep in mind two things: 1) leadership is influence - nothing more, nothing less, and 2) you can't be a leader if you don't have followers.

How to Develop Leadership in Your Closely Held Company

We can all agree that leadership development is important, and we know myth from reality. How then do family and closely held business executives begin to train and develop family members and key non-family managers to be more effective leaders? The first piece of advice is to understand that leadership development is very hard and time consuming work. It's hard to hold on to leaders; they're go-getters and entrepreneurial, and they want to do things their own way. It's not easy, but who ever said growing a business was easy in the first place?

Not everyone, not even the members of your family, will respond positively to leadership development initiatives. Goldsmith writes about one of his clients who asked a perceptive question: "Does anyone who goes to these leadership development programs ever *really* change?" He ultimately researched a pool of 86,000 course participants. 100% said that following leadership development training they would go back to their jobs and apply what they had learned. However, 3 out of 10 direct reports of the leaders who had received training said that their bosses had returned from the experience and "done absolutely nothing." When Goldsmith wondered about the disconnect between people who had claimed they had taken the training to heart versus people who actually undertook an effort to change, he found a stunningly simple answer consistent with our observations about family businesses: *the executives were simply too busy to implement the things that they had learned.* Goldsmith wrote:

> "This taught me a lesson: there's an enormous disconnect between understanding and doing. Most leadership development revolves around one huge false assumption: if people understand, then they will do. That's not true. Most of us understand, we just don't do. What was missing on the part of the executives was follow through. Part of follow through in leadership development is showing followers that a) you've undertaken a self and leadership development process, and b) you're actively beginning to implement some of the things you've learned. When leaders consistently follow up, their followers' perceptions of them go up dramatically."

What's the best kind of leadership development training? According to *Family Business* magazine, 85% of human resources professionals surveyed said they use formal workshops or training seminars to develop leaders. Yet leaders themselves said that *special projects* were more effective than formal workshops. 69% of those surveyed rated projects within their job responsibilities as highly effective compared to 55% who gave that rating to special projects outside their job responsibilities, and only 42% who said formal workshops were highly effective. Hands on assignments or special projects coupled with accountability are the best methods for developing next generation leaders.

As we discussed before in this chapter, a first step in developing leaders is to adopt Socrates' 2 word admonition: *"Know thyself."* While it's important to know what your strengths are, it's also important to know where you have weaknesses and even blind spots. As Mickey Rivers tried to convince Billy Martin, a person who's always focusing on his weaknesses will get more of them and can't inspire much "followership" in others. The purpose of knowing weaknesses and blind spots isn't to focus on improving them, but to gain greater perspective for where your strengths truly are so they get most of your time and attention.

Another aspect of leadership development is communication. Most entrepreneurs are so caught up in the day to day tasks of working in their businesses they don't devote nearly enough time communicating with their people. I can hear our readers now, "Wayne, that's silly! I talk to my people every day, and we're in constant communication." That's probably true, but simple day to day communication about the tasks at hand doesn't inspire confidence and isn't a leadership ingredient. The kind of communication we're talking about is the big picture work of communicating your vision exhaustively until all of your people – or at least as many as it's humanly possible to recruit – subscribe to it with as much passion and vigor as you do. A simple exercise is to make a conscious effort to double your face to face frequency with your people. Some management gurus call it MBWA – management by walking around. It's fine to talk about Aunt Sally's sore back and the youngster's piano recital, but in terms of your organization and your followers, it's most important to talk about your vision for the company, the values for which the company stands, and holding yourself and others accountable for producing the results you want.

Second, it's important in developing leaders to seek out training opportunities. Aptitude and personality testing should be a part of this initiative. For example, one of the leading tools psychologists use to analyze personality is the Myers Briggs Type Indicator (MBTI). *The Journal of Small Business Management* reported on a study that asked the following question: "Are certain personality characteristics of firm leaders more conducive to successful transitions?" The researchers found that "successful intergenerational transitions in family firms seem to involve collaborative family and participative business cultures. Furthermore, this cultural configuration seems closely related mostly to extraverted-sensing-thinking-judging leaders (ESTJs)." This study is not the final word on succession analysis, and it's not our purpose to turn this chapter into a discussion of MBTI theory; however, it does give some insight into how one might begin to use personality profiling instruments as very useful learning and leadership development tools. Other commonly used psychometric tools are: DISC (Dominance, Influence, Steadiness, Conscientiousness), the Kolbe A Index, and the FIRO-B (Fundamental Interpersonal Relations Orientation).

A third important consideration in developing current and future leaders is to conceive a development plan or an integration plan. We were asked to develop and integration plan for a 29 year-old successor, Sarah, so that she could one day fill the role currently held by her 63 year-old father, Joseph. We helped develop a 10 year plan which was coordinated with the company's culture firmly in mind. The plan called for Sarah to work in specific jobs in various departments in the company over various periods of time. Her employment was not an entitlement program; she would be evaluated frequently by non-family professional managers. The plan included psychometric testing and formal education which enhanced the undergraduate education she already had. We also designed into the plan that Sarah would have supervisory roles and, eventually, profit and loss responsibility for various departments. We allowed for a contingency component if Sarah ultimately decided to leave the company's employ for whatever reason. In other words, she needed "an escape hatch" so there would be no business or family ramifications if she elected to terminate her own employment. While developing Sarah, we also recommended that the company undertake a process of developing other high potential leaders so that she would not be isolated and that she would be part of a team on which she could lead, follow, and participate. We also arranged to communicate the integration plan to other executives and managers who would come into contact with Sarah; we didn't want her integration to de-motivate other managers or executives or even cause their departure. We added 360° evaluations of Sarah (supervisor, peer, and subordinate views) at various stages of the plan in order to gather ongoing and updated feedback. Finally, the plan specified coaching for both Sarah and her strong-willed father on how to deal with each other in healthy, assertive, adult ways rather than simply as daughter and father.

This sort of balanced personal development plan or integration plan sounds like a lot of work, and it is. However, the typical integration plan of starting an aspiring family member at the bottom of the organization in order to slowly work her way to the top doesn't necessarily teach young, aspiring executives about where they'll need to go in the future. Future leaders have to prepare for a job that doesn't really exist yet and develop a different kind of business for a different future. Keeping them trapped in 60 to 80 hour per week jobs only ensures that they'll continue the cycle of working IN the business rather than working ON it. Any integration plan has to contemplate time away from the tasks of the business so that the leaders can develop themselves and their strengths. An integration plan also must have milestones and checkpoints to ensure accountability. Simply running an individual through various departments in the company without real jobs and real responsibility and little accountability is a shell of a plan, and other leaders and managers in your company will see right through it.

Fourth, when it comes to developing future leaders it often pays to hire someone else to do it. Leadership training, not being part and parcel of the growth experience of most of today's senior generation executives, may not come very naturally to them. They don't have a past or a track record upon which to fall back. Therefore, a consideration might be to hire "bridge management" to not only help run the company, but also to help groom and nurture future leaders. Especially when family members are considered for future leadership, it's difficult for Moms and Dads to evaluate objectively. A non-family executive can be more dispassionate and analytical and can do a more objective job of helping the junior generation candidate develop more quickly.

Fifth, leadership development requires that the senior generation leaders step back and allow the junior generation candidates to fall and skin their knees from time to time. Rushing in repeatedly to help next generation managers avoid mistakes sends the wrong signals to the rest of the team and to the young people themselves. It's simply natural for human beings to learn more from their own mistakes than from being counseled not to make mistakes by others. As long as the oversights don't put the company or key relationships in jeopardy, it's wise to turn a blind eye to them and let your developing leaders learn their lessons the hard way.

Sixth, because many family businesses in the future will be led not by one founding or "strongest sibling" entrepreneur, but rather by sibling teams (or teams made up of part family, part non-family managers), it's important that their leadership training cover team and collaborative decision making. Most family companies, in their quest for family harmony, are absolutely awful at making controversial decisions. When asked, they say they make decisions "by consensus," but upon closer examination what they mean is that they make challenging business decisions *unanimously*. For example, if 4 siblings are considering developing property in a new territory, and 3 of the siblings vote yes to move forward with one voting no, what do you think the ultimate decision will be? The vote is 3 to one; therefore, it seems pretty clear that this initiative should move forward. However, experience teaches us that this family will *not move forward* with this development initiative. They are likely to be so focused on meeting the needs of the dissenter that the wishes of the 3 who voted yes will be voided. It's important that management teams develop decision making criteria upon which they can all agree. This allows them in times of disagreement or controversy to have a built-in system that will prevent them from wallowing in deadlock and developing frustrations.

Seventh, because most senior generation managers, especially in family companies, didn't have formal integration plans or leadership development training, they won't always know where to begin. Therefore, it is incumbent upon the younger generation to take steps to develop its own leadership plans. They may need to approach senior generation executives with a proposal – maybe even more than one approach will be necessary – for taking a few steps on the path to leadership development. In doing so, it's important to walk before they attempt to run. It may not be wise to go to Dad with a fully developed 10 year integration plan like the one described above. Rather, it might be better to go with a very modest proposal for a 3 month learning initiative and go back with a second (and third and fourth) proposal later on. In other words, the junior generation should not wait for the senior generation to dictate a path. If the junior generation doesn't have enough drive and ambition to initiate the leadership discussion herself, one has to call into question whether she has the drive and ambition to be a future leader at all. This may sound harsh, but don't for a minute think that the senior generation isn't looking for the signs of passion and commitment from the younger generation!

Eighth, when thinking about next generation leadership development, don't make the fatal mistake of thinking that the goal of leadership development is to clone the current leader. First of all, cloning isn't possible – at least not with human beings yet. It also fails to see a fact of today's business world: the skills that it took to get the business to its current place may not be the skills it takes to move the business to a new level. Furthermore, many companies today which have one clearly defined leader will have 2 or more in the very near future. Therefore, the needs for communication, shared decision making, the development of a common corporate vision, and collaboration will be multiplied in the future.

Finally, get next generation leaders involved in the process of strategic planning. At the risk of giving away some of the wonderful benefits of strategic planning in store in Chapter Nine, planning provides immense educational *and* relational benefits including:

- Next generation alignment with the firm's vision
- Improved knowledge of the firm's culture, history, and traditions
- Project management training
- Improved understanding of the company's value drivers
- Awareness of financial constraints
- Development of teamwork

Conclusion

Future leaders won't look like the authoritarian "all-powerful bosses" of the past. Due to the shifting attitudes of followers, they'll need to develop a team and service mentality to get the most out of themselves and their companies. They'll need to be much more open to embracing change and to re-engineering and reinventing their companies as the business cycle shortens and the pace of change quickens. They'll need to develop their self-awareness, communication skills, team building skills, and conflict management skills more than ever before in order to be effective. They'll need to have a crystal clear vision of where they'll want to take the company in the future; if there are multiple leaders, executives, or owners, they'll need to have a common shared vision. They'll need a consistency to their lives which keeps them moving toward achieving their vision in spite of the chaos which goes on around them. Leadership development requires time, energy and effort. It takes time to reflect, to work on yourself, and to work with and on the people around you. On the subject of leadership Winston Churchill said: "You must continually drive the vast machine forward at its utmost speed. To lose momentum is not merely to stop, but to fall." Passion and a well developed sense of urgency must be parts of the mix.

Building Block #2 – Self Management and Leadership Development

Executive Summary

⇨ Good self management is a must for an aspiring business leader. Don't rely only on yourself to make the determination of whether or not you're a good self manager. Use objective tools, instruments, or professionals to assess and improve. If you can't manage yourself, you can't manage anything!

⇨ A key component of self management is time management. Keep a time log for a business week or 2, and you'll be shocked at how little time you actually spend on high payoff activities

⇨ Learn time mastery tools and techniques, and apply them

⇨ Determine what your highest payoff business and family activities are and DO THEM FIRST!

⇨ Develop your own leadership skills and those of other high potential family or closely held business performers

⇨ Be wary of some of the pervasive leadership myths which may hold you and your company back

Chapter Four
Building Block #3 – People Management

If it's true that family and closely held businesses fail at an alarming rate and fail to reach their potential at an even greater rate, surely one of the biggest reasons is not having the right people on the team who can help an entrepreneur steer the ship properly. Most closely held companies are severely constrained by their inability to get great talent to complement that of the founder or the founding family. Among the very biggest constraints on maximizing family business potential is the lack of know-how on how to get great talent. Without great people, an entrepreneur or a family can only go so far. Since, as we've established, most entrepreneurs manage tasks and activities, they rarely focus on hiring the right kind of people or managing them for maximum performance.

Good To Great has proven to be one of the all-time biggest business blockbusters. If an executive came to me and asked me to give him a one-line synopsis of the entire book, I'd say it comes down to this: **get the right people on your bus – and get the wrong people off!** Collins says flatly, "People are not your most important asset. *The right people are.*" He also says:

> "The good to great leaders understood three simple truths. First, if you begin with 'who' rather than 'what', you can more easily adapt to a changing world. Second, if you have the right people on the bus, the problem of how to motivate and manage people largely goes away. The right people don't need to be tightly managed or fired up; they will be self-motivated by the inner drive to produce the best results and to be part of creating something great. Third, if you have the wrong people, it doesn't matter whether you discover the right direction; you still won't have a great company."

Attracting and managing the right people, people who are passionate about being excellent at what they do, will ultimately differentiate the sustainable closely held company from those that flounder.

In order to achieve this goal of getting the right people on the bus, you will need to develop a completely new "degree of sheer rigor" in order to ramp up your recruiting, hiring, management, and communication processes. Getting the right people on your bus doesn't happen by accident; it requires intelligent design. Treating HR in your company as a necessary evil is no way to build a sustainable business. In fact, Collins found another model which competed with the Good to Great one. He called it the "genius with a thousand helpers" model. In this form of business:

> "The company's a platform for the talents of an extraordinary individual. The towering genius, the primary driving force in the company's success, is a great asset – as long as the genius sticks around. The geniuses seldom build great management teams for the simple reason that they don't need one, and often don't want one."

Collins was describing leaders of public corporations, but he could just as easily have been describing the typical entrepreneur in a closely held business. Entrepreneurs, especially first generation entrepreneurs, do have a type of genius that allows them to formulate a vision, work tirelessly toward it, and juggle an inhuman number of responsibilities in order to make their visions reality. As an aside, one interesting tidbit in Collins' research was that:

> "The good to great executives received slightly less total cash compensation 10 years after the transition than their counterparts at the still mediocre comparison companies! We found no systematic pattern linking executive compensation to the process of going from good to great. The evidence simply does not support the idea that the specific structure of executive compensation acts as a key lever in taking a company from good to great."

We don't believe that Collins' research in any way indicates that executives don't feel that they should be paid competitive wages and have competitive opportunities. However, the theory that monetary compensation alone motivates managers to greater heights simply doesn't hold water.

If entrepreneurs could do it all themselves, they probably would. They trust themselves, their instincts, and their talents more than they could ever trust anyone else – even other family members. According to Harnish, 96% of all firms have fewer than 10 employees, and a majority has fewer than 3. Apparently, the decision to grow isn't an easy one.

At speaking events, we have challenged and confronted audiences with the statement, *"What most of you in this audience have is not a business but a job!"* Most leaders of family and closely held companies have operations which are completely dependent on them to make every decision no matter how small. Most take little, if any, vacation time, and even when they're on vacation they're still tethered to their companies by cell phones and email. The business is front and center in their brains, 24 hours a day, 7 days a week, 365 days per year. If they were removed from their positions for whatever reason, the company would stand very little chance of continuing, and you can bet that senior managers – even family managers – would be polishing up their resumes and seeking employment elsewhere. The traditional organization chart shaped like a rough pyramid actually looks like an *inverted* pyramid for most of these entrepreneurs. The continued success of the organization rests squarely on their shoulders, and unplugging the chief executive from the model would cause the entire house of cards to collapse.

The purpose of this book is to change this model from entrepreneurs having jobs to having real businesses, that is, businesses that are not dependent on one or a tiny handful of people for their continued success. A business, by definition, is perpetual. It's not easy to help an entrepreneur transition from having a job to having a sustainable business, but it can be done, and one of the building blocks is getting the right people on the bus.

Maxwell talks about how assessing and changing the people around him led to explosive growth in a church he headed. Looking at his leadership team, he determined that some weren't of the quality necessary to help grow the church. He removed weak leaders in favor of stronger ones. He said:

> "Almost as soon as I made the initial staff changes in 1981, we started growing again. In fewer than 10 years, the church became 3 times the size it had been when it started. And the annual budget, which was $800,000 when I arrived, grew to more than $5 million a year."

He realized that the biggest determinant of the church's success was not him as the entrepreneurial minister; it was the impact of the quality of the leadership team beyond just him. Whether you're building a church or a company, this iron law of business building is the same.

There is a "war for talent" afoot. Part of the reason that attracting and retaining good people is difficult and will become even more difficult in the

71

future is simple demographics. Growth in the economy at the rate of about 2% over the next 15 years will increase demand for executives by about one-third. However, the supply of executives is moving in the opposite direction. According to McKinsey and Company, "The number of 35 to 45 year olds in the United States will decline by 15% between the years 2000 and 2015. Moreover, no significant countervailing trends are apparent. Women are no longer surging into the workforce, white collar productivity improvements have flattened, immigration levels are stable, and executives are not prolonging their careers." Another demographic trend is job mobility. In previous generations, talented executives may have changed jobs only once or twice over their whole careers. Now, executives average working for 5 companies; as time goes by, they may work for 10 or more. Finally, recruiting and retaining top talent hasn't always been the highest priority of closely held companies. While a closely held business owner may have a rigorous maintenance schedule for vehicles and machinery, the maintenance schedule for evaluating, encouraging, and coaching talented employees is usually non-existent. It's one of those things that happens "whenever I get around to it."

Getting the right people on the bus has to become an absolute burning passion. Interestingly, one of McKinsey's research findings actually notes a significant advantage small companies have in attracting top talent. Big companies today find themselves competing for executives with entrepreneurial organizations. An executive at AlliedSignal said, "We're competing with start-ups, not General Electric." When we seek talent at The Family Business Institute, we always ask the question, "Why would you want to work for a small company like ours when someone with your talent, background, and resume could go work for virtually any Fortune 500 business?" The answer almost always points to one thing: *impact*. Today's talented executive wants to be in a role where she can directly see the impact her effort produces. That's sometimes very hard to do when you're simply a cog in a great machine. In a company with only 50 or 500 employees, impact is much easier observed than in a massive organization. This is certainly a hopeful fact for small businesses.

Most entrepreneurial companies have comparatively little structure in place in order to attract, retain, and manage talent. Usually the HR job falls to the entrepreneur herself or a trusted senior manager. Since we've already learned that the number one constraint for most closely held business leaders is time, this is simply one more job they don't have time to do the way they would like it done. The question arises, how many people can a talented executive manage directly? Today's family business leader usually manages *all* his employees directly for all practical purposes. Danco, pioneer of the family business consulting industry, concluded that most family businesses have organization charts that look like giant rakes; all employees report directly to the owner. This model of organization chart – irrespective of how elaborate the chart may look on paper – still prevails today. Most businesses hit a ceiling at around 20 to 25 employees. That's the point at which even the most talented entrepreneur can no longer manage every employee and every corporate function directly. The military has spent decades and millions upon millions of dollars studying span of control, and, depending on which branch of the service you ask, an effective leader can manage no more than 8 to 14 people at any given time. In order to develop the capability of getting the right people on the bus, closely held company leaders must develop a system for adequately recruiting, evaluating, hiring, managing, and communicating with top talent. There must be infrastructure in place, or these critical human resources tasks can't get done effectively. The beauty of having a system coupled with intense self and time management (Building Block #2) is that the talent level in an entrepreneurial organization will rise quickly, and the leaders will find less pressure on themselves to do everything, be everything, and manage everything. Getting the right talent on the bus is as liberating a thing as any entrepreneur can hope to do. The difference is either to work, work, work, or to create a business that works.

Family business leaders should give thought to how they represent their jobs to next generation family members who may be interested in coming aboard. 80 hour work weeks and obsessive attention to every detail in the organization no matter how small may not seem like a very attractive career to young people today. As one next generation family business candidate put it:

> "The more I watched what my father does for a living and the way he does it, the less enthusiastic I got about joining the company. The sacrifices he has to make in order to keep all the balls in the air at the same time are just amazing. It really isn't a very attractive position."

To develop a sustainable closely held company, entrepreneurs must realize that they will not, in all likelihood, be able to clone themselves. Simply substituting a daughter who needs to work 80 hours per week for a senior generation family member who currently works 80 hours per week imprisons her in the same job (not business). Senior generation family members must be careful how they market the attractiveness of entry into the family business. If they are continually complaining about long hours, unappreciative employees, cutthroat competition, and fickle customers, those teenagers and young adults may not find the family business a very desirable place.

If closely held company leaders spend too much of their valuable time working IN the business versus ON the business, where *should* they spend their time? We discussed this issue in Chapter Three where we outlined the top 10 duties and responsibilities of a business-building CEO. Reviewing and compiling the recommendations of several time management and executive coaching gurus, here is an additional guideline for where leaders should spend their time:

- 10% finance and "administrivia"
- 20% working in the business (helping sell new business, evaluating new equipment purchases, managing projects directly, designing systems and processes, etc.)
- 30% hiring, coaching, evaluating, managing, and training others
- 20% client relations
- 20% marketing and business development.

This recommendation isn't meant to be hard and fast. Some entrepreneurs may spend a bit more time on one function than another. However, this is a good guideline; it would be easy enough to keep a time log for a couple of weeks and compare the way you actually spend your time with these guidelines. Another disclaimer about this list: if, as Covey recommends, an executive is to spend about 20% to 25% of his time in Quadrant II (planning and preparation), where does that fit into this list? Planning, preparation, and strategy development will be part of the 30% of the time you spend in hiring and coaching. Also, certain activities of the 20% of your time you spend in marketing and business development and client relations could fall into Quadrant II time. Our list doesn't in any way conflict with Covey's admonition. Rather, we agree that planning and preparation are key elements to have a successful business and a successful life.

If the point of all this is to create a sustainable closely held business, then doing things the way that Granddad and Dad did them – even though those things may have been successful for them – will likely prove less useful in the future. Over the years, dozens upon dozens of prospective clients have described their family and business situations as being "at a crossroads." The crossroads, even though they may not have strictly identified it as such, is that tipping point where they realize that they're maxed out, spend all their time working IN the business, have not found the entrepreneurial freedom they so crave, and need a new how-to manual for how to get it done. Blasting past this tipping point requires getting the right people on your bus.

Myths and Misconceptions about People Management

The Definition of Stewardship

Most family and closely held business owners feel a real sense of stewardship about their companies and their employees. This presents a double-edged sword. On the one hand, stewardship requires thrift and a constant effort to keep expenses down. Hiring new people and adding staff means spending money for which the entrepreneur can't expect a rate of return right away. On the other hand, there is natural human reluctance to fire or discipline an under-performing employee because the owner knows him at a personal level; he knows the employee's wife and children and may attend the same church or be in a civic club with the employee's father. Letting the under-performing employee go might be defined as a failure of stewardship ("maybe we could work harder to make him successful, maybe he just needs another opportunity, or maybe it's my fault for not motivating him properly or giving him the right tools to do his job").

We'll look at the first side of the stewardship responsibility in another section, but let's take a moment to focus on the second half of the equation. A more realistic, purer definition of stewardship was recently related to us by a Methodist minister. He had just taken over a new church, and the staff was populated by managers who had been in their positions a long time, had become quite comfortable and routine in their view of their jobs, and cost the church money in salary, benefits, etc. The pastor said it was a *violation* of stewardship to use scarce and valuable church resources on people who weren't committed to their jobs or performing at a high level. It wasn't fair to the other members of the administrative staff, the congregation, or to the church in general to have these people in positions of responsibility where they became choke points and created more problems than they solved. It was a better definition of stewardship to let these people go so they could enjoy their retirement or find other positions more suited to their talents and energies. As Collins wrote: "Letting the wrong people hang around is unfair to all the right people. To let people languish in uncertainty for months or years, stealing precious time in their lives that they could use to move on to something else when in the end they aren't going to make it anyway – that would be ruthless." For many business owners, a transformation of their definitions of stewardship is in order to get the right people on the bus.

Looking at Hiring Employees As a Cost, Not As an Investment

A construction company owner had built his enterprise from the ground up to about $15 million in sales per year. As the company grew, so did the demands on the owner's time. When the company was smaller, he could personally estimate and project manage virtually all of the work. Now that the company had grown, he had hired competent superintendents to oversee the work in the field, but he was still retaining almost 100% of the estimating duties while simultaneously being the company's only business developer and the head of administration, IT, HR, customer service, planning, safety education, etc. In short, the owner was overwhelmed with all his responsibilities.

To compound matters, his wife and children were feeling ignored, and there was significant pressure from home to cut back on the 90 hour work weeks in favor of investing time and love in the family and watching the children grow up. When we asked why he was reluctant to hire a full time estimator who could relieve him of a minimum of 20 to 30 hours a week, he said he was currently making about $450,000 a year. The way he viewed a new hire is that he would have to spend between $65,000 and $80,000 per year to get a good estimator in place not to mention the time it would require to recruit, hire, and train. He viewed the expense of adding the new employee as a direct reduction in the profitability of the firm which had a direct impact on his own personal compensation.

There were many questions which required discussion: What would the impact of hiring a new employee be on the owner's family and home life? Why is it so important to have a high personal compensation level when you're never at home or away from work to enjoy it? What's the real economic benefit of hiring a full time estimator? Let's look at a side-by-side Return on Investment (ROI) analysis of the economic benefits of a new hire relative to a marketplace investment that the owner could have made with his high personal compensation (*Figure 4.1*).

The company owner had sufficient personal income to make a $50,000 speculative investment. He estimated the "cost" of a new, full time estimator at $65,000 per year. The investment had to be paid all up front with after tax dollars. The new employee could be paid for with pretax dollars and, furthermore, could be paid in bi-monthly installments. If the employee failed to work out in 90 days, the entrepreneur would be out about $16,250 instead of $50,000. He had little opportunity to control and supervise his investment, but he had enormous ability to control and supervise the new employee. His guaranteed rate of return with the speculative investment was technically zero. His guarantee of return with a new employee was quite high assuming proper orientation and training. His ROI goal for an investment was about 15% over time. His ROI goal for a new estimator was about 300% within 12 months. In other words, the estimator should produce gross sales above and beyond the cost of his salary within 12 months. The outside investment would have no immediate impact on the owner's work or home lives, while the new employee would allow the FBO to spend 20 fewer hours at work per week or 20 more hours at home pursuing the quality of life he and his family desired. Other benefits for hiring a new estimator were that there would be fewer estimating mistakes due to the specialization and time devoted to the task on the part of the new employee and the freedom, if he so chose, for the owner to focus more of his time and effort on his primary talent - business development.

Figure 4.1

ROI Analysis		
	"Investment"	*"Cost"*
Dollars expended	$50,000	$65,000
Tax status	after tax	before tax
Cash flow requirement	all up front	paid in bi-monthly installments
Control and supervision over investment	None	high
Guarantee of return	None	reasonably high
Return on investment goal	15% over time	300% within 12 months
Impact on FBO's work life	none in short run	20 fewer hours in work week
Impact on FBO's family life	none in short run	20 more hours pursuing quality of life
Other benefits	feelings of importance as a big ticket investor	fewer estimating mistakes due to specialization and sufficient time to devote to task freedom for FBO to focus more on business development, other CEO activities

Can a company be too fat and have too many employees? Of course it can. However, most family businesses tend to be on the opposite end of the spectrum and have too few productive employees which requires entrepreneurs to wear too many hats. Getting the right people on the bus means right-sizing the company and distinguishing between what's truly an investment and what's really a cost.

The Ceiling of Complexity

Most entrepreneurs run into Dan Sullivan's Ceiling of Complexity™ many times during their entrepreneurial careers. The Ceiling of Complexity™ refers to the point at which the entrepreneur feels trapped, dislocated, anxious, and overwhelmed by all the many and varied tasks he must do in the course of a typical work day. He's just not able to put his hands on all the things that need doing in the growing business, and, no matter how hard he works, the job simply becomes too much.

There are only 2 ways to break through the Ceiling of Complexity™. One is to make a conscious decision to retreat and take the $15 million construction company (in the example above) back to a manageable level of $3 million or $4 million in sales. The other alternative is to burst through the ceiling by investing in people and delegating responsibilities so the owner is free to focus more of his energy and talent on the things he does best. Doing that requires getting the right people on the bus.

Lack of Knowledge About How to Hire Great People
(or "We've tried to hire people in the past, but they never seem to work out")

Most entrepreneurs think they know how to hire people; after all, they hired a couple of other key employees when the company was getting off the ground. However, entrepreneurs are poor indeed at hiring *great* talent. They're not good at attracting the next superstar; they're not good at finding their Scotty Pippin to complement Michael Jordan. One reason they're not good at hiring top-level talent lies in the typical closely held business hiring process which looks as follows:

1. Due to an HR need, the business runs an application in the local newspaper resulting in 4 or 5 applicants
2. The owner interviews the 4 to 5 applicants. Only one or 2 meet minimum standards
3. The applicants take a drug test, and one hopefully passes it
4. The entrepreneur makes a call or 2 to check references. Sometimes these calls are returned
5. Due to the need to put a warm body in place, the owner hires the least offensive of the none too impressive candidates
6. With minimal orientation, training, or supervision, the owner hopes for the best result for this new employee. A certain percentage of hires do manage to hang on to their jobs, and the owner attributes high turnover to the economy, the industry, or life in general without any objective measurement tools by which to judge. Other business leaders brag about their low turnover, but this often means they are burdened with large numbers of marginal performers and don't often prune their talent trees

This is no recipe for finding great talent! The owner treats the hiring process as a necessary evil which steals time away from the activities he loves to do whether it's building structures, producing machine tools, fabricating metal, delivering tax or planning advice, or developing new property. In the long run, no one can do it alone.

Part of the problem rests with the popular business press which talks about different methodologies for recruiting and hiring as if any one of them were a panacea. *Figure 4.2* discusses the various methodologies promoted by the business press and the pros and cons of each methodology.

78

Figure 4.2

Recruiting and Hiring Methodology		
	Pros	**Cons**
word of mouth	1. simple 2. inexpensive 3. fast placement	1. limited reach 2. does not take advantage of available talent pool 3. often gets square peg which FBO must shoehorn into round hole 4. no attempt or assurance of team "fit"
networking	1. simple 2. inexpensive 3. fast placement	1. limited reach 2. does not take advantage of available talent pool 3. often gets square peg which FBO must shoehorn into round hole 4. no attempt or assurance of team "fit"
headhunter	1. someone else screens 2. some have track record	1. expensive 2. no attempt or assurance of team "fit" 3. no personality or quality assessments
newspaper advertising	1. simple 2. inexpensive	1. limited reach 2. no attempt or assurance of team "fit" 3. often gets square peg which FBO must shoehorn into round hole 4. generally poor results 5. limited space to describe job, company, etc
web based resume services	1. unlimited, global reach 2. inexpensive 3. room for full position and company description 4. virtually instantaneous resume results	1. no attempt or assurance of team "fit" 2. no screening or assessment of applicants beyond resume 3. perhaps too many choices 4. produces many unqualified applicants
21st century recruiting and hiring	1. extensive analysis of company needs 2. extensive development of "ideal" 3. extensive personality and quality assessments 4. extensive practical assessment of candidates 5. proven methodology for determining fit 6. reduction of failed hires and turnover	1. complex 2. time consuming 3. expensive 4. requires patience and deliberation 5. requires team involvement

The first 4 methodologies, word of mouth, networking, headhunters, and newspaper advertising, are the methodologies most typically used by private business owners to find talent. The list of pros for these is relatively short while the list of cons for each one is relatively long. The main issue for each is that they don't have reach beyond the locality or resources of the entrepreneur, newspaper, or headhunter, and, while they sometimes find talented people, they provide no methodology for assuring a good fit with the specific job and with the existing company culture and team. They also have the shortcoming of not providing any sort of practical or personality assessments to assure a good fit.

The final two methodologies are rarely used by the family and closely held business owner, but, taken in combination, provide an incredibly powerful tool for getting the right people on the bus.

I Could Never Train a New Hire To Be as Effective as I Am

This is a common lament. Consider the example of an executive who does 100% of the business development work for his firm. He says, "I'm the best salesman we could possibly have; I could never teach anyone else to be as good as me because I know everything about this business." He may be right. Let's undertake an analysis of what it would mean to hire a salesperson who is considerably less talented than the family business executive.

Referring to *Figure 4.3*, the entrepreneur, because of all the spinning plates he has to manage, only has about 10 hours a week available for business development. A new hire would have an entire 40 hour work week to devote to the task. The executive has an average value per closed deal of $10,000. The new hire's average value per closed deal is 40% less or $6,000. The entrepreneur can close a deal in only 5 hours whereas it may take 10 hours for the new hire to do so. And finally, the entrepreneur can close 2 deals per week in the 10 hours available while the new employee, even though much less efficient than the entrepreneur, can close 4 deals per week. That means the gross revenue per week is $20,000 for the entrepreneur while it is $24,000 or 20% higher for the new employee. Working 50 weeks per year in this simplified example, the new employee creates $200,000 of additional gross revenue in the first year while costing the firm $80,000 in compensation and benefits. The net improvement to the firm is $120,000.

Will the entrepreneur be able to cease all business development activities immediately upon hiring the new employee? Of course not. There will be a gradual process of the entrepreneur reducing his effort while the new employee ramps up. One must also expect that the new employee will become more efficient in his job as he learns more about it. Therefore, he eventually should approach the entrepreneur in terms of value per closed deal and in time required to convert a prospect into a paying customer. In other words, in future years the new employee should become more and more valuable to the firm. This example deals only with sales; consider if it was applied to other departments. The point is that busy entrepreneurs, while amazingly good at the variety of tasks they undertake in a given work week, simply can't be everywhere doing everything. Bringing on talented new employees who can focus their efforts more precisely pays dividends all around.

Figure 4.3

The Power of FOCUSED Effort		
	Self	Potential Employee
Time available to sell	10/hrs week	40 hrs/week
Value of deal closed	$10,000	$6,000
Time required to convert suspect into a customer	5 hrs	10 hrs
Sales per week	2	4
Gross revenue per week	$20,000	$24,000
Additional gross revenue year 1	n/a	$200,000
Additional "cost" year 1	n/a	$80,000

All the Books Say That the Most Successful Companies Promote From Within.
That's What We Want to Do

The reason this is a problem for most middle market companies is they simply aren't large enough. Think about it; taking a typical $10 million company with 60 employees, there probably isn't enough talent on board to help the company grow to $25 million. Furthermore, it's likely that no one in the company has ever managed a $25 million company before; they simply know neither what it would take to run a company which is 2.5 times larger nor how to get there. In addition, most of the people are already working at their limits. It's unrealistic to ask them to work at their limits and, oh by the way, take on important new responsibilities as the company embarks on an accelerated growth path. Most of the articles people read about promoting from within are written about extremely large companies which have talent pools of hundreds if not thousands of executives. In order to go from the current level to a new one, closely held companies are generally going to have to seek talent from outside their current employee base.

The Best Way to Hire New Talent Is to Evaluate the Applicants' Credentials.

This is a dangerous myth. There's probably nothing more common in the business world than a highly credentialed underperformer. Furthermore, credentials speak absolutely nothing about how the individual is going to fit with your existing and future company cultures. Credentials tell you nothing about the person's ability to execute (other than getting advanced degrees and certifications). Larry Bossidy, former CEO of AlliedSignal says, "I feel strongly that the interview is the most flawed process in American business." That's a perceptive statement, and interviews are often based – you guessed it – on what appears in a person's resume. As we'll see later, an executive who aspires to build her company from its current condition to a sustainable one will need to learn to embrace a new system for getting the right talent on the bus, and, in that system, credentials are just the tip of the iceberg.

A 21st Century Recruiting and Hiring System

There are 5 discrete steps in the 21st century recruiting and hiring action plan (followed immediately by a 6th which calls for creating a separate orientation and training action plan). There are between 2 and 9 specific action steps in each of the 5 priority objectives. In walking through the action plan, some family business owners have been intimidated or surprised by the sheer number of steps necessary to get great people on the bus. It does seem daunting on initial examination; however, each step has a specific purpose leading toward the goal of hiring an outstanding new team member who'll be committed and focused on company goals for the foreseeable future. Ultimately, rigorous screening, interviewing, assessment, and evaluation will lead to a higher quality hire, and the front end investment of money, time, and energy will be well worth it.

What about older employees who have been on board for a long time, and who weren't hired using such an extensive plan? The new 21st century hiring process isn't a reflection on anything you've done in the past. Rather, it's a new way of finding people who are going to fit with other employees and the team culture you've created. It's not meant to upend or upset anything or anybody currently on the payroll; this is simply a new tool to use as you create a different business for a different future.

The 5 specific priority objectives are:

1. Write a job description
2. Define the target candidate
3. Determine the search process
4. Develop the candidate interview, screening, and review process
5. Evaluate and hire

A typical action plan for hiring a middle manager or higher could take between 35 to 40 man hours and should have direct costs from about $1,000 to $3,000 not including the time invested by the leader and his team interviewing the candidates (nor the costs of using outside resources like consultants or other advisors). The action plan usually takes about 90 days from start to finish. That seems like an awfully long time, but it takes that long to deliberately go through all the action steps and to have the candidate properly evaluated and screened. The process could be shortened to 45 to 60 days in the event of an urgent need for a critical hire.

We will now take each priority objective in order and flesh out the action tasks that support the objectives.

Write the Job Description

We can hear the snorts of derision now: "Why should we write a job description for this person? If he's experienced, he'll know what to do." Or "why should we go to the trouble of writing a job description? We'll merely put it in a drawer and never use it after we get the person on board." The job description isn't merely a piece of paper that you put into a personnel file and never refer to again! THE JOB DESCRIPTION IS A TOOL TO MANAGE AND EVALUATE YOUR EMPLOYEE.

A good job description (*Figure 4.4*) is a 3 to 4 page document which is exhaustive in job details, what the working conditions are like, what the essential functions of the job are, what the measures of performance are, and the specific job duties and tasks the candidate will be expected to perform along with a timeline of when she'll be expected to perform them. The job description is a valuable management tool which keeps both the employer and the employee on the same page and mutually accountable. That's not to say it's engraved in stone and can never change or be adapted; however, when a new employee comes on board everyone needs to be crystal clear about what's expected and when it's expected. The following is a discussion of what a good job description should

83

contain with some brief comments so you'll be in a position to take it and create your own job description template.

The first step in writing a job description is to brainstorm what is necessary for successful completion of the job. In fact, a step prior to that may be brainstorming what sort of job would most benefit the company and the management team. If you have previous versions of job descriptions which served you well, they could be used as templates for developing the new one.

Step 2 is to actually draft the job description. The outline found in *Figure 4.4* can be used as a guide.

Step 3 is to design the compensation system for the position. If the compensation for the position is all base, it's a fairly simple task. If you're not sure what competitive base pay is for the position you're seeking to fill, it's easy enough to do a bit of internet research via the U.S. Department of Labor or other internet services to find out what constitutes competitive pay for employees in your area.

If the job is an incentive position such as a general manager, a marketing or sales executive, project manager, or others, it's important to design and test the incentive system. The system can be tested by simply running different spreadsheet scenarios. Closely held business owners are often surprised when, after designing a compensation system they thought quite reasonable, the employee is making $200,000 or $300,000 per year because they exceeded the expectation of the owner. Compensation systems should be tested for extreme success, modest case success, and worst-case scenarios so that you will be well versed in the full range of outcomes depending on the employee's actual performance. All 3 steps above could and should be brainstormed with the senior management team to get the benefit of everyone's thinking and experience.

Step 4 is to rough out the job description and then edit it until it's in satisfactory form. Ultimately the job description will go into the position manual which you'll hand the employee on his first day on the job as the first tool to use in orientation and training.

Define the Target Candidate

If the hire is for a position you've already filled several times in the past, you should already have a successful target candidate "model" in mind. It's easy, for example, to think of your top 2 or 3 salesmen and wish for a clone that could be reasonably expected to replicate their successes. To take it a step further, if you have several successful employees on board in a particular position, there are assessment instruments that allow you to zero in on the skills and talents that make them successful and quantify those characteristics. That will give you a predictor of future candidates' prospects for success. Those that don't meet the profile of the existing employees must have a compelling case to get hired. Otherwise, you'll rely on the template of successful employees to be your indicator.

If it's a new position, you'll need to define the qualities you seek in the candidate. An employer needs to have a picture in his mind of what a successful candidate looks like. While one shouldn't be rigid in this area, it is helpful to know what you're looking for in order to maximize your chances of finding it.

Determine the Search Process

The first step is to write an ad. If it's an old-fashioned newspaper classified ad, you'll need to write a short, concise description because print media charges by space to run the ad. If you're going to use electronic media for posting the ad, your space requirements are virtually unlimited. Electronic and internet job postings have revolutionized the ability to search for employees. In the past, a newspaper ad could produce a half dozen to a dozen applicants for a particular job; it's not unusual now to get 50 to 150 applicants for that same position. All other things being equal, the bigger the talent pool at your disposal the better choice you're likely to make; you're more apt to find a Michael Jordan from a talent pool of 150 than you are from a talent pool of 6. Using the internet based job search engines can allow you to expand your geographic scope for hiring from your locality to all over the world. An employer posted a white-collar job on the internet and found that he was getting applications from as far away as Sri Lanka! He certainly didn't expect to cast his net that wide, but was extremely pleased to find that his posting presented that kind of visibility.

It's often best to set up a blind email box and have all applicants respond with a cover letter and resume via email. You don't want dozens of applicants ringing your phone and faxing you night and day!

For some employers, the thought of getting 100 to 150 applications is quite intimidating. To reduce the intimidation factor and to make this task manageable, the next step is, based on your development in the previous step of the ideal target candidate, screen the resumes into 3 categories: A, B, and C. The As are the closest matches on paper to the ideal target candidate. The Bs could work in a pinch, and the Cs don't appear to have the right qualifications. Ideally this step will trim down the applications to about 20% of the overall total.

Following the resume screening process, the employer should develop telephone interview questions for use in the next step. These questions could be quite general or quite specific; it's a matter of personal preference. A list of 10 telephone interview questions is generally sufficient because you'll limit the telephone interview time to about 30 minutes in order to be efficient.

Figure 4.4

Job Description (Sample)

A. *Title for the Position*
B *Department*
C. *Reporting Relationships*
   1.   To whom is the employee accountable? If more than one person, be sure to list all of them.
D. *A three or four line description of the job…*
E. *Requirements*
   1.   Education
      a.   Minimum required
      b.   Preferred
   2.   Licensing/Registration/Certification/Credentials
      a.   Minimum required
      b.   Preferred
   3.   Experience
      a.   Minimum required
      b.   Preferred
   4.   Skills, Knowledge, and Ability
      a.   Minimum required
      b.   Preferred
   5.   Physical
      This is the description of the physical requirements of the job. For a truck driver, as an example, the physical requirement is the ability to sit for extended periods of time. If there's heavy lifting or specialized skills like typing involved in the job, they should be listed and enumerated here.
   6.   Mental
      In this section the employer should list the required mental skills such as language skills, mathematics skills, industry or job specific skills, or other mental processing skills that are necessary for successful performance.
F. *Working Conditions*
   Describes extended periods out of town to make sales calls on prospects, for example. Some jobs require time outdoors while other jobs are exclusively office environments.

G. *Essential Functions - Authority*

The authority section should clearly delineate the functions in which the employee has sole or shared authority to make decisions. The employer could place dollar limits or scope limits on the employee with respect to his responsibility.

H. *Other Requirements*

Here the employer could list any other requirements he thinks are necessary for the successful applicant. There could be specific references here to team play and successful interaction with other employees, or there could be references to periodic requirements to work weekends or other long or unusual hours.

I. *Key Measures of Performance*

Here the employer lists the criteria with which he's going to measure the employee's success. These could entail any number of different things: for a CPA, one of the items could be realization rate. For a construction project manager, an item could be percentage of jobs completed on time and on budget. For a sales and marketing executive, the number of new client relationships developed each month is a measure, and for a general manager the target could be adherence to budget numbers and/or profitability targets. There should be 5 to 8 measures of job performance. They should be easy enough to calculate so that the employee can periodically keep up with her own performance and know how things are progressing whether there's direct feedback from the manager or not.

J. *Job Duties and Task List*

This is a matrix with 5 columns. The first column is "duties and tasks performed" followed by a vertical list of all duties and tasks expected from the position. The next 4 columns are labeled "daily," "weekly," "monthly," and "other." The employer can then put a checkmark in the appropriate column so that the employee will know when the respective duties are to be performed. For example, in the case of hiring a marketing executive, there might be a weekly meeting with the FBO to discuss new business, new developments, problems that may have arisen, etc. There may be other meetings which take place monthly or quarterly. This simple, one page matrix allows the employer and the employee to literally be on the same page with respect to the execution and timing of job duties and tasks.

The Candidate Interview Screening and Review Process

For that top 10% of attractive candidates, it's now time to schedule 30 minute telephone appointments with each of them to further whittle down the talent pool. Since all the candidates have sent their cover letters and resumes to you via email, it's easy enough to reply that they've made the initial cut and you'd welcome the chance to talk to them on the phone. Block off a day or 2 in specific 30 minute chunks of time, and give those dates and times to the prospective interviewees. They'll then select a time that is mutually convenient. For those applicants who don't respond, don't worry; your talent pool should be sizable enough to not be adversely effected if you never hear from one or 2.

Using the telephone interview questions you developed, conduct the telephone appointment. Ask the applicants the same questions in order to develop some consistency of response. Batch the telephone interviews whenever possible. For example, it's better to get them all done on a Tuesday than doing one Tuesday followed by 2 on each of the following days of the week. By the end of the week you won't remember who've you've talked to or who seemed attractive relative to the others. In case you haven't already figured it out, it's vitally important to take good notes. The old cliché is that even the dullest pencil is sharper than the best memory.

After you've done the first round of telephone appointments, you should be in a position to reject about half of those who made the first cut. For example, if there were 100 initial applicants, and you were about to cut out 85% of the resumes for one reason or another (placing them in categories B or C), there are 15 applicants still in the mix. After conducting the telephone appointments, the ideal scenario would be to cut that group down to 6, 7, or 8 final applicants which you'll interview face-to-face as soon as possible.

Handle the personal interviews in the same way you handled the telephone interviews; block off days and times when you're available. Since you cast your talent search wide, many applicants may have to travel to you for their interviews. It's customary for the employer to pick up the travel and overnight lodging costs of those who have to travel. Those expectations are reflected in the costs discussed previously and should not be budget-busters.

Conduct the first round of personal interviews; each interview should be approximately 90 minutes to 2 hours. Using the list of interview questions you've developed, add to it by developing resume-specific questions based on the candidate, experience, and previous positions. You'll also need to give the applicant a brief thumbnail of what your company is, does, and seeks to become. The goal of the first round of personal interviews is to cut the list of applicants from 7 to about 3. Don't notify the unsuccessful applicants quite yet; you might want to come back to them depending on how you perceive the quality of the rest of the interviews.

For those who have made it to the next round, have them come back for a second visit and interview. At this point you've developed your businessperson's intuition, and you think you know what you're dealing with. Put those feelings on hold, and be very thorough in asking questions. It is also appropriate at this stage to conduct any sort of psychological profiles you want to do. Among the most common are the Myers Briggs Type Indicator, the FIRO-B, the Kolbe, the DISC, or other commercial psychological profiling instruments that can give you a glimpse into how your applicant thinks and behaves. If you're not familiar with these instruments or haven't used them in the past, there are many professionals available who'd be happy to help you understand and complete the instruments and provide interpretation and guidance in the hiring process. Again this should not be a budget-buster. Now is the time to send kindly worded letters of rejection to the applicants who did not successfully advance.

If you're happy with your final talent pool of 3 or 4 applicants, give them assignments, evaluations, or skills tests. For example, give them an assignment that might take them 2 to 5 hours of their personal time; this is a test to see if they really want the job and can really produce the kind of output you're looking for. Don't skip this step even though it might seem like you're imposing on the applicants. Experience shows that most applicants who are professional and credible welcome this opportunity to show you what they can do; they know it helps set them apart from the competition.

Following the interpretation of the personality instruments and review of the skills test assignment, it's time to have the candidate back one more time to be interviewed by other team members. Why would a business owner have other employees interview a prospective hire? Isn't it the job of the owner of the business and well within this authority to hire and fire at will? Of course it is; but it's vital to have others visit with someone who may be joining the team to look for good fit and chemistry, background, skills, etc. Even if your mind is made up, and you choose a candidate against the advice of your other employees, you've still included them in the process and shown that you value their counsel and input. In other words, you're acting like a team leader as opposed to a dictator. Often, your employees will come back to you with insights and observations which you didn't expect and which may have an impact on your hiring decision. They also have networks of resources to allow them to check out the new applicant in ways that you had neither considered or been able to before.

Evaluate and Hire

After the 3 rounds of personal interviews, the personality assessments, and the skills tests, now is the time to check references provided by the applicant. Be advised that you're not going to get very much out of the references for most applicants. Everyone in today's society is afraid of being sued or saying something detrimental to the career of a former coworker. For the great applicants, you'll have no shortage of kind references which should give you confidence. However, if you can't find those outstanding references, alarm bells should be ringing.

It's also a good idea at this point to undertake a criminal background check. Let's face it; some people are great at hiding their past. One employer was sold on the skills of a potential sales manager candidate only to find out during the background check that he had a felony conviction for embezzling from a previous employer! It's a shame that he made such a mistake when he was younger, but that is an important piece of information that an employer must have in order to make a sound hiring decision.

After the references and background check, it's time to make a formal written offer. If you've used formal letters in the past for hiring, you can use those previous versions as your template. If not, a short, warm businesslike letter offering the top candidate the job is easy to produce. Again, don't throw out your second and third choices quite yet. There may be a reason why you and your top choice can't get together (i.e. because of money or because the applicant has taken another job). Assuming candidates 2 and 3 are well-qualified and good fits, there should be little if any fall off between your first choice and your third.

Things can get a little tricky here. There's a period of one to 2 weeks at this stage which will require negotiating the position. Most employers want employees who will work for a low base wage with high incentives. Most employees prefer a high base and low incentives so they can enjoy more predictability in their incomes. Don't be afraid to negotiate, and stick to your guns on what you think is right and appropriate. As Collins says in *Good to Great,* "If you have the right executives on the bus, they'll do everything within their power to build a great company, not because of what they will get for it, but because they simply cannot imagine settling for anything less." Great employees are motivated by the job itself, not by whether they can get a few dollars more.

If you don't feel good about the tone of the negotiations between you and the top candidate, move on to candidates 2 or 3. If they're as good as you think, they are likely getting job offers from other sources, so don't wait too long, or they may all get off the hook. That's not a crisis (especially because you have such a powerful new action plan), but it could represent an opportunity cost if you're not diligent in managing the process and in respecting the time and other needs of your candidates.

Depending on the position, it may be wise to have a non-compete agreement, non-solicitation agreement, or a confidentiality agreement with the new hire. Your attorney should have forms which he can draft in short order to cover any of these contingencies. If you intend to use one of these types of agreements, you should let the employee know that during the process.

During the negotiation period, you should be developing (or have already developed) the orientation and training plan for your new hire. If he's experienced, you can expect him to come in and be productive very early, but no employee feels comfortable leaping into a job without any sort of company orientation. Make sure you do all in your power to see to it that your time and energy investment in this new hire pays off and that he feels he's welcomed and a valuable member of the team from day one.

The 5 step action plan works best for middle management applicants and above. It has not proven to be as successful in attracting rank and file or low level employees; the traditional methods of seeking workers seem to work better with that particular cohort. However, if you're looking to take your company from good to great, simplify your life, have more freedom and quality in your life, this action plan can be a life saver and produce millions of dollars of results for you over time.

Now That You've Got Great Talent on Board, What Do You Do With Them?

Once you've got talented people on board, things just don't stop. You have to manage, communicate with, and evaluate them. This is the magic triumvirate of strong employee relations. In conducting employee surveys and employee meetings over the years, you'd be shocked at how many closely held company employees are crying out for evaluations. They truly want to know how they're doing and how they fit into the big picture of the company. Since, as Buckingham writes, "Confusion retards everything," every employee should have a thorough job description describing his scope of authority, how you will measure his performance (how you will hold him *accountable*), what his compensation system looks like (including variable and fixed compensation), and when you'll be meeting with him.

McKinsey and Company researched 115,000 employees at 231 companies around the world. They found there was one combination of practices which, utilized together, increased organizational effectiveness more than any others. The first of these organizational effectiveness practices was having "clear roles and responsibilities with accountability." That means that the job description typically used in most closely held companies – "whatever it takes" – isn't good enough. Having crystal clear roles and responsibilities supported by high quality job descriptions eliminates overlap, creates sound accountability measures, allows employees to self-manage, and makes disciplinary or firing actions much easier by removing subjectivity from the decision. The process takes time and energy, but the payoff is enormous, and, in today's increasingly complex world, you can't afford not to do it.

Developing clear roles and responsibilities is an across the board management task. In terms of individual management and how one relates to employees at a person to person level, Buckingham writes that the "one thing all great managers know about great managing is this: discover what is unique about each person and capitalize on it." Every employee is unique in his own way. They won't be motivated by the same things, aren't good at the same things, don't aspire to the same things, don't think in the same ways, and won't respond to you as a manager in the same ways. Identify and isolate the uniqueness in each employee, and appeal to that uniqueness in the context of how you encourage them to do their jobs; you'll find your management job is much easier. Doing this will require that most precious executive commodity: time. You'll have to invest a little more time in management by walking around and in getting to know people at an individual level. You'll have to invest time in coaching and observing to help them put your coaching tips into practice. You'll give your most responsible and productive performers more responsibility and more challenge. You'll get away from the habit of reserving every decision for yourself, and you'll refrain from second-guessing employees when they make minor mistakes. The job as a manager (which is quite different, as we have seen before, from the job of a leader) is to build your employees' self assurance and confidence. *Business Week* reports that this kind of individual investment in employees pays off. Employers who emphasized energy, engagement, and morale experienced 5 times the growth rate of employers with poor morale. If your goal is to build a sustainable enterprise, investing more of your executive time in building your people is a must.

Buckingham outlines some outstanding questions for you to use as a management engagement tool:

1. What was the best day at work you've had in the last 3 months? What were you doing? Why did you enjoy it so much?

2. What was your worst day at work in the last 3 months? What were you doing? Why did it grate on you so much?

3. What was the best relationship with a manager you've ever had? What made it work so well?

4. What was the best praise or recognition you've ever received? What made it so good?

5. When in your career do you think you were learning the most? Why did you learn so much? What's the best way for you to learn?

He notes that this "mini interview" will only take about half an hour, but it should be rich in terms of the information it produces.

The second task for developing a management system is to figure out how you're going to communicate with them. Let's first take a look at how *not* to communicate with them. A common way for executives to communicate with others on the team is to send out the dreaded memo, or today perhaps an email. Bosses think that if they send an email to everyone in the company, surely all will read it and take it to heart. But you have to ask some questions about how well memos – electronic or otherwise – work. Think through this cycle: how many actually received the memo? How many actually opened it? How many actually read it? How many actually read it with a high level of comprehension? How many agreed with the points made in the memo? How many internalized it? How many actually put it into practice along with all the other things they had to remember during that busy day? Written memos are certainly one way to communicate to others on your team, but it's not the only way, and it shouldn't be something on which you over-rely.

Over the years, several family business owners have said to me with glee in their voices, "I don't believe in meetings, and we don't have them here." They may even attribute their flexible management style as a factor in their success. I've never understood this. How can you communicate with 5 or 10 or 500 employees in your business effectively if you don't have meetings? Certainly there can be an overabundance of meetings, but they remain the most effective way to simultaneously deliver information to groups of people and to solicit the views and input of those people in a collaborative and efficient way. Harnish writes:

> "The predictable winners are those that have established a rhythm and a routine of having meetings. The faster they're growing, the more meetings they have. I'm talking about short, punchy meetings with a structure, time limits, and a specific agenda. This type of meeting doesn't leave you feeling bogged down. On the contrary! This type of meeting routine actually sets you free."

Most companies have staff meetings on a weekly or monthly basis. What they lack, however, is a full complement of meetings, each of which has a slightly different intended purpose which gives them an opportunity to communicate big picture items as well as routine, day to day items. We recommend that companies have the following 4 types of regularly scheduled, recurring meetings (scheduled well in advance):

1. *Weekly meetings*
   Weekly meetings can bring together an entire company if you're small. If your company is larger, the meetings will need to be done at the department level.
2. *Monthly meetings*

93

Monthly meetings should be used to deliver the company's "president's report" which lets everyone know how the company has done in the last 30 days, how the company is doing relative to goal attainment for the current year, new information that may positively or negatively affect the company in the coming months, and other important information. If the company shares financials with everyone, this should be done on a monthly basis. In lieu of financials, some companies share performance data (percentage of on-time deliveries, improvements in scrap rate, new business contracted during the month, etc.).

3.   *Quarterly team meetings*
The purpose of quarterly meetings is to review the performance in the previous quarter and the year to date, make any necessary adjustments to the strategic plan (What? You don't have a strategic plan? Shame on you! We'll talk more about that in Chapter Nine), and make any short term adjustments necessary for the coming quarter. If this meeting threatens to be too big and to get out of hand, department leaders could be the attendees, and they should be charged with formally reporting the results of the meeting to their respective staffs.

4.   *Annual strategic planning*
The annual meeting – actually a series of meetings for the top brass – is a meeting of the minds of the best thinkers in the organization from various departments in order to analyze where the company has been and to develop new strategies for where it's going. For companies with one year plans, this meeting will be the foundation for building next year's strategy. For companies with 3 or 5 year plans, the meeting will be for the purpose of making adjustments to the short and long range forecasts, developing new strategies, and deleting old strategies which have proven unsuccessful.

It's a good idea to get these meetings on the calendar a full 12 months in advance. They should be sacred; a key manager or family member shouldn't even think about trying to get away with, "Oh I can't make it. Our customer called and he needs me to be out of town that day." If people won't respect the rhythm and importance of these regular meetings in order to effectively communicate among the team, you really have to ask yourself if they are a good fit. Meetings will have greater and greater impact as you make the transition from being the kind of business you are now to the kind of business which is sustainable over time. The issue of how much or how little participation necessary in some of these meetings is an important consideration. The continuum of participation ranges from no participation in which the CEO keeps all plans and makes all decisions between his ears, and, on the other hand, having all employees participate in all decisions all the time. These represent the two extremes, and obviously the best solution for you and your company lies somewhere in between. The old saying, "2 heads are better than one" is true in almost every case. Take advantage of the brain power inherent in your organization; get people involved down to the lowest possible level and take advantage of their energy, know-how, and creativity. Even if you're not having them participate in your annual strategy meeting, create a system of weekly department meetings where they can participate, be informed, and pass information back up the chain of command.

Employees wish to be, and must be, evaluated from time to time. Holding people accountable – especially family members – is difficult. However, if you're going to transition from being a doer to being a teacher, mentor and coach, evaluations will provide you with the stopping point you need in order to be effective. Believe it or not, evaluations are a way of showing that you care for people. Less than a third of people report that they frequently receive praise or recognition for good work. Evaluations are not only a time to recognize deficiencies in employees' performance, it's a time to praise and reward outstanding performance. Praise isn't just a recognition of good performance; it's a contributing factor. Too many closely held business leaders practice the Vince Lombardi type of management; if an employee does well, you say nothing because you expected her to do well. If, on the other hand an employee fails, there's much weeping and gnashing of teeth. We're not advocating that you be soft on your people, just that you recognize a job well done with the same intensity that you'd recognize a job poorly done.

The reason for doing evaluations is obvious. If people are performing poorly, they'll need corrective suggestions and coaching in order to become more effective. On the other hand, if people are doing well, they'll need encouragement and new direction as they reach higher and higher goals and are rewarded with greater responsibility. We at The Family Business Institute have adopted the philosophy "Change is fragile and must be protected." This is true with respect to employee evaluations. If you have given corrective recommendations to an employee, you'll have to follow up and check back on that employee to make sure the coaching has taken hold and is producing better results. If the opposite is true, and an employee has succeeded with greater responsibility, you'll need to follow up in that situation to offer new guidance and reassurance. People at every level of the organization get better with follow up and coaching. The absence of follow up causes people to stagnate or to meander aimlessly in their jobs. Zig Ziglar said, "You'll get everything in life you want if you help enough other people get what they want." In terms of today's employees, it's not enough to think that they have fully subscribed to your compelling corporate vision; you must understand how their personal ambitions intersect with your vision and how you can come together as a win-win unit in order that both may prosper. Regular evaluations provide a one-on-one check-in time for both sides to assess where they are in the deal.

One of the key skills a good manager or evaluator needs is to be a good listener. Sadly, most closely held business leaders have so many balls in the air at any given time that their listening skills have eroded. If they've engaged in conversation with another person for more than 5 or 6 minutes, they inevitably check their cell phones for messages, glance at their email to see what's new, or look at their watches to see how late they are for the next function. If you're shuffling through the mail or glancing at your watch every few minutes, you'd probably be better off not having the meeting at all. You're sending all the wrong signals:

- I'm not listening
- You're wasting my time
- I've got somewhere else I need to be that's more important than being here with you
- I don't care what you have to say

We'll close this section of the chapter with another management tool; it is an employee evaluation tool readers may reproduce and use. Most performance reviews are one sided and "boss administered" and are pretty dysfunctional. The mindset of the boss is to discuss deficiencies which require improvement. The mindset of the employee is to justify performance in order to secure a pay increase. There are risks for both sides, and reviews are generally uncomfortable.

The alternative to a one sided, uncomfortable employee evaluation is a 2 way review. To accomplish the goals of performance reviews, evaluating employee performance, gaining employee perspective, and improving future performance, many companies have instituted a "shared evaluation" process.

The shared evaluation process involves getting feedback from both the manager and the employee. Both compare the employee's performance against the job description goals and objectives, and how the employee's performance can be improved. These observations are grouped into 2 categories, those accomplished in a satisfactory or better manner, and those which need improvement to be considered as satisfactory. In addition, both parties prepare recommendations to improve areas deemed unsatisfactory. The result is that the employee and manager get a much more accurate and inclusive picture of the employee's strengths and weaknesses and jointly determine how to improve performance.

The employee fills out the employee review form prior to the meeting listing those items he feels he has accomplished satisfactorily and those that have not and what might be done to improve. The manager fills out the manager's review form in a similar fashion.

The manager and employee meet for the review; the manager asks the employee to discuss items that he feels are satisfactory. As the employee lists the items, the manager adds them to her review form. When the employee has completed his list, the manager introduces any items which the employee has not mentioned. The manager then asks the employee to discuss areas that are not satisfactory. As the employee lists the items, the manager adds them to his review form. When the employee has completed his list, the manager introduces any items not mentioned. The discussion then focuses on how to make improvements. The employee and manager share their thoughts on the subject and select the highest priority items needing improvement, a maximum of 3, and develop a plan to improve them. The manager reviews the improvement plan periodically with the employee, at least once a quarter, to ensure that the goals mutually decided are accomplished.

In those cases where the employee's performance is not acceptable for continued employment without changes, the manager prepares a 30/60/90 day action plan. This plan details the areas where performance is not acceptable, those actions necessary to remain an employee, and the consequences of failure to meet the action plan requirements. Senior management approves all action plans of this type prior to the employee review.

Here are some basic instructions to keep the process positive and constructive.

Instructions to person being reviewed:
- Review your job description
- Review specific goals and objectives
- Review specific assignments
- For each area of responsibility, determine goals, objectives, and specific assignments which were performed satisfactorily or better and those which were not
- List those which you feel are above average on the Employee Review Form
- List those areas in which you feel you need to make improvements on the Employee Review Form
- Prepare a list of training or other aids which will help you improve these areas and list them on the Employee Review Form
- Take the Employee Review Form to the review meeting
- Approach the review with an open mind

Instructions to manager preparing a review:
- Review the job description for the person you are reviewing
- Review specific goals and objectives
- Review specific assignments

- Determine which areas the employee performed satisfactorily or better, and list them on the Manager's Review Form
- Determine which areas the employee performed unsatisfactorily or better, and list them on the Manager's Review Form
- Prepare a list of training or other aids which you feel will help improve these areas and list them on the Manager Review Form
- Take the Manager Review Form to the review meeting
- Approach the review with an open mind

Instructions to manager giving the review:

- Have the person being reviewed list areas that she feels she performs in an above average manner
- Add to that list those items on your list
- Have the person being reviewed list those areas in which improvement is needed
- Add to the list any areas on your list, if any
- With the person being reviewed, develop a plan to address improvement areas
- For those performers that are lacking in the basics of the position, prepare a 30/60/90 day action plan

Finally, we can't explore getting the right people on your bus without taking a glance at the obverse: *getting the wrong people off your bus.* McKinsey reports that only 3% of executives say their companies "move low performers out quickly." Perhaps the concept of getting poor performance off the bus can best be illustrated by a couple of true life stories.

Case Study: Creatively Pruning the Employment Tree

A family business run by cousins had a 70-something year old employee who had been with the firm 38 years. While at one time he was quite a valuable part of the team, in the last few years he had become an obstacle to any new initiatives, was a constant morale buster, and wasn't earning the money the company paid him. For several years, the cousins discussed this problem employee at their management meetings. However, because he had been employed by the company almost as long as they had been alive, and because they always thought he would retire soon, they never had the heart to take action to move him out and get someone more productive in his place. What the cousins ultimately decided to do – with a strong dose of assistance from their consultant – was to give the employee an end of the summer retirement party. The company president went to him, thanked him for his many years of loyal service, presented him with a generous gift, and told him of the plans to have an all-hands company retirement party for him in a few weeks. The dreaded event, the one avoided for so long because of the potential for negative reactions, was a non-event. He understood the need for the company to move on, had the resources he needed to retire, and was very pleased at all the kind comments and warm sentiments he received at his going away party. Since then the cousins have used this approach in turning over older staff in favor of younger, more energetic people.

Case Study: Firing a Family Member

An owner was having real problems with his son's poor job performance. He was often absent from work, when he did come to work he was habitually late, and he often left early. When he set his mind to it, he could do high quality work; the problem was that he rarely seemed to be in the right frame of mind. In addition to the direct cost of lost productivity, the other employees were having serious problems with the kind of favoritism shown to this young man. His mom was adamant that he have a position in the family business; perhaps she knew that with his poor performance he wasn't fit to work for an employer that would hold him truly accountable. The pressure on his father inside the business eventually (after about 2 years!) overrode his family concerns, and he began to develop a strategy for resolving the matter. The first thing he did was arrange for a 3 month paid sabbatical for his son. That satisfied Mom's concerns about how he'd pay his rent and buy groceries and also gave the son more time to think about his direction. His passion was in the field of auto racing, and that's where he spent a great deal of his time outside the workplace. He was encouraged during the period of his sabbatical to explore all possibilities that might relate to a career in auto racing about which he could be passionate and enthusiastic. Next, the parents agreed that they would fund, for a period of time, additional education which would relate directly to the racing field. In addition, if he got a job in that field which paid less than his modest salary in the family business, the parents would, out of their own pockets, make up the difference for a period of time. As his compensation in the new career began to increase, they would reduce their stipend proportionally. The maximum duration for this offer was 24 months.

Some readers may think it ridiculous to jump through this many hoops in order to simply "fire a son." Others, on the other hand, may think that removing a family member from the business would be like cutting off their own arms; it could never be done. The reality is that it's often necessary to prune the family tree in order that the business – the goose which lays golden eggs for the family and everyone who works for the company – may be strong and healthy. Just as gardeners prune rose bushes for maximum health, so the family company needs that sort of tender loving care. Due to concerns of the family, however, it's not always as simple as just sending the employee home and mailing him a severance check. The concerns of other stakeholders come into play: mothers-in-law, siblings, and grandparents.

Whether it's a family or non-family employee, getting the wrong people off your bus is just as important as getting the right people on it. The wrong people hold you back, create morale problems, and create an element of self-loathing quite unlike anything else. It's amazing to hear closely held business owners say after the fact, "I should have let him go 5 years ago!" Getting the wrong people off the bus is one of the most liberating things a closely held business can do to maximize productive behavior and create the framework for building a sustainable company.

Building Block #3 – People Management

Executive Summary

⇨ Without great people, even the most talented and energetic business leader can only go so far. Unfortunately, most closely held companies have woefully underdeveloped systems for attracting high quality talent

⇨ Most family business owners don't actually have *businesses*; they have *jobs*!

⇨ There is an ongoing war for talent, and demographic changes are making getting great talent harder

⇨ The quality of your system for getting the right people on the bus – and for getting the wrong ones off – is the greatest determinant for how successful your closely held company can ultimately be

Chapter Five
Building Block # 4 - Marketing and Sales Management

We once met with a group of CEOs who were considering retirement and possibly selling their businesses. One of the CEOs asked, "If I were to put my business on the market, what is the one thing that a prospective buyer would most want to see?" We thought about the answer for a few minutes. Surely a prospective buyer would want to see high quality products or services, a solid management team, strong financial performance and a sound balance sheet, adequate facilities, etc. These are all givens; no buyer would want to purchase a decrepit, run down, wheezing business. However, the thing that struck us as being the most desirable in the eyes of a prospective buyer is a *well developed and robust marketing and selling system.* Think about it; nothing is more common than the underdeveloped business which has outstanding product or service quality but lacks an adequate number of customers. If a company, on the other hand, has a well developed marketing and selling system, it can put the right kind of suspects into the pipeline, convert them to prospects and eventually customers, keep product prices high by careful customer qualification and selection, and keep the production side of the business busy and engaged in virtually any economic climate.

Most family and closely held businesses are dependent on the enthusiasm and charisma of the top executives to push marketing and sales forward. In the early days of the business, the owner was the only salesman, and the likelihood is that even today the owner or her direct descendents are still the most effective marketers of the company services. Furthermore, because the owner was also the lead production person, the company benefited from a direct, unambiguous conversation between her and customers that made conversion from sales to production that much simpler. For the closely held company to grow and become sustainable, it's incumbent on the leaders to develop the marketing and sales functions so the company is not dependent on her for its sales. The business has to extract the information held in her head and somehow catalog it in a way that allows other talented marketing people to gradually take on her former business development role.

Whenever we ask business owners why they are successful, they almost always come back with 2 answers: high quality and hard work. Neither of these answers is accurate, and here's why. First, virtually every closely held business began with a founding entrepreneur who worked devilishly long and hard hours; the personal sacrifices founding entrepreneurs make are the stuff of legend. If your competition has executives who are working the same 60 to 80 hour work weeks you are, doesn't that cancel out the hard work assumption? Second, as I write this I'm sitting in my office conference room. Looking out the window, I can see 7 commercial buildings. All of these buildings are of high quality and built to high specifications. Each building was proudly delivered by an architect and contractor who were extremely proud of the finished product. However, the reality is that any one of 50 or 100 architectural firms or contracting businesses could have erected the structures with virtually the same level of quality. So much for the quality and hard work arguments for why closely held companies are successful. They cannot be successful *without* hard work and high quality, but those arguments are simply cancelled out by the facts.

The truth is that people buy things not because of promises of hard work or quality, not because of promises of technical expertise, and not because of the quality of printed brochures or other collateral marketing materials. People buy things from other people. Because of the difficulty the typical consumer has in understanding and evaluating the technical excellence of a product or service, the personal relationship between the seller and the buyer takes on great significance. Consumers of products and services – even if it's business to business selling – are looking for trust, peace of mind, confidence, and reassurance. Management consultant David Maister has a formula for defining customer satisfaction: satisfaction = perception - expectation. He says: "If the client perceives service at a certain level but expected something more or different, then he or she will be dissatisfied." In the good old days of selling, just being there was enough: make the sales calls, be friendly, dress well, do lunch. The demand for products and services was high, price wasn't always a major concern, and there was enough business for everyone. The average salesperson knew the features and benefits of his product and maybe even the competitor's product. To get ahead, ambitious sales people simply worked more hours and made more calls.

Times have changed. Customers are much, much more sophisticated today, competition is tougher and more intense, selling cycles are longer, and pricing pressures are intense. Now, instead of just selling products, the competition sells assorted value added services to go along with them. There's continual pressure on margins, and it seems buying decisions are more fickle and less predictable than ever.

Most family and closely held businesses have poorly developed marketing and selling functions. In a recent survey of a small group of CEOs (*Figure 5.1*), they rated the "importance of marketing to your company" at a 4.0 on a 5 point scale. However, they rated their "satisfaction with sales efforts" at only a 2.38, their "reach and ability in comparison to that of your competition" at a 2.13, their "satisfaction with market share" at 2.25, and their "use and formality of sales methodology and processes" at 1.88. For this group of CEOs, the disconnect between the desire for world class marketing and the execution of that function was glaring.

Figure 5.1

Importance of marketing to your company	4.00
Satisfaction of sales efforts in comparison with competition	2.38
Reach	2.13
Use of sales methodology	1.88
Satisfaction with market share	2.25

Our experience tells us that it is reasonably fair to extrapolate these discouraging numbers from this group of CEOs to family and closely held businesses in general.

Part of the difficulty in being effective at marketing is the simple lack of market focus. Too often family business leaders will take any business opportunity; prospects are so rare that every sow's ear looks like a silk purse. They have to bid, quote, and propose for every potential customer because they don't know who or what their ideal customer really looks like. They also don't know their true cost for marketing and sales and don't associate opportunity cost with proposing on Project A related to how it might impact their ability or inability to propose on future Project B. It's a fact that as a closely held company grows, the leader's time is more in demand and becomes more fragmented. Therefore, when the company was very small and the executive could have direct, unfiltered sales time with the customers and direct, unfiltered time with the production folks to translate the customer's wishes into product or service realities, things worked well. As his time became less available and the organization became more complex, his attention moved *inward* towards putting out company fires rather than outward toward the customer where it once was. This is exactly the time when closely held business owners should be *focused outside themselves* and their companies; they should be focused on their customers, without fail, all the time.

In order to be sustainable, closely held companies need a *system* to translate the passions and selling charisma of the owner to other people. Failing to create this system is dangerous; the majority of companies don't have anything remotely like the "XYZ Company Way" of marketing and selling. If they have half a dozen marketing and sales people, there are probably half a dozen different mixed – and sometimes conflicting – messages trickling out into the marketplace. Mission statements say one thing on the wall in the company's lobby and another on the company's website. A brochure developed in 2003 says things and makes claims that are quite different from the marketing materials produced in 2009. Salesman A assures customers that shipping can take place in 2 weeks, whereas Salesman B tells prospective customers that shipping within the next 6 weeks is impossible.

If an entrepreneur is serious about building a marketing and sales system in order to have a sustainable business, she ought to be aware that there could be a fight – even from family members and executives whom she thought shared her vision. Why is this? Well, effective marketing and selling will only bring more customers and more business in the door. This puts more pressure on the production people (one of whom might be Brother Billy or Sister Sue). Jimmy, the salesman, thinks it's great to have more customers, but Billy, as the head of production, can't see how he's going to work any harder or get any more done than he does right now. New customers mean more work, more pressure, more expense and possibly debt, more moans and groans from production people, longer delivery times, etc. More customers mean a greater need for customer service and more potential headaches for Sister Sue. Some closely held business leaders either consciously or subconsciously fear and loathe these potential changes, and that's why they, in spite of their assertions to the contrary, never really develop marketing and selling systems. If the leaders elect to go that route, be prepared for a few fights.

Marketing Management

Marketing and sales are different. They're used interchangeably – even by writers who should know better. Marketing is a strategy supported by action plans which creates leads and deal flow. A sales system gathers those leads and converts them into paying, happy customers. Marketing is what you do to get people to knock on your door, and sales is what you do when you're turning those people into customers. It's as simple as attracting and converting. The American Marketing Association defines marketing as:

"Marketing is an organizational function and a set of processes for creating, communicating, and delivering value to customers and for managing customer relationships in ways that benefit the organization and its stakeholders."

In order to get potential clients and customers to knock on your door, you as leaders must invest time, money, and energy into attracting that deal flow by developing a strategy.

Developing a marketing and selling strategy is extremely people-intensive. The traditional framework of marketing involves the "4 Ps" (product, price, promotion, and place). The 4 Ps model is most useful when marketing low value consumer products and is often referred to as the "marketing mix." A better marketing framework is what we refer to as the "6 Ps of sales and marketing" (*Figure 5.2*).

Figure 5.2

1.	**Purpose**	The anticipated results which guide actions, goals, and objectives
2.	**Value Proposition**	A business or marketing statement summarizing why a consumer should buy a product or service
3.	**Plan**	Strategies and action plans for products or services. Price, promotion, place, and physical evidence
4.	**Process**	The processes involved in customer acquisition and customer relationship management.
5.	**People**	Any person having contact with customers and how they behave
6.	**Persistence**	The act of persevering, continuing, or repeating behavior; doggedness, tenacity, tenaciousness

These 6 Ps represent a more useful marketing framework for most family and closely held companies. We'll undertake each of the 6 Ps in context as the chapter unfolds.

PURPOSE relates to Covey's *"Habit 2:* begin with the end in mind." It has a great deal to do with visualization and prior planning. Think about the purpose of the marketing plan. Is the purpose to grow sales? Grow profits? Are you trying to land bigger clients or bigger projects? Are you trying to move into a new area of business (i.e. from automobile sales into heavy truck sales)? Are you looking to expand into different regions or geographies? Are you planning to hire your first marketing and sales team? Are you planning to develop deeper relationships with your existing clients? Are you looking to build a system which translates the passions and selling charisma of the current leaders into a group of new and different ones?

The most valuable research you can do in the initial steps for planning your marketing function is to better understand your customers needs and wants. When we ask business owners about how they measure the quality of their products or services, the answer almost always comes back something like, "Well our customers aren't complaining, so they must be happy." That simply is not quantifiable or actionable data. Just because they haven't complained doesn't mean they're not dissatisfied; they may be considering moving their business from you to your competition at this very moment! Worst of all, you wouldn't be in a position to know it until after the fact!

There are several ways to get to know your customers better. Here are a few:

1. Take some time out of your busy schedule; go and sit down with your customers. Buy them lunch or dinner, and ask them for their considered and thoughtful feedback. Prepare for the meeting; develop a short script of important questions to ask your top dozen customers. That way, since you're asking each the same questions, you'll be getting feedback on consistent areas of your business. The answers obviously won't be the same, but you'll be exploring what you and your team have determined to be the most important marketing issues you face. At least talk to a few of your customers on the phone; this will put you back in touch with customers in the same way your father and grandfather had direct, unfiltered contact with them in the early days of the business.

2. Engage in "Voice of the Customer" research. This is taking the concept of talking to your customers to a sophistication level several orders of magnitude higher. In this case, you'd engage a third party source – and you'd better believe your customers will give more blunt and truthful feedback to an objective, independent third party than they will to you directly – in order to ask questions and compile the answers for you. The researcher would help you select among your customers and design the

type of research best suited to get the answers you want (quantitative information gathered through surveys, qualitative information gathered through direct one-on-one contact, or both). The researcher would analyze the data noting themes and patterns contained therein and help you translate the information into a marketing strategy and tactics for your use. Voice of the Customer research is an incredibly valuable marketing tool to help you listen and learn and to burst through any limiting or incorrect marketing assumptions.

3.   A third way of knowing your customers better is to install a formal quality assurance program. Anyone who bought a new automobile in the last 20 years has seen quality assurance work directly in action. After buying a vehicle, someone (or more than one person) from the dealership calls within the first few days to assess your level of satisfaction with your interaction. In addition, you get a written customer satisfaction survey. Some dealerships take the quality assurance function to an extremely high level and check back with you 90 days or 6 months after your purchase to reassess the quality of your experience. Automobile dealers take this to be gospel truth: dealers with higher CSI (Customer Satisfaction Index) scores have higher sales and more repeat customers. Isn't that what everyone in business wants?

How can you translate the automobile dealer's customer satisfaction index experience into your business? It's easy. Assign someone to follow up with customers immediately after they purchase from you. Initially, the contacts should be done by a senior executive; it's nice to get a call from the boss or at least a VP in the organization. There should be a "quality assurance script" so no matter who on staff conducts the quality assurance questions they are consistent and directed. If your volume of sales prohibits one-on-one calls, electronic surveys are also useful and can be substituted in the quality assurance function. The main point is that you have some way of following up with your customers after the sale to make sure that they are happy and satisfied. If they're not, don't treat their objections or frustrations as bad news! They're helping you by telling you where your assumptions are incorrect in terms of quality or service or both. They're giving you the raw material you need to make your business better.

4. A fourth way of understanding your customers better and especially in helping you refine your internal customer selection process is what Sullivan calls the "cloneable client" exercise. Using a large whiteboard and a matrix format, list your top 20 clients down the left side. Across the top, list demographic, psychographic, and other kinds of characteristics which may help you define why this small list of individuals and companies are, in fact, your best customers. Demographic and psychographic characteristics you might consider include education, age, location, type of business, type of locality, spending habits, products or services purchased, number of outlets or locations, or types of team members, executives, or support people. The purpose of this exercise is to help you determine why your best customers have ascended to that level. An obverse of that exercise is to list your worst customers and do the same analysis. Taken together, the 2 exercises will tell you where to focus your marketing efforts in the future and, just as important, where to avoid putting marketing time and effort.

If you undertake one or all of these investigative activities, you'll find new information – often shocking information – that will raise your marketing effort to an entirely new level. For more information on this topic, please read *The Trojan Horse and Inside Positioning* at www.familybusinessinstitute.com/8blocks/.

The purpose of the exercises above is to help you understand and think more clearly about what it's like to be a buyer in today's world. Buyers of your products or services experience the following feelings:

Figure 5.3

Insecurity	How do I really know this is the right product?
Risk	If I make a bad decision, what happens?
Impatience	I have so many things on my plate I really don't have time to devote my full attention to this choice
Ignorance	I really don't understand all of the technicalities associated with this product or service
Skepticism or Cynicism	I've been burned before. You better make sure it doesn't happen again
Fear	This all sounds great up front, but will I be able to get these people on the phone when I need them after the sale is consummated?
Vulnerability	If we bring these people aboard, I'm going to have to share confidential information, and I'm not sure I'm comfortable with that
Fear of Remorse	What if I'm wrong? Will Dad or my partners still believe in me?

It's the job of the sophisticated marketer and the purpose of market research to identify how best to answer the clients' fears and concerns and to place your organization at the top of the heap when it's time to investigate a purchasing decision.

In developing a marketing strategy, it's important to consider what your **VALUE PROPOSITION** is. If you can't differentiate between yourself and your competitors, your marketing is useless. Your customers can almost certainly give you this information; after all, they specifically chose you over other marketplace alternatives. Your employees may also be able to give you insight into what makes you unique and what constitutes your "unique selling proposition."

Your value proposition is a statement that summarizes why a business or consumer should buy your product or service. It should convince a potential consumer that you can add more value or better solve a problem than other similar offerings or competitors. You should also be able to clearly demonstrate that your customer gets what he pays for. An example of what some closely held companies use as their statements of value proposition are:

Figure 5.4

Duration	"We've been in business 106 years."
Execution	"We have 98% same day deliveries." Or, "96% of our projects are delivered on time and on budget."
Technology	"Not only can we deliver the service in the way you want, we also do it in an environmentally friendly way that does not add cost to your project."
Personal Attention	"At our company you'll be dealing directly with the owners and not with hired guns who may move into another job in 6 months or a year."
Claims to Fame	"We built the State Capital building." Or, "We created the first widget."
Specialization	"We only work with a well-defined, homogeneous, carefully selected group, (i.e. regional insurance companies, private developers, or retirees)."

There are many ways to state your value proposition. One way is to develop what marketers call the "elevator speech." For example, the Family Business Institute's elevator speech is, "We help family and closely held businesses make more money in less time with fewer headaches and a higher quality of life." The goal of any elevator speech (it's called that because it can be delivered in about 10 seconds to someone on an elevator) is to get the person to say, "Oh. That sounds interesting. How do you do that?" If that's the response, you now have permission to go into a more lengthy description of who you are and what you do; the inquirer has opened the door for you. Ultimately, your elevator speech, unique selling proposition, or value proposition must relate directly to the purchase preferences of your target market. You are intentionally and deliberately positioning the perceptions you want in the minds of your prospects.

Figure 5.5

Questions to ask about how best to market your products and services:

⇨ What is the entrepreneur really good at and really passionate about? Why did he start this business in the first place?

⇨ What makes us unique and different from our competition? How can we differentiate ourselves so that we're not just another commodity?

⇨ What kind of customers should we pursue? What kind of customer should we shy away from? Which customers should we fire right now in order to improve profits and our sanity?

⇨ What's wrong with our marketing and selling processes right now? Are they too complicated? Are they too simple? How can we sketch out (process map) our marketing functions?

⇨ How much cleanup, scrap, waste, or customer complaints are we having to endure right now? Is it in line with industry standards? If not, why not?

⇨ What do we need to be doing to innovate so that our customers will be satisfied with us in the future?

⇨ What marketing tactics have worked for us? Which of our marketing tactics has recently failed? Why have the successful tactics worked, and why have the unsuccessful ones failed?

⇨ How do we measure our marketing output and return on investment (ROI)? Do we use media visibility, inbound customer inquiries, quality assurance or customer satisfaction measures, new business acquired, old business expanded, or other measures? What are our marketing KPIs (Key Performance Indicators)?

Make this a team effort; engage your staff to assist in evaluating these questions. It also might be wise to bring in an objective third party in order to dig out answers.

If you've listened to your customers, determined the purpose and value proposition of your marketing strategy, and invested the time, energy, and money necessary to convert marketing from an ad-hoc function to a strategy which can help you sustain your business into the future, you'll need ways to appeal to potential customers and to occupy a position in their minds when they realize they have a need. This gets to the **PLANNING** stage of developing the marketing strategy.

113

There are a host of marketing tactics. It's difficult to pinpoint which one or ones are most effective given the sheer number of industries occupied by family and closely held companies. The following are a few generally accepted marketing practices proven to work over time. It will be up to you and your team to select which are best for you and how you may go about employing them.

1. Public speaking (After all, if you are anointed as a speaker to a group, small or large, you must be an "expert." If you have a really compelling message, you can even get paid as a professional speaker and create a new stream of income).
2. Company newsletters
3. Trade show exhibits
4. Direct mail campaigns
5. Email campaigns
6. Referrals from satisfied customers
7. A compelling website with "data capture" capabilities and search engine optimization
8. Networking (civic, religious, and social organizations)
9. Writing articles in customer-centered press (usually in trade or industry publications)
10. Doing proprietary research which customers can access or which may generate free publicity for your firm
11. Video or audio brochures
12. Advertising
13. Sponsorship of industry events
14. Brochures

All of these tactics fall under the general heading of business development efforts, and all are tactics which can be undertaken by many people in the organization, not just the chief executive. A quick note on one of the tactics: I have always been amazed at how much time and effort family and closely held business leaders put into the development of brochures. A brochure is an excellent digest of things your company can and will do for customers. However, the way they are handled by customers is no different from junk mail. Somewhere a marketing myth grew up that "you have to have a brochure." I've never seen a brochure sell anything, and I really believe the time, effort, and money used to develop the typical brochure could be expended much more usefully in the pursuit of other strategies and tactics.

Finally, as part of the marketing plan, all this brainstorming and information must get synthesized, cataloged, and written down. Having it exist vaguely between someone's ears is inadequate when the ultimate goal is to build a marketing strategy which can sustain your business over the generations.

Sales Management

A sales system is distinct and different from marketing: The purpose of your sales system is to gather leads and convert them into happy, paying customers. Let's take a closer look at how to do that. Academically, sales is thought of as merely a part of marketing. However, sales usually requires a separate functional person or group of people in a business organization employing that often reviled, usually misunderstood category of people called *sales people*. While sales may be considered more of an art than a science, successful selling is usually characterized by a systematic process of repetitive and measurable milestones by which a salesman relates his offering of a product or service enabling a buyer to achieve his goal in an economic way. Marketing plays a critical role in selling by driving qualified leads through the door and providing suspects upon whom sales people can call. In the absence of marketing driving leads, sales people have to spend the majority of their time "prospecting" which is simply searching for people to whom to sell. Most organizations put the cart before the horse by putting their sales people in charge of marketing or by making the marketing function a requirement of the sales people. Having an effective marketing strategy as a part of your overall system allows salesmen to do what they do best, namely, establish relationships in order to help the company achieve its sales goals.

We have established that the founding entrepreneur was generally the company's first and probably best sales person. In building marketing and selling systems, the closely held business moves forward on the path of professionalism by recreating what the entrepreneur did in sales, translating it, and training one or more other people to do it. One of the fundamental necessities of building a sustainable closely held company is to eliminate the unfortunate dependence that most have on one or a tiny handful of people. If sales (or any other vital function for that matter) comes to a grinding halt in the absence of the chief executive, that's a sure-fire sign that, while the company supplies jobs, it's not really a business.

Most companies spend 75% of their marketing dollars on scouring the marketplace for new prospects with only 25% of their budgets devoted to their existing customers. And yet it's a given in marketing that it costs 3 to 10 times as much to win business with a new client versus winning new business or extending old business with an existing customer. Most firms simply don't pay enough attention to nurturing existing customers as opposed to developing new sales leads. If this is the case, why is there a comparative neglect of existing customers in favor of new customers? There are several reasons. The first is that pursuing new business probably gives a greater sense of "the thrill of the chase." Maister writes,

> "Pursuing a new client proposal opportunity usually has the characteristics of a well-defined, finite project with relatively clear tasks and specific deadlines. Nurturing an existing relationship often has few inherent deadlines, little obvious structure, and more ambiguous tasks. Consequently, it is reported to me, it is a less-satisfying activity: it doesn't provide the same 'rush of adrenaline'."

It also might be said that pursuing new clients is less intimate; that is, it doesn't require the same degree of closeness that nurturing existing client relationships requires. It might be characterized as the difference between "liking" customers and learning to "love" them. There are rewards associated with selling new business versus extending old business; most commissioned sales people receive a clear cut and definable compensation for bringing a new customer on board. On the other hand, sales commission residuals tend to be lower for retaining or extending old business. Therefore, most companies have a built-in financial bias toward pursuing new versus extending old business. There's also the internal "newsworthiness." Here's an example: What have you heard more about in the news in the last 12 months? Did the press report that a new company promising 1,000 jobs has relocated to your state, or did they report that 100 existing businesses grew and each added 10 employees? The net jobs result is the same; however, it's just not as sexy to report on the latter. Many companies treat new business with excitement while they give a bored, ho-hum response to "upselling" old clients.

We got an email from a CEO recently, a man who's been running his company for over 25 years, asking, "I have heard that I need what is called a 'sales funnel'. What is it, what does it look like, and how do I get one?" While it's easy to think that this entrepreneur is behind on the learning curve, his request for information is the rule, not the exception. Most family and closely held businesses simply do not have well defined sales functions. While there are elaborate software programs that would track a sales funnel, it's easy enough to design and conceive with pencil and paper or a simple spreadsheet. The classic sales funnel appears in *Figures 5.6 and 5.7.*

Figure 5.6

← Calls

← Contacts

← Appointments

← Selling Presentations

← Successful Closes

Here's an example: a construction company executive makes 20 calls to architects and/or building owners. His entreaties lead to 14 contacts resulting in 7 interested parties who open the door for a selling presentation. Of the 7 who open the door, the executive is able to actually schedule 5 of them in the near term. Of the 5, 2 actually elect to do business with the executive during the course of the next 6 months. The executive's hit rate, therefore, is 10% (*Figure 5.7*) which is an outstanding rate if he is "cold-calling" the architects and building owners. If he was calling on existing relationships, his hit rate should be more like 20% to 30%.

Figure 5.7

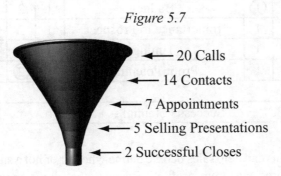

← 20 Calls

← 14 Contacts

← 7 Appointments

← 5 Selling Presentations

← 2 Successful Closes

2 (closes) ÷ 20 (calls) = 10% hit rate

Tracking the sales funnel requires patience because a selling cycle can be quite long. Once a sales person knows the ratios of calls to contacts, etc., she'll have a predictable model for how much business development work she needs to do in order to hit her targeted sales numbers. In order to jump start the process, she could do a back study to quantify previous year's sales activities; while it might not be 100% accurate, most companies should be able to get pretty darn close. Having a well-established sales funnel and being able to track sales success objectively over time puts one on a path of conducting sales and business development in a systematic, strategic way rather than doing it haphazardly "whenever I get around to it."

Another useful tool is the qualification worksheet (*Figure 5.8*):

Figure 5.8

Qualification Worksheet										
Date:						**Account:**				
Minimize						**Maximize**				
-						**+**				
5	4	3	2	1	Importance of Account	1	2	3	④	5
5	4	3	2	①	Business Fit	1	2	3	4	5
5	4	3	2	1	Personal Fit	①	2	3	4	5
5	4	3	2	①	Credibility	1	2	3	4	5
5	4	3	2	1	Attitude	1	2	③	4	5
5	4	3	②	1	Competition	1	2	3	4	5
5	4	3	2	1	Access to Decision Maker	1	2	3	④	5
5	4	3	2	①	Budget	1	2	3	4	5
5	4	3	2	1	Importance to Prospect	1	2	③	4	5
5	4	3	2	1	Timing	1	②	3	4	5
5	4	3	2	1	Profit Potential	1	②	3	4	5
Success Potential = +14										

Having a tool like this can help sales people define whether or not a suspect matches the company's desired customer profile. Suspects that don't appear to be high quality leads receive low priority and vice versa. Using a tool like this is a way to assure that the selling skills and knowledge of the entrepreneur gets translated to other people on the team in a crystal clear way. It also assures that sales people aren't wasting time and effort on low-payoff activities or wild goose chases.

In terms of the 6 step marketing and sales framework, using qualification tools of this type is **PROCESS** work. Questions for evaluating process work include:

- How do you manage relationships with existing customers including extending engagements and acquiring new business from them?
- How do you currently generate new leads and acquire new customers?

- How can marketing help sales do a better job and vice versa?
- Can you process map marketing (lead generation) and selling (converting leads into customers) in order to find weaknesses and inefficiencies in your processes? Refer to *Figure 5.9* for an example of a process map (we'll talk more about process mapping in the next chapter) for an inside selling system.

Many family and closely held businesses live and die with repeat and referral business. If that's the case, it is absolutely, 100% incumbent upon you to find the time and energy to make sure your customers are getting the nurturing and hand-holding they need. If you don't have a system for gathering referrals from happy customers and converting those referrals into sales prospects, that is a high priority task in building out the marketing and selling system.

PEOPLE are the most vital component of the 6 step marketing and sales framework. These are the people who come in contact with your leads throughout the process including everyone from the most senior executives to the person who answers the telephone. Everyone in the organization should see himself as a business development specialist and learn what he can about the selling and customer service processes in order to be more effective in relaying the company's brand and service potential.

The characteristics of successful sales people have been well documented, and utilizing psychometric tools and surveys can help you determine who among your staff has the raw material necessary for successful selling. Thousands upon thousands of books about selling are available with the click of a mouse; our intention is not to recreate that literature here. Suffice it to say that it is simply a poor idea to wake up one day, realize you need a better sales function, and make your nephew who just joined the company your lead salesman because everyone else is fully occupied. Defining the characteristics of a successful salesperson relative to your company's culture and to your customer's needs, fully evaluating who inside or outside your organization might best fit your selling needs, and hiring and motivating sales professionals is important work. Treating it as a necessary evil won't produce the results you want, will create frustration, and, because of the poor results, will sour you on developing a sound selling system later on ("we already tried that and it didn't work").

In terms of evaluating sales professionals, that could be done any number of ways, including by leads generated, closes, sales revenue generated, sales presentations made, profitability per account, customer satisfaction index scores, cost of sales, customer retention, etc. If you're building out your selling system for the first time, however, you may not have a good guideline for training your sales people on how they should be investing their time to produce maximum results. Here's a quick guideline subject to modification and

Figure 5.9

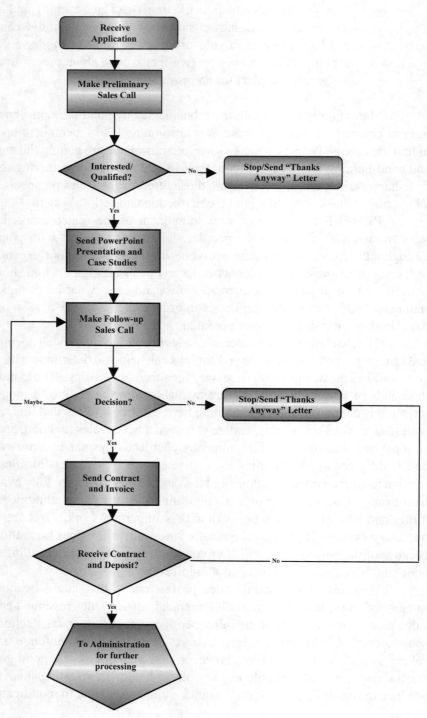

adaptation (depending on your existing sales system, company culture, and type of customer) for you to use. Sales people in mature businesses should spend their time roughly as follows:

- 30% of time should be spent with marketing people evaluating quality assurance and other types of market research and "hand-holding" activities to make sure their projects are being executed and their expectations are being met. This time should be spent nurturing existing clients and becoming the client's internal advocate
- 35% of the sales executive's time should be spent exploring whether old clients have new needs which might be satisfied by your company. There should be plenty of high payoff potential in this area generated, at least in part, by the 30% of the time above, which you spent being the client's advocate or what Maister refers to as "super pleasing"
- Finally, 35% of time should be spent developing and courting new client relationships

You may need to adapt the numbers for your company, but this gives a sales professional a rough guideline for how to invest his time for maximum payoff.

Sales training has an extremely high ROI. A company which hasn't invested time and money into getting high quality training for its sales force is sending the team out with one hand tied behind its back. Surely some people are "born salesmen," but most, even the most magnetic person, could benefit from refinement. Tiger Woods, perhaps the greatest golfer who has ever lived, doesn't rest on his laurels. He is constantly seeking new training, new coaching, and new information which will allow him to become even better. Why wouldn't you adopt the same approach to developing your selling function?

The final P in the 6 part framework is **PERSISTENCE**. Calvin Coolidge said, "Nothing in this world can take the place of persistence. Talent will not; nothing is more common than unsuccessful people with talent." Creating a selling system allows your people to be efficiently persistent. Keeping accurate notes and files on all leads, even if done with pencil and paper, can give you a tremendous advantage when the phone rings. A few years ago, we got a consulting assignment because when the prospect called, we were able to pull a file from 12 years prior and relate specific meeting details and conversations to the suspect who, when he dialed the phone, thought he was reaching out to complete strangers. Adequate record keeping is a factor of persistence. It's astounding to see what kind of fire drills take place in most companies when a lead comes in the door. There's a sense of confusion and chaos; no one's exactly sure what to do. There are all sorts of: "Didn't this guy call before in 2005, and didn't he put us through the ringer before electing to do business with our competition?" Information stored between someone's ears is fragile. Memories are poor, often confused, and if that individual leaves the firm for one reason or another, the data is lost forever. Developing a selling record keeping system eliminates this potential for mischief.

Another failure of most sales teams is a simple lack of persistence. If they make one sales call and don't get the business, they're out – and out for good. Most sales, especially high dollar, complex sales, require multiple sales calls, clarifications, and exchanges of information. A lack of persistence or an inability to finish jobs started plagues many family and closely held businesses.

Building Block #4 – Marketing and Sales Management

Executive Summary

⇨ Marketing and sales are NOT one and the same. Marketing is what you do to get people to knock on your door. Selling is how you successfully turn them into happy customers

⇨ A key characteristic which a company must have to be sustainable is a marketing and selling *system* which produces qualified leads and conversions in sufficient quantity

⇨ Closely held companies should focus on the "6 Ps" framework for improvement of business development functions

Chapter Six
Building Block # 5 – Operations Management

If one analyzes how most closely held business executives spend their time, they'd probably conclude that a minimum of 50% – and realistically a much higher percentage – is invested in the area of operations. Most business leaders got their start in – you guessed it – operations. Even if they are the founding entrepreneur, they worked for someone else – in production management, project management, or other technical areas of the business and one day decided, "Hey! I'm making a ton of money for the guys who run this company. Why can't I just start my own and make the money for myself?" And so they started. Their belief was and is that the secret to success and sustainability in business is to do the technical work they'd always done at a highly proficient level. They were blissfully unaware of the dozens if not hundreds of other requirements which go into *building a business which does the work the entrepreneur once did.* The trick to building a sustainable enterprise is to take the things that the entrepreneur was initially very good at, the reason he was able to build a business around his technical skills in the first place, and institutionalize them so that the business is no longer dependent on him for the actual day to day work.

The purpose of managing operations effectively and creating an operating system is to deliver goods and services to your customers on time with high quality at a fair price. If the operations system can do this consistently and predictably, and the marketing and sales system discussed in Chapter Five can create steady deal flow, the business has its raw materials for sustained success.

Before we fully embark on this chapter, it's important to issue a disclaimer. Because there are so many different types of companies doing so many different things in so many different industries, it's easy to over-generalize on the subject of operations. The differences in types of companies are enormous. There are:

- product vs. service companies
- inventory businesses vs. businesses which have no inventory
- businesses which receive and convert raw materials vs. businesses that don't
- businesses conducting e-commerce vs. companies with no e-commerce capabilities
- retail vs. wholesale
- business-to-consumer entities vs. business-to-business entities
- professional service firms
- technical professions like medicine, engineering, and law

And so on. What we'll do in this chapter is to explore operations improvement techniques which are universal. In being so broad, we run the risk of leaving out critical operations components which may be unique to any given reader's particular industry. If we have left out unique information about your particular industry, we apologize; we have made that decision in order to keep the book concise and to maintain its broad utility.

Thinking About Operations in a New and Different Way

Family and closely held business leaders are action-oriented doers. Unfortunately, their heroic obsession with the work of the business creates a limiting tunnel vision. Here's a story to illustrate:

> A group of researchers at Princeton University in the early 1970s produced what has come to be known as the "Good Samaritan Research." A group of theology students had an assignment to go to another part of the campus and deliver a sermon on the topic of the Good Samaritan. A portion of the students were told they were late for the sermon and needed to hurry. Unknown to the students, the researchers had hired an actor to play the role of the injured man in the parable. 90% of the late students passed the suffering person by and ignored his needs in the rush to get to the chapel. The study commented: "Indeed, on several occasions, a seminary student going to give his talk on the parable of the Good Samaritan literally stepped over the victim as he hurried on his way!"

Many family business owners, obsessed with the short term production needs of the business, are like these seminary students. They pass by opportunities to improve their operations. They ignore small steps which if employed today could produce big dividends later. They invest their time in fire fighting, and ignore opportunities for greater long term improvements. Because their intentions are, in fact, noble and they work so hard, they judge themselves by their intentions rather than the long term results their behaviors actually produce, and they perpetuate business practices which they'd surely change if they had the time to do strategic thinking and planning. They pay far too much attention to inputs like work hours and effort rather than back end results and measurable outputs. In short, they are doing work, but they may not be doing the right work.

As entrepreneurial companies grow larger, the entrepreneur is sucked more and more into the vortex of the business. McKinsey & Company states that in most industries 25% of the workforce is "knowledge workers whose basic means of production is the productive use of knowledge, rather than capital, land, or labor." Most small business executives today could – at least loosely – be labeled knowledge workers. Yet knowledge workers waste tremendous amounts of time searching for the knowledge they need; each upsurge, according to McKinsey, in the number of professionals working in the company leads to an almost exponential – not linear – increase in the number of potential collaborators and unproductive interactions. A measure of this largely unproductive type of exchange is that corporate email rose in volume from about 1.8 billion emails per day in 1998 to more than 17 billion per day in 2004. As a knowledge professional attempts to collaborate and pool information, he must go up the organization before he can go across it; that is, he first goes to the company leader in order to find out where the information he requires is housed. The leader is drawn into virtually every interaction between her subordinates; she is the clearinghouse for virtually all of the company's institutional information. If she wishes to create a sustainable company, she must develop a strategy and system for allowing her executives and knowledge workers to collaborate productively without drawing her continually into the mix.

Bringing a new operations management viewpoint to the company requires a significant shift in thinking. Closely held company executives have to ask themselves questions:

- What do we do?
- What do we not do very well?
- What should we quit doing?
- Can we outsource a task, or is it necessary that we do it ourselves?
- What *really* makes us money in operations?
- What do our customers *really* want?
- What are the results we absolutely must have, and how do we best hold people accountable?

Entrepreneurs should analyze closely what they do in operations that makes them money. Some family members are more favorably oriented towards money than others; for example, in one sibling team, 2 of the siblings, the oldest and the youngest, were very much what might be considered stereotypical business people. The brother focused on administration and operations, and his sister focused on marketing and sales. The middle sister, who worked primarily to earn a paycheck in order to support her artistic endeavors, was ambivalent to hostile in her attitude about money. She thought, in fact, that profit was evil and didn't really understand her sibling's constant dialogue about the necessity of making money. This is an all too common state of affairs in closely held companies. We often hear the sentiment: "It's not all about money to us." That's good; it's not normal for people to be obsessed with money. However, a business that doesn't produce sufficient profits is not a sustainable enterprise. The purpose of your company might not be to make profits any more than the purpose of your life is to breathe air. But in the absence of breathing air, there is no life. For businesses, the absence of profits over time means certain death. Profit may not be the purpose of the business, but it is a necessity. If this sort of discordant thinking doesn't exist among family members in your company, you can bet it exists among certain of your employees. The more people you can align towards the fact that it is a requirement of any business to generate profits and to educate them that profit is simply a health and wellness indicator, the better off everyone will be. It simply makes sense to have as many people's philosophies aligned as possible.

In the next part of the chapter, we'll explore 4 different operations management tools, why they are necessary, and how to use them.

Key Performance Indicators

Key Performance Indicators (KPI) help a company define and measure progress toward its goals. To utilize KPIs, a company first has to have goals; then, it needs a way to measure its progress toward the goals. That's what KPIs are for. The concept of KPIs is not new; it's been around for a long time. The percentage of closely held companies, however, using KPIs is quite small indeed. There's almost no operational process which couldn't be gauged and improved through the use of KPIs.

To use them effectively, KPIs, like goals, must be **SMART** (**S**pecific, **M**easurable, **A**ction-oriented, **R**ealistic, and **T**imely). KPIs stated as "get better every day" or "increase sales" won't work because they're simply not measurable. KPIs can vary widely depending on industry and company. Refer to *Figure 6.1* for a few examples of KPIs by category.

As this partial list illustrates, there's no shortage of KPIs. It's worth noting that KPIs can be used to measure things which are thought of as being quite difficult to measure (i.e. customer satisfaction, morale, or employee effectiveness). Don't try to utilize too many of them at any one time to assess the health of your business. Your "management dashboard" should only focus on about a half dozen KPIs at a time. Here's an example of how to think about and utilize a Key Performance Indicator:

> "When people talk about operations management, they are talking about the point at which all other corporate activities are proven out. Product development, marketing, and sales all assume that a product can be produced at a particular cost and that if the gross margin is met, earnings will result. They talk about efficiency, productivity, standard cost utilization, earned hours, absorption, etc. However, the key metric in good operations management is meeting or beating the predicted product cost. Unfortunately, most managers focus on hours used to make a product to the detriment of the other costs. In a typical manufacturing product, the cost at the gross margin line is about 70% of the selling price. Material cost is about 80% to 90% of the total production cost, or 56% to 63% of the selling price, leaving about 7% to 14% (typically 10%) for all labor costs. Managers tend to focus on labor costs only (10% of the total cost of production) because it's the easiest to measure. However, focusing there is simply not a winning proposition. In the case of a manufacturing company, the most important KPI, then, is predicted cost versus actual cost."
>
> *– Bill Provett, The Family Business Institute, Inc.*

Process Maps

In entrepreneurial businesses, processes are the least understood and least managed element of performance and, therefore, represent the biggest potential for improvement. Experts estimate that about one-half of the typical knowledge worker's time and energy is wasted. Waste occurs because people don't do the right work, do work the wrong way, or do work that shouldn't have been done in the first place. The biggest culprit in this waste is the poor engineering and management of processes. Processes are the beginning to end, left to right, horizontal flow of work that cuts across functional barriers. A process may involve everything from marketing through selling through purchase by a customer through paperwork and administrative processes through order

127

Figure 6.1a

	Current	Goal	Issues & Comments
Sales KPIs			
sales calls			
sales presentations			
sales closes			
sales close ratios			
gross sales			
sales/FTE employees			
units sold			
referrals			
referrals resulting in new business			
cost of sales per new unit sold			
sales growth rate			
Marketing KPIs			
customer satisfaction (QA)			
leads generated			
market share			
customer demographics			
competitive analysis matrix			
web traffic measures (unique visitors)			
web traffic measures (returning visitors)			
time spent per web visitor per visit			
conversion rate from web leads			
direct mail leads per mailing (leads/total)			
Operations KPIs			
inventory turns			
inventory costs			
billable hours			
billable hours/FTE employees			
billable hours/total working hours			
units produced/units of time			
scrap or defective products			
equipment utilization			

Figure 6.1b

	Current	Goal	Issues & Comments
Operations KPIs			
shrinkage or employee theft			
on time deliveries			
same day shipping (week, etc)			
safety measurements			
training: hours training/FTE employees			
payback period for cost recovery			
gross margin per product or unit			
predicted costs vs. actual costs			
call backs or warranty work			
Admin/Finance/HR KPIs			
employee turnover			
absenteeism			
employee morale			
family harmony (or employee harmony)			
ROI			
ROE			
ROA			
debt/equity ratio			
profitability			
collections days (AR aging)			
profit center analysis			
current ratio = CA/CL			
quick ratio = CA – Inventory/CL			
debt to equity ratio = debt/equity			
cash flow analysis			
break even sales (monthly or annually)			
EBIT or EBITDA			
valuation (fair market)			
net profit			
gross margin %			

fulfillment through delivery through customer satisfaction. Eliminating waste and increasing efficiency as this horizontal process cuts through all the vertical divisions of the company can add serious value.

The concept of process mapping is pretty unheard of in most closely held companies, but the idea is simple enough. In the absence of processes or systems, people do the work in entrepreneurial companies in the ways they deem best and easiest for them. If a construction company has 5 project managers, each project manager may undertake his job in a substantially different way. Furthermore, when a project manager leaves the company, and a new one takes his place, the new employee has virtually no place to start. He has to quickly engineer a new system of his own in order to meet company and customer demands. The entrepreneur is usually the custodian of the process in question which again sucks him into the vortex of operations.

In order to build a sustainable company, entrepreneurs must develop processes and systems that support their long term goals. There's an old saying that when a good worker runs into a bad system, the system wins the majority of the time. The obverse of this is true also: good systems produce good results in spite of average employees and mediocre management. In other words, *having good processes in place will make the entrepreneur less dependent on employees.* As cold as it may sound, employees become components which can be plugged in or unplugged as the situation demands without great harm to the system or the company at large. In today's world where employees shift jobs 5 times per career, it's unrealistic to assume that a manager who's a caretaker of Process A will be there by your side for the next 25 years; it's incumbent upon business leaders to build systems that make their companies less dependent on themselves *and* less dependent on one or a small handful of employees.

Here's a definition of a process: *an activity or a group of activities that takes an input, adds value to it, and provides an output to an internal or external customer.* Processes are measurable, repeatable, and sustainable. Just because a process is repeatable doesn't mean that it's a good process, and just because it can be measured doesn't mean it should be measured. Process mapping requires that an executive or a work team take a fresh look at all steps involved. Processes have definable boundaries with specific starting and ending places. They also have ordered, sequenced sets of activities that have to be performed. They cut across multiple business functions which are the vertical "silos" of sales, manufacturing, customer fulfillment, and administration. Process mapping as an exercise will be most valuable when a company is considering:

- Changing the way people do their work
- In the case of a merger, acquisition, or reorganization where

different departments have different approaches and the goal is that they have one common process

- When introducing new or revising old products or services and companies wish to understand the resulting effects on people, technology, equipment, and tasks
- When undertaking quality initiatives to reduce waste, reduce cost, or improve efficiency
- When an executive or a team is trying to get a handle with what's going on in an increasingly complex business or function of the business
- When a company is attempting to capture knowledge about processes for the purpose of creating operations manuals or training
- When customer needs are not being met (i.e. customer complaints are on the rise)

The benefits of process mapping are:

- It creates a visual of the process information flow
- It displays a complete visual of how an entire process works
- It provides a view of how horizontal processes flow through vertical functional areas
- It identifies operational goals and expectations
- It measures process lead time
- It identifies high cost activities
- It qualifies and quantifies value added activities
- It qualifies and quantifies non-value added activities
- It determines activity performance measures
- It provides information to establish visual management controls
- It provides a training, educational, and team building tool

Refer to *Figure 6.2* for an example of how a company might use process mapping to evaluate its system for hiring. This process map refers to the "get the right people on your bus" discussion in Chapter Four so the visual will have context.

Recession Planning

What's the first order of business in a recession? This is a very real question as this book goes to press. While everyone is concerned about the poor stock market, high fuel prices, the unsettled housing market, and the government

Figure 6.2a
Getting the Right People on Your Bus — Proccess Map

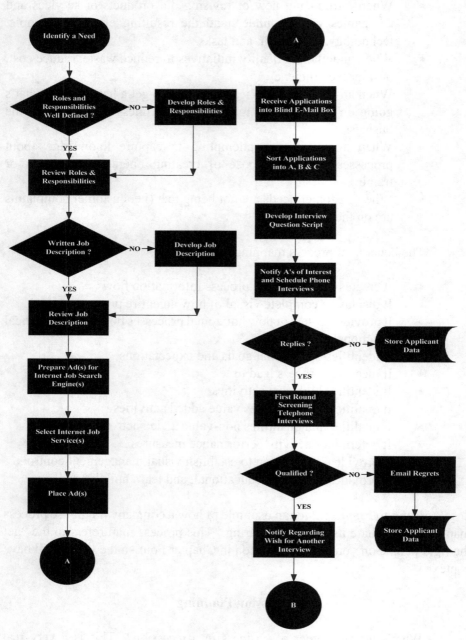

Figure 6.2b
Getting the Right People on Your Bus — Proccess Map

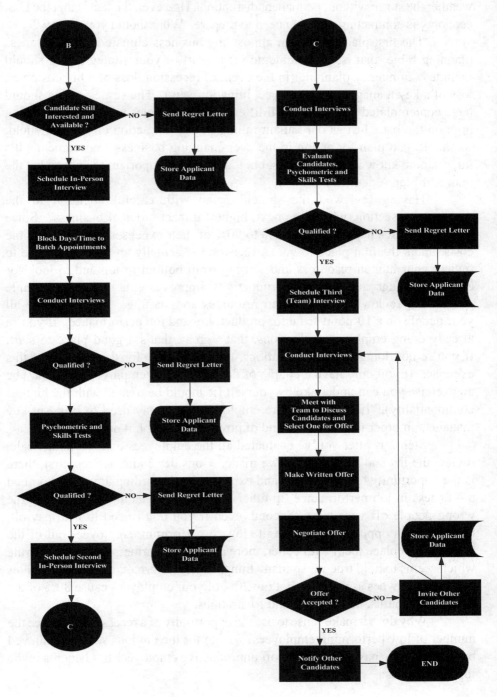

133

bailout of the financial industry, it's worth noting that, as scary as things seem right now, the average recession lasts only about 12 months, and most companies weather the storm without permanent disruption. However, the fact is that the U.S. economy is contracting, and you need to prepare. What should you do now?

The first place to turn in almost any business climate is your business planning bible, that is, your strategic plan. Part of your strategic plan should include contingency planning (in the event of recession, loss of a big customer, loss of a key management employee, litigation, etc.). The strategic plan should have contemplated any number of different contingencies with recession being high on the list. Just as our valiant military plans for action on the battlefield, so should you plan for action in the ever changing business environment. It's important to know what the plan is, but it's almost as important to know what the plan is if Plan A doesn't work.

Having reviewed the strategic plan with careful attention to the contingency section, what's the next, highest impact order of business? Since most businesses have between 35% to 90% of their expenses tied up in people costs, that's the first place to go. A recession is actually an opportune time to review your human resources and staffing from bottom to top and to look for expense savings and potential productivity improvements. Here's a simple process for reviewing your human resources and staffing. First, evaluate all your people on a 10-point scale for productivity and job performance. If you're already doing employee evaluations, that's great; that's a good place to start. If you're not doing formal evaluations, that's okay too for the purpose of this exercise. If you only have a couple of dozen or fewer employees, this may be an exercise you can undertake by yourself (it should be treated with the highest confidentiality). If you have more employees, you may need to bring in key managers in order to give it the kind of power and oomph it deserves.

Step 2 is after you've evaluated all the employees on a 10-point scale, review the list and the notes you've made. Consider 2 alternatives: first, there is the opportunity to trim payroll and expenses by discarding anyone who rated a 4 or less in job performance (in other words, you're taking action to get the wrong people off your bus). Second, even if you don't need to trim payroll, this is still an opportunity to take the lowest performing employees out of the mix and to replace them with better, more capable performers. If the 80/20 rule which seems to hold true for so many things in life is correct, it probably applies to your employees as well; the bottom 20% of your employees cause 80% of the headaches, snafus, bottlenecks, and frustrations.

Why does it make sense to use the opportunity of a recession to reduce the number of low performing employees? Aside for the obvious savings achieved by not having to pay them, laying off unproductive employees has benefits in the following areas:

- Eliminating unproductive employees increases morale. Most people think layoffs are poor for morale. However, if you have a few problem employees, eliminating them will have the positive effective of radically *increasing* morale. You know the old saying about a few bad apples

- Poor employees are drags on productivity. We once interviewed a gentleman who owned a building supply company. He had a counter salesman who was adequate and who had been with him a number of years. The salesman earned about $45,000 per year and generated about $250,000 a year in sales. I asked him to stop for a minute and brainstorm what would happen if he could replace this below average "4" performer with someone who performed at an "8" level. He said he thought that, realistically, a better salesman could increase sales by about 50% to $375,000, would generate fewer customer complaints, would increase customer satisfaction, would generate fewer internal complaints, and would produce higher energy among those who worked alongside him. The point is that a "4" employee, while known and adequate, really couldn't compare in terms of productivity to what a genuinely motivated employee could produce. Moving poor performers out in favor of better ones is a winner all around

- Getting rid of lower productivity employees demonstrates your commitment to company excellence rather than simply adhering to the status quo. It increases accountability among employees and points out to everyone that you are steering the ship responsibly and actively as captain

- Eliminating lower productivity employees simply will make your life easier. You'll have fewer headaches, and you'll have more people on hand to whom you can reliably delegate

- Eliminating lower productivity employees will increase trust of the leader among employees. Engineering constructive layoffs, far from reducing morale in the organization, actually increases the confidence of the people in the organization who are highly productive. Many family business owners cling to long term employees out of a sense of stewardship. But what is the highest definition of stewardship? Should you be hanging on to one or 2 bad apples in the name of stewardship, or should you be looking after the other 30 or 300 employees who are the most committed and dedicated to your long term success? Where does your stewardship duty actually lie?

- Eliminating low productivity employees can produce serious money savings. Here is a simplified example:

> A company with $20 million in sales has a 5% net profit margin. Of the $19 million of business costs incurred annually, 50% of that number is payroll. Almost all companies wish to increase sales; look at what an increase in sales does for this organization. A 10% increase in sales pushes the top line upward to $22 million. Assuming the same net profit margin of 5%, the company now has $100,000 of additional funds at the bottom line.

> Now let's look at the same company if it is able to trim payroll by 5% by eliminating lower productivity employees. Since the total people costs were $9.5 million, reducing payroll by 5% produces $475,000 of annual savings. Without increasing sales by *one dollar*, management has cut expenses by $475,000 which goes straight to the bottom line. It doesn't require a Ph.D. in economics to figure out that an increase of $475,000 beats an increase of $100,000. By strategically trimming payroll, the company has increased its net margin from 5% to 7.38%.

So what then is the first order of business in a recession? The first place to go is to look at your people costs to see if you can get one of 2 benefits: either you'll be able to increase top line sales by eliminating lower performing employees in favor of better ones, or you'll be able to generate savings by trimming payroll and lowering your costs. Either way your business gets healthier. There is a corollary to this recommendation. You can't always eliminate employees unless you have someone else to take over the jobs they were doing. Some jobs can be eliminated altogether or merged with others, but some people, as much as you might like to be rid of them, are performing essential functions. Therefore, in order to be able to allow those people to seek greener pastures elsewhere, you'll need a highly developed human resources system for "getting the right people on your bus." One of the unanticipated benefits of a recession is that other companies are cutting as well. That means that the available talent pool to enter your organization has increased. Take advantage of the opportunity to scour the marketplace for the best talent, and not only will you increase your bottom line, you'll make your life simpler, better, and more fulfilling as well.

Coping and Communicating In a Recession

If examining people costs is the first place to go, what should one do next? What should the family business leader do in an atmosphere of relentlessly downbeat news; increasing anxiety among customers, suppliers, lenders, and employees; and overall gloom and doom? Here are a few tips that, individually or collectively, can help business leaders and their companies refocus on coping, and maybe even prospering in tough times.

1. **Meet with your family and staff as often as necessary.** Your people know what's going on in the world at large, and they often know as much as you do about what's going on with your customers. Sit and talk with them. Be candid about what the economic slowdown is (or could be) doing to your company. Especially if you've experienced a significant negative event (loss of a major customer, delay in a major project, departure of a key employee, etc.), you'd better get ahead of the gossip curve before things spiral out of your control. If you're not comfortable talking to your employees face to face, solicit their input via an employee survey. The long and short of it is that finding a way to communicate with and understand your employees in tough times is more important than listening and talking with them in prosperous times

2. **Acknowledge your shared fears.** Acknowledge that there are fears and concerns at many levels of society and business. Talk openly with your family members and employees, attempt to understand their concerns about the future, and do a bit of listening. Just allowing them to air their concerns is sometimes enough to change attitudes and to help people see a more positive side of the story

3. **Put things in perspective.** The large one-day drop in the Dow Jones Industrial Average in the fall of 2008 was big, but how big was it? It didn't even crack the top 10 worst days in terms of percentage decline. For example, in October 1987, the market dropped more than 22% in just one day! Most likely your business has weathered bad economic or industry news before, and it will almost certainly have to do so again. Take the long term view

4. **Engage your family members and employees in seeking creative opportunities**. In a client company, employees were asked to participate in a contest to cut expenses during the

recession of the early 1990s. Management pledged to pay a bonus based on the value of an employee's cost-cutting suggestion. One employee earned a $2,000 cash bonus by coming up with a money-saving idea in a manufacturing process. If things are going poorly, working on an expense reduction plan with your family members and key managers could produce tremendous benefits

5. **Review your strategic plan.** If you're on target with your plan for the current period, how do you stay on target? If you're off target, how do you get back on track? Does the plan need to be readjusted? If so, where and when? What are the specific action steps that you or others in your company should take (with accountability measures firmly in place – especially for family managers) to put the company on a more solid and success oriented footing? If you don't have a strategic plan (shame on you if you don't!), now is a good time to use the motivation of a recession to put one in place. Developing a strategic plan is an excellent big picture assignment for an up-and-coming family business leader and can help her better understand the family enterprise in its many facets

6. **Review your budget.** Are there other, non-people expenses that you could cut (remember to use a scalpel rather than a meat cleaver)? Can you bring in an outsider to review your expenses with an objective eye and to help you benchmark in order to find fat that could be trimmed where you may not have seen any before? If you don't know what your industry's standard numbers are, you have nothing to compare against, so make sure you have accurate numbers from outside your firm as well as inside. If your chart of accounts is a mess, and you haven't broken your numbers down into cost centers, those are things that you should do before undertaking serious cuts. Many entrepreneurs make the mistake of simply cutting costs across the board by 10% only to find that by doing so they cut off future opportunities. As an example, some cut marketing expenses during a recession only to find that when business conditions improve they've cut off lead generation opportunities and are starting from a point of disadvantage relative to their competitors

7. **Remind your team about previous successes in lean times.** Talk about the joys, successes, unexpected positive outcomes, successful new hires, etc., that have happened to the company in previous times of recession. Pat Joyce of Joyce & Associates,

138

an eastern North Carolina construction company, saw the handwriting on the wall prior to the recession of 1991. He rallied his team and undertook a rigorous business development process in order to secure work. Instead of the normal 8 to 10 project bids they'd generate in a month, they planned, prepared, and rolled up their sleeves to produce 40 in a single month! The intense work plan was a success, and they had a record year when other contractors found themselves in danger of outright failure. That tremendous success in the face of a serious recession gives Joyce & Associates the assurance that they can weather virtually any storm as a team and come out unscathed

8.   **Finally, be resolutely optimistic.** If you as the leader are down in the dumps, spend your time watching CNN for the next dose of bad news, and adopt a "woe is me" attitude, it won't be long before that negative vibe is a virus running through your company. If you can't be optimistic, stay out of the office until you can be. At the very least, show strength and resolve in the way you handle yourself

Here are some other ideas for improving sales and profit health during lean business times:

- Improve the quality, regularity, and frequency of your marketing
- Make greater use of outsourcing and subcontracting
- Undertake process mapping in order to avoid duplication of effort and better efficiency
- Drop unprofitable services or products
- Fire unprofitable or "pain in the neck" customers
- Bill more frequently (go to weekly invoicing instead of monthly)
- Improve the speed of collections
- Reduce space
- Invest in higher efficiency, lower cost equipment or machinery
- Add cost recovery clauses to contracts
- Generate cash by selling underutilized equipment, vehicles, or assets

Coping in a recession often comes down to leadership. What your employees want from you is a sign that, while things may be challenging now, they will

139

get better. If you've ever checked into a darkened hotel room, you know how difficult it is to take that first step into the room where you don't know exactly where your footsteps will take you. Flicking on even the tiniest light gives you the clarity to move with confidence into the room. Showing your family business team that light at the end of the tunnel will give them the confidence and clarity they need to move forward with you into more prosperous times ahead. For more information, please read the article *How To Turn Recession Into Opportunity* at www.familybusinessinstitute.com/8blocks/.

Turnaround Planning

Turnaround planning is different from recession planning in that, if a turnaround is truly called for, things are dire indeed. In general, "turnaround" refers to redirecting an underperforming or failing company versus project or department salvage which is a subset of this broader discussion. "Underperforming and/or failing" refers to a company's inability to generate cash flows sufficient to fund normal, recurring operations without drastic changes.

The turnaround of an underperforming or failing company requires a unique skill set that usually does not exist inside your company. It is often necessary to enlist the services of a turnaround professional to successfully develop and then execute a turnaround plan, or, at the very least, orchestrate the effort. A cautionary note: many turnaround consultants take a short term view of the turnaround process (like Al "Chainsaw" Dunlap) because their compensation incentives are often tied to short term gains in performance. In many cases, short term performance improvements are relatively easy to attain; however, without consideration to the impact of all strategic initiatives on the long term, short term plans may ultimately do more harm than good. Turnaround executives *must* keep their eyes on both short and long term objectives since ultimately the goal of an effective turnaround plan is to survive the short term cash flow crisis while building a bridge to long term success.

To begin a turnaround process, closely held company leaders must consider:

1. Whether the company possesses the assets, infrastructure, revenue opportunities, leadership, determination, commitment, and intangibles required to implement a successful turnaround
2. Whether it can garner the support of key strategic partners required to assist with an effective turnaround effort such as attorneys, accountants, consultants, bankers, and others
3. Worst case scenarios such as bankruptcy in order to make sure owners understand the range of possible outcomes and the financial

140

implications of each
4. Whether there are viable merger and/or acquisition opportunities that, assuming required synergies, would add value sufficient to the troubled organization and advance ownership's long term (though likely modified) financial, family, and other life objectives
5. Evaluate the current pool of knowledge regarding competitors (and expand it if necessary), and, for those that are consistently successful, evaluate the differences between their operations and yours to determine opportunities for quick improvement
6. Evaluate other external factors such as current and forecasted economic conditions to determine whether the turnaround effort will be conducted at the top or bottom of the economic wave

As with any and all important decisions, ownership and management must remove emotion from the decision making process and make a prudent business decision based on risk and return. Some companies (though very few) *cannot* be turned around.

The company must come to grips immediately, and before anything else is done, with the adequacy of control over cash, cash flows (both historical and forecasted), and the cash management function. While there may be varying degrees of expertise inside an organization regarding financial statement preparation and analysis, the first signs of trouble generally appear with cash flows, and even the most informed readers of financial statements may have difficulty drawing precise conclusions regarding the condition of cash flows. Traditional financial statement presentations (i.e. those financials that are the product of an audit in compliance with GAAS and deliver financials that are GAAP compliant) can leave readers grasping to understand the intricacies of the company's precise cash flow condition.

In a turnaround, it is likely that financial and accounting personnel will come under fire for "allowing" the problem to occur unless they've been very publicly delivering timely information to executives who ignored the warning signs. In any case, executives must be able to count on the delivery of accurate, timely financial data by accounting and finance personnel and follow that with prudent decision making and strict accountability. Poor or dated information will undoubtedly lead to poor decision making, and the company can ill afford that during turnaround.

Regarding cash, cash flows, and cash management operations, companies facing a turnaround challenge must:

1. Ensure there are adequate physical and tactical controls over cash, cash equivalents, and any other assets easily converted to cash –

presumably most current assets
2. Look to accounting, finance, and other executive personnel to develop firm, precise controls over cash forecasting capabilities and constantly adjust assumptions until forecasting capabilities are completely reliable. It is critical that ownership and management be able to count on a strong, steady, and uncompromising financial executive to steer the turbulent waters associated with turnaround
3. Examine and evaluate sufficiency of credit facilities to ensure access to levels of cash sufficient to execute on a prudent turnaround strategy. It is often necessary, particularly in smaller companies, to bring in skilled outside experts that understand the lender-borrower dynamic well enough to make an effective pitch to the lender that financial restructuring serves everyone's best interest
4. Determine immediate steps that can be taken to alleviate cash flow suffering such as obtaining extended terms from critical vendors to improve (stretch) average days to collect
5. Look for opportunities to convert non-earning assets to cash without compromising the company's ability to generate revenues for the long term

It is incumbent on executives involved in the turnaround process that there is unequivocal consensus regarding the underlying goal which is to *preserve cash flows*. To do so, they must ensure that everything possible is done to remove constraints and convert products and/or services to cash as quickly as possible. This discussion falls under the category of constraints theory and is generally beyond the scope of this book; however, suffice it to say that executives must understand it is imperative to remove all impediments to a lightning fast conversion of products and/or services to cash.

Executives must endeavor to examine – and then adjust – short to near term goals and related operating strategies to ensure complete focus on turnaround related tasks while repositioning the firm for long term success.

Markets and industries are littered with failed companies that executed successfully on a turnaround plan that delivered improved short term performance, but a false sense of security retarded long term results due to the short sighted nature of the proposed solutions or initiatives. Additional turnaround initiatives are to:

1. Evaluate existing business, strategic, and other operating plans to determine what changes are required to deliver improved cash flows in the near term while repositioning the company for sustainable success for the long term

2. Develop consensus regarding the required changes to operating tactics and strategies, then develop the summary turnaround plan to deliver on required modifications
3. Examine burn rate to determine what measures (if any) can be taken to lower break-evens without compromising the company's near or long term abilities to deliver successfully on products and services. As used here, "burn rate" refers to the amount of expense that will be incurred (usually measured in monthly increments) without regard to revenues over the short term or inside the bell curve or normal range of activity. This will, once recalculated to reflect the new (turnaround) reality, tell executives and owners what revenues will be required to cover non-discretionary spending
4. Examine the impact of every strategic initiative on both the short term and then long-term to avoid selling out the long term in favor of the short term

The most effective turnaround plans are those that are prepared to address short term needs with an eye on the long term, and the turnaround should be viewed, to the extent possible, as a subset of the company's larger, longer term strategic business plan.

Companies must evaluate their current human resource pool to determine whether the talent exists in house to successfully execute a turnaround plan. Many of a company's best employees and skilled employees and advisors over the years will find it difficult to operate in a turnaround environment due to their inability to deal effectively with rapid or sudden change and the potential stresses associated with the sense of urgency inherent in the turnaround process.

Whether right or wrong, current cash flow failings are often linked inexorably to the existing accounting and finance team which can undermine confidence regarding their abilities to provide the strong, steady hands required to help steer the company out of trouble. Whether those assessments are fair or not, they are a reality of turnarounds, and banks and other stakeholders will press for change if they are to buy into proposed turnaround strategies. Pay particular attention to financial, accounting, and non-financial executive level positions that will play an integral role in the turnaround effort, and make changes where and if necessary; be realistic given the urgent nature of the current circumstance. This evaluation should also be extended to external or contract relationships such as legal and accounting. Many attorneys and accountants will find themselves outside their comfort zones when faced with the challenges associated with turnaround.

Executives facing the turnaround challenge must remain focused, unified, and consistent in their signals and messages to internal and external consumers of information about the condition of the company. Executives must ensure that important relationships remain intact. It is disconcerting to customers, vendors, or other stakeholders to receive misinformation from uninformed sources – or worse, misleading information from competitive forces. Executives responsible for turnaround must pull together an organized messaging campaign that sends the proper signals to stakeholders that the company is okay and is undergoing a "transformation" that all businesses face at some point as they grow and evolve. Executives must also take every precaution to communicate both short and long term goals effectively to employees who may be outside the turnaround process looking in. There is generally an elevated level of stress associated with companies facing the turnaround challenge, and while some matters are more for management's or ownership's consumption only, it is important to instill a sense of confidence in employees that there is a plan, that they play an important role in that plan, and that there is a light at the end of the tunnel. It can be difficult, if not impossible, to affect a functionally effective turnaround without solid, unwavering support from the workforce at large; when that support is not there, a well thought out turnaround plan can fall apart from within.

Executives must examine low risk (cost), potentially high reward (return) opportunities to advance revenue growth. It is counterintuitive to think about expenditure during a time of never ending cost cutting, but, the fact is that turnaround plans and companies can crumble from within if modest, strategically viable investment opportunities are blindly overlooked. The very word "turnaround" suggests cash flow difficulties; however, the company cannot afford to overlook opportunities to spend 50 cents to gain a dollar.

Finally, leaders must develop flash or other reporting systems that keep executives on top of metrics daily telling them how the company is doing against plan and to allow for quick, precise adjustments to strategies when needed. Information is always important, but perhaps at no other time is fast, accurate information more important than during a turnaround effort. The company and its executives will face a variety of challenges, some known and some unknown, as they proceed through the turnaround plan; one of those challenges should NOT be the inability to make effective, timely decisions due to poor, irrelevant, or outdated information.

Conclusion

There are a huge number of other universal operations issues and tools we could have taken up; handling paper flow, developing accountability and action registers, evaluating leasing versus buying hard assets, the correct uses and sources of capital, inventory turns, and lean processes to name just a few. What we've tried to emphasize and reinforce with the 4 tools presented is that family and closely held business executives should *not* be too involved in company operations but instead be focused on developing thinking, systems, and processes which translate their hands on work into tools which others can use – and so they can find the entrepreneurial freedom they've wanted for so long.

Building Block #5 – Operations Management

Executive Summary

⇨ Closely held business leaders should rigorously analyze their operations to determine precisely which parts of their operations actually make them money – and which don't

⇨ Key Performance Indicators help a company quickly assess progress towards goals and overall health. KPIs (not more than about 6) make up an executive's "management dashboard"

⇨ Process maps help eliminate waste, improve effectiveness, merge several ways of doing things into one common way, cut costs, and increase knowledge. Process mapping creates a visual flow of how an entire activity works across company functions from beginning to end

⇨ Recession planning is a high order tactic in tough economies. Among the highest payoff activities in a recession are to objectively evaluate company staffing with an eye to cost savings and to communicate frequently and clearly about future company plans

⇨ Turnaround planning is called for when company prospects for future success are dire indeed. Turnaround work almost always requires bringing in talented outsiders to redirect the business

Chapter Seven
Building Block #6 – Administration Management

The purpose of administration management is to coordinate all the "details" of running a business. Administration management is NOT a necessary evil or an afterthought – although many family and closely held business owners treat it that way. To have a sustainable closely held company, managers must develop more and better infrastructure and administrative support systems.

Think of all the items that can potentially fall under the heading of administration management:

- Finance and cash management
- IT, hardware and software
- Communication systems
- Vendor, supplier, and advisor relationships
- Compliance
- Physical plant and space
- Business correspondence
- Planning
- Budgeting
- Compensation planning
- Employee and asset controls and policies
- Knowledge and information sharing
- Record keeping and storage
- Maintaining efficient paperwork flow
- Training
- Problem solving
- Dispute resolution
- Being a resource to others in the company
- Employee benefit plans

- Events planning
- Customer care
- Equipment management
- Supplies management

The list above represents items which are necessary in order to have a smooth running business, and company executives will find themselves involved in every single one of them at one time or another. Few entrepreneurs start their companies because they wish to be consumed with compliance, vendor, supplier and advisor relationships, or maintaining their physical plants and spaces; they prefer, as we saw in the previous chapter, to be involved in the operations of their businesses. A plumber starts a plumbing company, a salesman starts a company to represent manufacturers, or a project manager starts his own construction company. None of those entrepreneurs started his own business because he dreamed of slogging through administering people and processes. He started the company because he loved the technical work of doing whatever it was he did. For an entrepreneur, however, to make the leap from having a job to having a sustainable business, he has to get comfortable with the idea of building administration management infrastructure (or at least he has to have someone on the team who can do it for him).

At what point does an entrepreneur need to develop this vital infrastructure? The typical case is to fall behind the curve in developing administrative systems. The ideal way to do it is to invest time, money, and energy just before it's actually necessary in order to support additional revenue and customer demands. The universal complaint of business leaders is that there's not enough time for them to do all the things they need to do; a corollary complaint is that they always find themselves "putting out fires." If they had the right kind of infrastructure and systems in place, they'd find their fire fighting responsibilities curtailed and would create more time to do more of the things they love to do – or to simply spend time on that underutilized boat they bought a few years ago. From a leadership perspective, one could say that managers work IN the business while leaders work ON the systems and infrastructure they'll need in order to have the business work for them. Covey writes: "When structures and systems are aligned, they facilitate empowerment; when they aren't, they work against it."

To create a sustainable company, entrepreneurs need to ensure themselves that their companies and employees can replicate the things that the entrepreneur herself was originally good at. Tatum writes:

"As businesses grow, they attract their first customers or clients on the strength of the entrepreneur's unique talents. At a certain size, however, the physical demands become so intense that the entrepreneur can no longer deliver on an individual basis the value he or she once did. As a result, misalignment arises, and the company experiences a number of breakdowns, including sales stagnation, quality problems, ineffective new product development, and customer service failures."

Here's an example: an entrepreneur with a small number of employees in a manufacturing job shop always promised customers 30-day production turnaround. In order to accommodate this aggressive promise, he often had to juggle the production schedule and put Customer B ahead of Customer A in the queue. This frequently upset his production employees, but they knew who was boss and did as he wished. Due to company growth, the entrepreneur hired a new production manager who had worked for several larger companies and had an impressive resume. The entrepreneur saw this as a freedom-giving hire, and he didn't expect to be involved in production much at all going forward. Things weren't quite that smooth, however. The new shop manager didn't have a detailed job description, didn't understand the necessity of continually juggling the production schedule, and had no real way of understanding what the entrepreneur was out in the field selling. In other words, there was no support and communication structure to help the production manager do his job in the exact way the entrepreneur wanted it done. Because the shop manager was trapped between his boss, who was constantly making sales promises the production manager wasn't prepared to keep, and his production staff which resented having a new work schedule every day, production faltered and delivery times lengthened. Because the entrepreneur realized promises to his valued customers were going unmet, he found himself spending *more* time in the production facility than before. His frustration grew; he simply didn't understand how hiring a production manager could result in this kind of chaos and customer dissatisfaction. He considered trying to replace himself as production manager a failure and resolved to never lose control like that again.

The entrepreneur failed to understand the potential ripple effects from this change in his organization. Furthermore, he failed to build out the job in such a way that his expectations were crystal clear so the new production manager could understand fully what was expected of him. This is an example – replicated in tens of thousands of businesses across America – of poor administration management and underdeveloped business infrastructure. Was the effort a failure because the new production manager was incompetent compared to the entrepreneur, or was it a failure because the transition had too little administrative and communications infrastructure?

Other problems that typically arise as a company grows beyond the capabilities of its founding entrepreneur are:

149

- Leaders become confused as new business decisions become more complex, and they don't have past experience to tell them which solutions are correct and which are fraught with danger
- The company doesn't really know which of its products or services make money and which don't
- The company faces a cash crunch to the shock of the owners ("Sales and profits are up 25%! How can we possibly be out of cash?")
- The functional and financial reporting systems don't give leaders or managers the necessary information in a timely way
- Confusion reigns as having more employees means an exponentially growing need for communication which usually isn't met
- Quality suffers as the entrepreneur simply can't keep all of the tasks of the company under his thumb anymore
- Customer complaints go up, and the entrepreneur finds his time spent at work increasing rapidly in order to placate disappointed buyers
- The entrepreneur comes to work in the morning with a short list of important things he needs to do, but he finds at the end of the day he's had no time to get to any of them because he's spent his entire time putting out fires, taking phone calls from employees who need his guidance, and meeting with customers, suppliers and prospects

The symptoms above indicate a company suffering through growing pains and in sore need of better systems. Most entrepreneurs find themselves in this frustrating period in their lives without knowing precisely how they got there. Building out the administration management of a company means quantifying and standardizing things the entrepreneur always did by intuition or feel. There's no room for "assumptions" here; leaders simply can't afford to expect others to read their minds or have the same level of intuitive understanding about production or sales or process. Leaders must push the information and wisdom they've accumulated over the years out of their brains and onto paper for the benefit of those who will follow them. Withholding information and failing to disseminate it out of mistrust or a desire to hold power by having everyone on a "need to know basis" only serves to suck an entrepreneur deeper into the vortex of administration and prevent him from achieving the wonderful goal of entrepreneurial freedom.

If an entrepreneur isn't alone – if she has siblings, parents, or cousins in the ownership or leadership group alongside her – they'll need to have serious discussions about where the business is going. As we discussed in the previous chapter, they'll need to have a meeting of the minds about money and the meaning of money. They'll need to question whether their obsessive, long-standing devotion to tax avoidance really serves the company well in terms of its future administrative needs. They'll need to have heart to heart discussions about what people and systems changes confront them as they move from being an entrepreneurial organization to a more professionally managed one capable of sustaining itself. They'll need to critically and objectively evaluate themselves and their current management team in order to see if they truly have what it takes; if they find serious capability gaps, they'll need to determine how to close them.

We'd like to explore 2 areas where family and closely held businesses seem to have difficulty in the lion's share of cases. The first is benchmarking and the second is cash management.

Benchmarking

Benchmarking is the process of comparing the cost, time, or quality of what one organization does against what other organizations do. Sometimes benchmarking is referred to as "best practices" analysis. Benchmarking can be applied to corporate practices, individual performance, processes, finances, and other areas. Benchmarking can sometimes create anxiety; what if we don't meet the standard? Some egos are too fragile to risk undertaking a rigorous benchmarking process. Even some who do undertake the process dismiss deficiencies which show up in the analysis and rationalize them away: "I know that the benchmarking shows that our receivables are 75 days on average while our competitors collect their money in 35 days, but we like to treat our customers right, and we're not obsessed with money around here. Quality's the name of the game for us."

The purpose of benchmarking is to find gaps between your company's performance and the performance of a group of others. To be valid and accurate, it's best if benchmarking is done against a homogeneous sample. For example, it might not make sense to compare a funeral home to a manufacturing company or a construction company to a wholesale distributor. Different industries require different benchmarking standards and practices. The idea of doing benchmarking and identifying gaps is to allow entrepreneurs to find areas which need improvement in their own companies and guidance about where specifically to improve performance. Benchmarking is ideally done as a part of an ongoing continuous improvement plan and should be revisited from time to time.

It's done in virtually all industries. For example, the New England Patriots are the gold standard benchmark these days in the National Football League. Everyone who wants to win the Super Bowl benchmarks his team against Coach Bill Belichick's system:

151

- Strong defense
- Controlling the ball with few turnovers
- Strong special teams play
- Having interchangeable parts (players) which are subsumed within a larger egalitarian system
- Drafting and trading for players who fit Belichick's philosophy of team play over individual statistics and glory

If you don't benchmark, you don't truly know where you stand relative to your competition and your industry. The hundreds, if not thousands, of people who say, "Our quality is the best in the industry" usually have no data on which to base that statement. How do they know? Against what standards do they judge themselves? Where is the evidence which supports their claims? If a potential customer asked those questions, the silence which followed would prove embarrassing. Benchmarking also allows business leaders to know where their competition is. If you find that the scrap rate average for your industry is 5 units per thousand and your scrap rate is 2 units per thousand, that's a wonderful piece of information that may help increase your sales, raise your prices, or take some other tangible action. If, on the other hand, you find yourself in the opposite situation, you know you have to roll up your sleeves and get to work.

The table in *Figure 7.1* is a real life example of a benchmarking study, some of the conclusions we were able to draw from the study, and some of the results which followed. This family came to us in serious condition as a result of the unexpected death of the 67 year old founder of the company. 2 of his 3 adult children and his son in-law worked in the company while his wife and one child did not. Analysis of their financials painted a challenging picture indeed. The first thing we noticed was their debt to equity ratio was seriously out of kilter; the company basically had no book value. One of the reasons for the company's poor financial performance revealed itself in the Collection Period line. The industry upper quartile has a Collection Period of 6 days while this company had an average Collection Period of well over 30 days! However, when looking at the Payables Period line, they actually were in the habit of paying their bills *faster* than the industry norm. Paying bills quickly while collecting debts slowly is a recipe for financial disaster in any company! The Operating Profit on Sales line paints a bleak picture as well as the Working Capital to Assets line. Neither generation had ever undertaken this sort of financial benchmarking analysis. Dad, an accountant by training, kept all the numbers to himself and shared none of them, not even the most basic financial information, with his children or key managers. Frankly, the family was distraught; they had assumed from Dad's lifestyle and behavior that the company was in excellent financial condition. Getting in touch with these numbers for the first time was quite a blow to

Figure 7.1

XYZ Supply Company, Inc.				
OPERATING RATIOS				
SOLVENCY RATIOS	Industry Upper Quartile	Year 4	Year 3	Year 2	Year 1
Current Ratio	1.8	1.3	1.2	1.1	1.7
Acid Test	0.9	1.3	1.0	1.0	1.1
Debt to Equity Ratio	1.3	27.4	51.2	-6.6	13.4
Fixed Assets to Equity	0.2	4.8	7.3	-0.8	2.2
Interest Coverage (times)	4.5	0.0	0.0	0.0	0.0
EFFICIENCY					
Collection Period (Days)	6.0	35.1	36.3	35.8	38.0
Sales to Assets	60.4	7.3	6.0	7.5	5.6
Sales to New Working Capital	10.0	38.1	50.0	78.2	17.3
Payables Period (Days)	32.0	25	27	21	27
Inventory Turns	14.9	0	0	0	0
PROFITABILITY					
Operating Profit on Sales (%)	3.0%	-1.6%	-0.6%	-5.2%	-0.1%
Operating Profit on Assets (%)	13.7%	-11.8%	-3.6%	-39.5%	-0.8%
Operating Profit on Equity (%)	45.8%	-335.1%	-188.2%	220.8%	-11.1%
Owners Comp to Sales (%)	0.8%	0.0%	0.0%	0.0%	18.2%
FINANCIALS					
Industry Averages					
Accounts Payable to Sales (%)	6.2%	7.1%	7.5%	6.1%	7.3%
Working Capital to Assets (%)	2.4%	19%	12.0%	10%	32.0%
Cost of Goods Sold as a % of Sales	59.6%	72.9%	72.0%	74.4%	69.5%
Gross Profit Margin (%)	40.4%	27.1%	28.0%	25.6%	30.5%
Current Liabilities to Inventory	2.0	15.8	34.8	-4.0	7.1
Inventory to Working Capital	1.8	0.1	0.7	1.3	0.8
Current Assets to Total Assets (%)	74.0%	74.6%	78.7%	81.5%	81.5%
Sales to Inventory	8.8	312.2	66.9	61.7	21.7
Current Liabilities to Inventory	1.2	23.9	7.4	5.9	1.9
OTHER TRENDS					
Working Capital		287	214	127	461
Working Capital as % of Sales		3%	2%	1.0%	6%
Working Capital % Increase		34%	69%	-72%	n/a
Working Capital Required ($000)		834	1,182	947	703

153

everyone.

In terms of turning things around, the most obvious place to start was to begin an aggressive campaign to collect money owed this company. We also slowed down the payables period; we understood their desire to be perceived as "nice guys" in the industry, but they needed a great jolt of reality in order to get their financial house in order. The next area where we provided focus was to get company expenses down as the most direct way to drive profits up; we needed the gross profit margin to be more in line with industry average. We worked with the junior generation on creating a clear, common vision for the 3 employee family members and then worked on a sales plan to drive the top line higher. Finally, we helped the family with a little "tough love" by easing Mom out of the office she had occupied since her husband's death. Not knowing what else to do, she had tried to assume a role as a leader in order to fill the vacuum created by her husband's death; unfortunately, that only made family and business relations suffer.

Benchmarking is not a panacea for every business problem, but it is important to know where you stand relative to your industry and competition. Even if the financial benchmarking isn't as bleak for your company as it was for our friends at XYZ, it's still information you need to have in order to operate efficiently. The data helps with a commodity which is often missing in family and closely held businesses: objectivity. When it comes to numbers, there are 2 schools of thought. One is, "The numbers don't lie." The other is to view the numbers as Mark Twain did: "There are lies, damn lies, and statistics." With respect to Mr. Twain, failing to undertake strenuous financial analysis and rigorous examination of your business financials most decidedly means that you're swimming upstream when it comes to the administration management of your company.

Cash Management and Cash Flow Planning

Cash flow seems like a simple concept, but it's not. As we said before, entrepreneurs don't start or build businesses because they love the idea of administering income statements and balance sheets. They often treat accounting as a necessary evil and hand it off to a junior family member or staff person while paying scant attention to what's likely to happen to their cash if the business grows or shrinks in the future. Furthermore, the accounting profession, the most relied upon outside professionals for family and closely held companies, is almost entirely focused on *historical* reporting. Their job is to collect data, put the data into generally accepted accounting conventions for the purpose of reporting, minimize taxation, and provide a conduit for government and regulatory compliance. We know what you're saying: "My CPA isn't like that." We have 2 thoughts. First, how do you truly know that in the absence of benchmarking professional services? Second, if that's the case, as virtually every closely held company leader states, why do we not see better financial and cash flow planning in more than a precious few client cases?

Cash is king in business, and no company can survive for very long without generating positive cash flow. Cash flow is simply a company's cash inflows minus its cash outflows over a given period of time. Most closely held business owners think of cash as revenues less expenses. This simply is not the case. To comply with generally accepted accounting principles (GAAP), financial reports and filings generate a great deal of "accounting static." It's quite difficult to tell from an income statement or a balance sheet how a company's cash is actually utilized and the condition of the company's current and future cash flows. Cash is required for everyday things like payroll, purchases, debt service, lease payments, inventory purchases, and materials. A profitable company doesn't necessarily have positive cash flow, and a company with positive cash flow may not necessarily be profitable.

There are three kinds of cash flow:

- Cash flow from operations
- Cash flow from investments (from the purchase or sale of assets)
- Cash flow from financing (utilizing a portion of a company's line of credit, for example)

A cash flow statement is a sort of a compressed corporate check book analysis. For a closely held company – especially one which anticipates strong future growth – projecting future cash is vitally important. Cash flow analysis is simply an administrative management tool which helps a company anticipate and avoid liquidity problems going forward.

Cash flow does have a link to the balance sheet. The simple balance sheet analysis of:

$$CA + NCA = CL + NCL + OE$$

Current Assets + Noncurrent Assets = Current Liabilities + Noncurrent Liabilities + Owners' Equity can be restated breaking down the Current Asset (Cash + Accounts Receivable + Inventory) component as:

$$Cash + AR + INV + NCA = CL + NCL + OE$$

Cash + Accounts Receivable + Inventory + Noncurrent Assets = Current Liabilities + Noncurrent Liabilities + Owners' Equity.

155

If one rearranges the equation using eighth grade algebra, it's easy to isolate cash:

Cash = Current Liabilities + Noncurrent Liabilities + Owners' Equity – Accounts Receivable – Inventory – Noncurrent Assets.

This helps one understand how changes in any of the asset classes will affect the company's future cash position. For example, looking at the equation above mathematically, an increase in inventory requires a corresponding decrease in cash (unless, of course, offset by the use of debt). Conversely, an increase in a current liability also increases cash on the other side of the equation. Utilizing credit which may increase debt to a supplier company simultaneously frees up a company's cash to use for other purposes. Maybe this helps one understand why cash flow analysis can sometimes get pretty confusing.

Growing companies sometimes find themselves in cash flow trouble because they have to invest money before they receive it in exchange for their product or service. For example, a farmer must utilize cash to improve or upgrade equipment, buy seed, and pay employees with the understanding that he won't be able to sell his crops until several months in the future. As is always the case, investment comes first and return comes later (one certainly hopes). Relying only on income statements creates a false illusion; income statements tell how much cash a company will *eventually* create. If a company – especially a growing one – doesn't have a well developed capability for predicting future cash flows, they'll find themselves in trouble.

Figure 7.2 presents a simplified example of a company that is growing and profitable and also happens to be heading for a cash crisis. In month one, the company had revenue of $1,300,000, cost of goods sold of $1,100,000, and a gross profit of $200,000. After deducting expenses, the earnings before tax was $135,000. That is an excellent margin. Let's look at the effect, however, on cash flow as the company grows. In month 2 and in each of the following months, sales increase 25% per month. This would be an idyllic time for most small businesses! By month 5, monthly sales are at $2,930,000 and gross profit is up to $220,000.

Let's take a look at some other telltale numbers, however. In month one, gross profit margin was over 15%. The new sales in months 2 through 5 have a much lower margin which could be a reflection of a tight economy, increased competition, decisions on project or job selection, or other factors. Employee costs have risen to be able to produce the new work, but employee costs as a percent of sales actually falls.

Referring to "Free Cash Flow," AR payment received grows, but not at a rate as fast as revenue has grown. This is an indication the company has taken its eye off the ball in terms of staying on top of collections. As a result, net cash flow in month 2 falls from $135,000 to zero and actually becomes negative in months 3 through 5! Companies often suffer simultaneously from sales growth, declining margins, and lengthening collection periods, and this is a recipe for disaster! The company in our example shows a $499,000 net profit while at the same time its cash balance drops from $165,000 to negative $495,000! The company has two choices: it could either try to finance the negative cash flow from its retained earnings – obviously a poor idea – or it could seek outside financing. In either event, the firm must address its margin and collections issues to return to good health. To compound this cash crunch, if this company is an S corporation, the owners owe tax for the profits they booked. From where will the cash come to pay the tax liability?

Since top line sales growth is the dream for most entrepreneurs, why didn't this company see trouble coming? The most common reason is because they looked at their corporate finance function as a historical reporting requirement, and they didn't have tools for peering into the future. In order to head off the potential of such an ugly scenario, we'd like to present a simple tool (*Figure 7.3*) for anticipating future cash flow needs. This cash flow budget worksheet can be adapted to virtually any business of any size. Assuming one has a pretty good handle on future inflows and outflows (and this might take a bit of homework especially on the part of businesses which haven't undertaken this kind of analysis before), it's reasonably easy to forecast cash flows and anticipate potential problem areas. This tool, while readily available and easy to use, is incredibly *underutilized* in most entrepreneurial companies. Building administration management infrastructure requires that closely held company leaders become intimately familiar with concept of cash flow and able to predict it with unerring accuracy.

A word about utilizing professional advisors for closely held companies: There are 3 simple criteria for what you should expect from your legal, accounting, and financial professionals. They should be able to:

- Speak plain English (or whatever your language of choice might be) in a manner you can understand
- Be highly proficient in their field (and, while it may sound mercenary, you should shop your professional services around periodically)
- Turn their work around quickly

We live in constant amazement that most professionals advising family businesses fall short in at least one of these areas. And yet the business leaders make

Figure 7.2a

How to Go Broke While Making Profit 25% Sales Increase For 4 Months ($000)				
	Month 1		**Month 2**	
Income Statement		Percent of Sales		Percent of Sales
Revenue	$1,300	100.00%	$1,500	100.00%
Cost of Goods Sold	$1,100	84.62%	$1,375	91.67%
Gross Profit	$200	15.38%	$125	8.33%
Expense Detail:				
Employee Costs	$30	2.31%	$40	2.67%
Operating and GS&A Expenses	$35	2.69%	$35	2.33%
Total Expenses	$65	5.00%	$75	5.00%
Earning Before Taxes	$135	10.38%	$50	3.33%
Year to Date Earnings Before Taxes				
Free Cash Flow				
AR Payment Received	$1,300		$1,350	
AP Paid	$1,100		$1,275	
Employee Costs Paid	$30		$40	
Operating and GS&A Expenses Paid	$35		$35	
Cash Received – Cash Disbursed	$135		$0	
Beginning Cash Balance	$30			
Ending Cash Balance	$165		$165	
Balance Sheet				
Current Assets				
Cash	$166		$165	
Accounts Receivable	$1,300		$1,500	
Long Term Assets				
Fixed (Less Depreciation)	$225		$225	
Total Assets	$1,690		$1,890	
Current Liabilities				
Accounts Payable	$1,100		$1,375	
Short Term Loans	$10		$10	
Line of Credit	$0		$0	
Long Term Liabilities				
Notes	$150		$150	
Total Liabilities	$1,260		$1,535	
Owners Equity				
Paid in Capital	$10		$10	
Retained Earnings	$420		$345	
Total Liabilities & Owners Equity	$1,690		$1,890	

Figure 7.2b

How to Go Broke While Making Profit 25% Sales Increase For 4 Months ($000)					
	Month 3		**Month 4**		**Month 5**	

Income Statement		Percent of Sales		Percent of Sales		Percent of Sales
Revenue	$1,875	100.00%	$2,344	100.00%	$2,930	100.00%
Cost of Goods Sold	$1,720	91.73%	$2,160	92.16%	$2,710	92.50%
Gross Profit	$155	8.27%	$184	7.84%	$220	7.50%
Expense Detail:						
Employee Costs	$40	2.13%	$50	2.13%	$50	1.71%
Operating and GS&A Expenses	$35	1.87%	$35	1.49%	$35	1.19%
Total Expenses	$75	4.00%	$85	3.63%	$85	2.90%
Earning Before Taxes	$80	4.27%	$99	4.21%	$135	4.60%
Year to Date Earnings Before Taxes					$499	
Free Cash Flow						
AR Payment Received	$1,675		$2,000		$2,500	
AP Paid	$1,720		$2,160		$2,710	
Employee Costs Paid	$40		$50		$50	
Operating and GS&A Expenses Paid	$35		$35		$35	
Cash Received – Cash Disbursed	($120)		($245)		($295)	
Beginning Cash Balance						
Ending Cash Balance	$45		($200)		($495)	
Balance Sheet						
Current Assets						
Cash	$45		($200)		($495)	
Accounts Receivable	$1,875		$2,344		$2,930	
Long Term Assets						
Fixed (Less Depreciation)	$225		$225		$225	
Total Assets	$2,145		$2,369		$2,660	
Current Liabilities						
Accounts Payable	$1,720		$2,160		$2,710	
Short Term Loans	$10		$10		$10	
Line of Credit	$0		$0		$0	
Long Term Liabilities						
Notes	$150		$150		$150	
Total Liabilities	$1,880		$2,320		$2,870	
Owners Equity						
Paid in Capital	$10		$10		$10	
Retained Earnings	$255		$39		($220)	
Total Liabilities & Owners Equity	$2,145		$2,369		$2,660	

Figure 7.3

Cash Flow Budget Worksheet

Cash Flow Budget Worksheet	[Month]	[Month]	[Month]	[Month]	[Month]	[Month]	Total
Beginning Cash Balance							
Cash Inflows (Income):							
AR Collections							
Loan Proceeds							
Sales & Receipts							
Other:							
Total Cash Inflows							
Available Cash Balance							
Cash Outflows (Expenses):							
Advertising							
Bank Service Charges							
Credit Card Fees							
Delivery							
Health Insurance							
Insurance							
Interest							
Inventory Purchases							
Miscellaneous							
Office							
Payroll							
Payroll Taxes							
Professional Fees							
Rent or Lease							
Subscriptions & Dues							
Supplies							
Taxes & Licenses							
Utilities & Telephone							
Other:							
Subtotal							
Other Cash Out Flows:							
Capital Purchases							
Loan Principal							
Owner's Distribution							
Other:							
Subtotal							
Total Cash Outflows							
Ending Cash Balance							

excuses for their professionals; they simply don't hold their advisors to the same rigorous standards to which their customers hold them! To be fair, many closely held business owners don't use their professionals as planners and preventers of problems; they use them as firefighters. Perhaps these decisions are made out of thrift or simply a lack of awareness, but having outstanding professionals and utilizing them in a proactive manner can help closely held business executives keep a host of problems at arm's length.

The prospect of building out an administrative management system and the associated infrastructure will not warm the hearts of most entrepreneurs. However, in order to achieve the goal of having a sustainable business rather than simply a job, it's necessary. Undertaking this building block will help entrepreneurs eliminate headaches, reduce fire fighting, and increase the quality of their lives. They'll find themselves more able to break through Sullivan's Ceiling of Complexity™ and find a new state of simplicity which will allow them to refocus energy from being a doer and a worker to being an owner and investor. That's the payoff for developing a healthy administration management system.

Building Block #6 – Administration Management

Executive Summary

⇨ Administration management – the act of "running a business" – is not an afterthought and deserves to be thought of in systems and process terms

⇨ The absence of well developed administrative systems and talent means that a company can face cash, profitability, communication, customer satisfaction, and other potential crises

⇨ Benchmarking is the process of measuring and comparing the cost, time, or quality of one organization against others. The purpose is to find gaps between your company's performance and that of others. Benchmarking is best done as part of an ongoing continuous improvement process

⇨ Cash management and cash flow planning are vital administrative processes. Enlightened companies utilize accurate cash flow forecasting and budgeting to avoid unpleasant surprises

Chapter Eight
Building Block #7 – Family Management

If the title of this book is *The Top Nine Reasons Family Businesses Fail – And The Eight Building Blocks for Creating a SUSTAINABLE Closely Held Company*, why did we place family management among the final building blocks rather than as the primary one? The answer is best illustrated by a thought and memory experiment. Think back to younger days. Many of you played sports on various teams; some of you were lucky enough to be able to participate actively in sports through college and even into adulthood. Thinking back on the experiences of your sports life, try to recollect the instances when harmony on your teams was at its very greatest. Then, try to remember the experiences when the teams had absolute disharmony, fractiousness, and contentiousness. Now match those recollections with your team's won/loss records. People almost inevitably find that the teams they played on with outstanding, winning records experienced little disharmony. On the other hand, the teams with poor or losing records had quite a bit of disharmony. This concept isn't perfectly transferrable to family businesses; some family businesses are quite successful and still experience disharmony. However, the lack of harmony tends to be inversely correlated with a family company's success. Putting the 6 building blocks previously discussed into place dramatically increases the chances that a family business will be successful. Having a successful and profitable company removes a massive potential source of friction and disharmony.

The Family Business Institute library has dozens of books written by our peers and friendly competitors on the subject of getting along and preserving the family company. We won't, in this chapter, be attempting to synthesize the wisdom found in those works. Our mission in this chapter is to provide brief background and discussion followed by 3 support structures for successful family and closely held business management: trust, harmony, and conflict resolution.

For us, the terms "family business" and "closely held business" are virtually interchangeable. For example, 2 unrelated partners who come together to create and build a closely held company eventually begin to take on the characteristics of a sibling partnership or a cousin consortium. As their children grow and mature and express interest in the closely held company, the enterprise could easily morph into a stricter definition of family business. 3 unrelated closely held business owners once engaged The Family Business Institute with the outright acknowledgment that, while they weren't technically a family company, our experience working with families in business together could help them avoid the difficulties many of their peers, true family businesses, had experienced. Owners and leaders in closely held companies share many more commonalities than differences with family businesses.

In *First Things First*, Stephen Covey writes, "Our greatest joy – and our greatest pain – comes in our relationships with others. The fact is that quality of life is, by nature, interdependent." Families are paradoxical; they're usually the sources for our greatest joy while simultaneously being the sources of our greatest pain. The interplay between family and business presents even more paradoxical relationships. Love is unconditional in the family while in the business "love" – if it can even be called that – is conditional *(Figure 8.1)*. It's much easier to love a salesman who exceeds his quota every month than one who constantly underperforms. The family focuses on relationships and the emotions at play in the relationships while the business, in theory at least, is an impersonal place. If you produce, you are welcome; if you fail to produce, the impersonal nature of enterprise means you must move on. Families are places of stability and permanence; when it comes to family, you can always go home again. Businesses are, in theory, perpetual entities, but the fact is that the people who populate the business tend to come and go with some regularity. You and a coworker may be as close as brothers, but if he gets a job offer at twice his current compensation rate, he will likely move on to advance his own career and to benefit his nuclear family. The family changes constantly. People are born, age, die, get married, get divorced, develop new interests, discard old interests, suffer health setbacks, etc. In *Prescriptions For A Healthy Family Business*, we discussed at length the fact that adults consider themselves to be relatively unchanging, but Dr. Daniel Levinson disproved that theory in his remarkable book *The Seasons Of A Man's Life*. Businesses, on the other hand, change sporadically. The growth curve for most closely held companies isn't a steady 10% per year. Most businesses grow in leaps and bounds, plateau for a period of time, and enter another period of rapid growth later. Their growth curve looks more like a stair step than a smooth line. Finally, families avoid or suppress conflict (more on this later in the chapter) while businesses are continually engaged in competition. Competition can't technically be called conflict, but it shares many of the same components. Given the vast differences between the needs and functions of a family and the needs and functions of a business, it's amazing the 2 ever blend very well at all, and yet families working together in business are hardly the exception.

Figure 8.1

The Interplay of Family and Business	
The Family	**The Business**
Love is unconditional	"Love" is conditional
Focus on relationships	Impersonal
Stability and permanence	People come and go
Changes constantly	Changes sporadically
People centered	Profit Centered
Avoid or suppress conflict	Seeks competition

Family and personal considerations have a tremendous effect on closely held companies. The *Wall Street Journal* reported in 2007 that significant events in the personal lives of CEOs such as a relative's death or the purchase of a large new home affected the performance of the companies they managed. Following the death of a CEO's child, profitability declined by 21%. A spouse's death resulted in a roughly 15% decline in profitability. When a CEO bought or built a home larger than 10,000 square feet or sited on more than 10 acres, a company's financial performance also fell. Closely held company CEOs may consider themselves rock ribbed, bulletproof leaders, but the fact is that abrupt changes in relationships or lifestyle habits can't help but find their ways into the workplace and affect performance. For more on this subject, please read *Business Focused Families vs. Family Focused Families* at www.familybusinessinstitute. com/8blocks/.

Some family business writers estimate that about 85% of family business crises arise around transition issues. Upon analysis, it's easy to see why. Some of the things that have to take place during a transition process are:

- Changing the culture from urgency addiction to planning, preparation, and prevention
- Developing and training future leaders
- Finding a meaningful role for departing leaders
- Handing off of day to day management responsibilities
- Dealing with ownership transition issues
- Planning for senior generation retirement or withdrawal

- Modeling of corporate finances for the benefit of senior and junior generations
- Updating, conceiving, or implementing "drop dead plans"
- Developing a new vision which suits both senior and junior generations
- Handing off of customer, professional, and vendor relationships

And – oh by the way - the company must continue to run profitably while all this is taking place! If it takes 60 work hours a week for the CEO to assure that the company runs profitably, the burdens of transition planning could easily add another 5 to 10 hours per week. In fact, engaging in transition planning may be likened to taking on a part time job!

One of the transition issues that family and closely held companies seem to struggle with is distinguishing between what it is to be an *owner* and what it is to be a *manager*. The lines are almost always blurry. In the founding generation, Mom and Dad were both owners and managers; the old cliché was that they could have a board of directors meeting in a telephone booth. As family enterprises move down among the generations, the original model persists. While some subsequent generation family members are employees of the company and own shares of stock, others elect to pursue different careers and are owners of shares only. However, they usually fail to clarify the rights and responsibilities of ownership versus the rights and responsibilities of employment. One CEO defined an owner as "somebody who thinks he can enforce gratuitous control." The following example illustrates.

Case Study: Am I an Owner or a Manager?

3 brothers in their early to mid-fifties (the same three brothers of whom we spoke in Chapter One) contacted The Family Business Institute; their communication had broken down completely. Even though their offices were side by side in the same corridor, they only communicated with each other through email. This situation had been building for many years, but the trigger which pushed them over the top is illustrative. The 3 brothers, Scott, Doug, and Richard, each had specific responsibilities in the company. Scott was in charge of engineering and production, Doug was in charge of finance and administration, and Richard was in charge of sales and marketing. One Friday afternoon Richard, returning from a sales trip, walked into the plant to find a trusted, long time employee expressing outrage and disgust. When Richard asked what was the matter, the employee said, "Your so-and-so

brother came out here and changed a process we've been using for 20 years. He claims the process will save us time and make us more efficient, but it's taking me much longer to do it this new-fangled way!" Richard asked a few more diagnostic questions and concluded with the following advice: "Well then, just go back to doing it the way you always have."

At our retreat, Scott related this story in a voice filled with anger and disbelief. He had worked on this new process for hours and was 100% satisfied that it would, over time, save the company significant time and production costs. He couldn't believe his brother had cut him off at the knees, overturned his directive, and undermined his authority in the plant. When asked about his reasoning behind the incident, Richard replied, "I OWN JUST AS MUCH OF THIS COMPANY AS YOU DO."

We all own shares of stock in public companies either outright or in our retirement plans. Would you ever dream of walking into a General Electric, IBM, or Microsoft plant and issuing orders to people in the production area? That's exactly what Richard did; he let the fact of his ownership override his rights and responsibilities as a manager and blundered into his brother's area of responsibility. His justification absolutely did not hold water. He did what he did not out of malice but out of ignorance; he simply didn't recognize what should be a very clear boundary between management and ownership. Richard isn't alone. This type of myopia – the failure to distinguish ownership rights from management rights – is present in the vast majority of family and closely held companies, and it causes no end of confusion and conflict.

Trust

A father and son in business together were having trouble seeing eye to eye during their period of transition. One of the very first recommendations we had for them was to schedule a weekly breakfast or lunch with a written agenda in order to communicate necessary information between them (this sounds unbelievably basic, but like most closely held companies they lacked even the simplest communication structures and systems relying instead on informal "hallway meetings" or family functions to transmit information to one another). The procedure went well for a couple of weeks, and there seemed to be an ebb to the intergenerational tension. Shortly thereafter, one or the other began to call at the last minute and cancel meetings. Inevitably the cancellation was due to a customer's request to meet or an internal requirement that something get done under a tight deadline. Communication – and consequently trust – began to erode again between the father and son. The message they were sending to each other was "customer work is more important than working on our relationship and our abilities to communicate effectively with one another."

They had taken some – but not all – of our recommendations. The specific recommendation was for them to have a weekly *sacred, inviolable* planned and scheduled meeting. Cancelling meetings due to the latest fire in need of water undermined the entire communications system. Covey, in *The Seven Habits Of Highly Effective People*, has a wonderful diagram illustrating how closely trust relates to differing levels of communication:

Figure 8.2

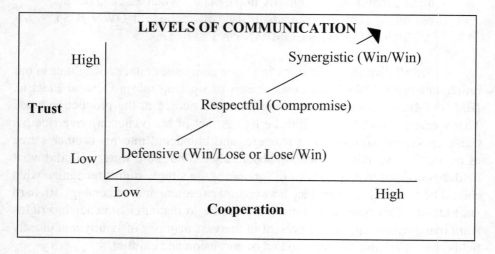

Simply put, there can't be trust and cooperation in the absence of sound, consistent communication.

For purposes of working with family and closely held businesses, we offer 2 definitions of trust: 1) belief in and reliance on the integrity, strength, or ability of a person or thing, and 2) to do something without fear. From where does trust come? Trust beliefs are based upon definitive evidence, past experiences, and that there are repeated fulfillment of promises or obligations by those asking to be trusted. In order to increase trust, one must, as Edward Deming stated, "Drive out fear so that everyone may work effectively for the company." Family members who are shocked by reports of low trust in their company environments say, "We're all family here. We love each other. What would anyone here have to fear?" They underestimate the great emotional risk in family business. Disappointing your non-family boss while working for XYZ

Company is one thing, disappointing your boss who also happens to be your dad and who has for your entire lifetime been your hero figure is something quite different. Other fear factors in family businesses are:

- Angering other family members
- Negative outcomes
- Looking foolish
- Losing money
- Getting laughed at
- Making mistakes
- Making a decision which may be reversed by others
- Failing to live up to the successes and standards of other family members
- Being left behind or left out
- Not having all the answers

Fear is a business killer! Fear in the workplace stops the creative process and makes problem solving, risk taking, and sound decision making suffer. When fear is used as a disciplinary tool or threat, employees and family members work at removing the threat and neglect the necessary work of the family and organization. Fear and anxiety have a chilling effect on performance.

When there's low trust in the business or the family, people begin to ask all sorts of questions:

- What are his motives?
- How will I be affected?
- Can I rely on what she says?
- Is it safe?
- Who will benefit?
- What's the level of support?

The lack of trust leads to a lack of forthrightness which fuels the cycle by leading directly back to a lack of trust, and so on. Trust is lost in a family or a business through a lack of follow through, a lack of ethical behavior, a lack of free information flow, continual negative feedback, failure to listen, lack of empathy, lack of sensitivity, and lack of integrity. When trust is low, people become defensive and argumentative instead of open to feedback and new ideas.

When trust is high, leaving the status quo behind and breaking through to new levels of respect and performance are easy. People can more readily subscribe to the vision of the future of the company. The motivations, processes, and plans for moving forward find easy acceptance among family members and

169

employees. People become invested in the benefits of change and have a stake in the outcome. Continuous improvement can become the rule of the day.

Trusting others in the workplace or in the family is risky. It makes it easy to take advantage of someone, and there's potential for hurt and disappointment. 3 things are essential to building trust equity. The first is an agreement to be open and honest both individually and as a group. Next, honest and forthright feedback is an essential component. Finally, accountability systems have to be in place; holding people accountable – a key function of management – is a huge factor leading towards a trusting environment. Providing accountability in an organization sounds easy, but there are several reasons why people may not behave responsibly, in spite of their good wishes, when left on their own and must therefore face negative consequences when held to account (these may sound familiar and hit perilously close to home):

- They're not organized
- They're not clear about roles and/or levels of authority
- They have trouble managing their workload or priorities
- They have trouble delegating
- They have been over-promoted and don't have the talent or skills to do the job
- They do not possess the proper training
- They lack motivation or initiative

Accountability reinforces trust by applying support, training, and external motivation when needed to allow people to be their best and accomplish more. It allows your best people to know that all are held accountable for their work, and that those who don't meet accountability standards will be dealt with proactively so the talent level of the organization rises over time.

In a trusting environment, doors are usually open (the common interpretation of "open door policy" that doors must *never* be closed is foolish. Certain circumstances and deadlines require closed doors for maximum work efficiency). Communication between people flows freely; people smile, express joy, and are happier in the workplace. People in teams feel encouraged; problems and issues are discussed and resolved in timely and constructive ways. Being able to trust allows people to function naturally and directly; it enhances interpersonal relationships. It helps to work through conflicts and makes people willing to be influenced by others in the group they trust. Trust allows for and promotes straightforward communication. People in the workplace hear statements like:

- "I'm here to support you"
- "I trust you"

- "I want you to have responsibility for this project"
- "What do you need?"
- "How can we help?"

If trust seems to be rare in your family or business, or it's been eroded over a period of time, how do you work to regain it? First, admit errors of the past, both to yourself and to those who have been affected. Apologize genuinely; looking back, it's all too easy to think of times when you were brusque, inattentive, or preoccupied with a job. Let others know that you are genuinely sorry for not meeting their needs and that you're working with intentionality to regain their trust. Commit to behaviors that promote trust, like open and honest "no B.S." communication. Show genuine interest, and become involved in the activities, projects, and concerns of others. Solicit and accept genuine feedback, and, once you have it, don't try to evaluate it, simply say "thank you." Share information with others; hoarding information benefits no one in the long run, and it tells other people that you don't trust them to handle the information responsibly. Listen to other people without talking (for strong family business leaders, this is a difficult challenge indeed. They're simply used to telling people things and having others listen rather than the other way around). Practice active listening and paraphrasing so that the other people will know that you've actually heard and understood what they've said. Follow through on your commitments; if you can't do it, or you can't do it by the deadline, don't take on the project or responsibility! Learn to say no! If you're one of those types who never says no, people will readily acknowledge how hard you work and how pure of heart you are; however, it serves no one's interest to be unable to refuse responsibility only to let others down by not finishing the job on time or doing poor quality work. Write down and keep track of your commitments. If you have trouble organizing yourself, get help; surely there are others in your family or organization who could help you stay organized and focused.

Building trust in a family or closely held business is hard work. Paradoxically, family companies – where people have known each other intimately for decades and who love each other – often suffer from the lowest levels of trust. Rather than viewing this with shame, recognize it for what it is – an opportunity to get better by acknowledging the situation as it truly exists and by rebuilding the levels of trust and communication in order to strengthen both the business and the family simultaneously. As Patrick Lencioni wrote in *The Five Dysfunctions of A Team:*

> "Trust is the foundation of real teamwork. And so the first dysfunction is a failure on the part of the team members to understand and open up to one another. And if that sounds

171

touchy-feely, let me explain, because there's nothing soft about it. It's an absolutely critical part of building a team. In fact, it's probably the most critical."

The Preoccupation with Harmony is Counterproductive in the Long Run

One of the goals of any family, whether in business or not, is to have a sense of harmony and well being. Families in business together, however, often raise the desire for harmony to unreasonable and unattainable highs. Lencioni writes: "If we don't trust one another, then we aren't going to engage in open, constructive, ideological conflict. And we'll just continue to preserve a sense of *artificial harmony*." For more on this, please read *The Seductiveness of "NO"* at www.familybusinessinstitute.com/8blocks/.

In our experience, families in business together can usually agree on problems at hand, and they can agree at times to solutions. Yet, because of the inflated desire for harmony which exists in the family business system, they push off decisions to do anything about problems for fear that one or more family members may object. In effect, they give any one family member a veto over new initiatives which can be used at any time. The failure to have clear decision making processes – processes which may challenge the sanctity of their artificial harmony states – is a substantial reason why family companies fail to reach their potential. When family businesses say they usually make "decisions by consensus," what they really mean is they make decisions *unanimously*. Let's get real! It's almost impossible to get a group of 5 or more to agree on what movie to go see on a weekend; how can it be possible to consistently get 5 business people or family members together unanimously? The difficulty of creating unanimity in family groups is a contributing reason for why many family decisions are made in a unilateral, dictatorial, or authoritarian fashion.

As we will see in the next section of this chapter, it's all right to have conflict periodically. Harmony can't truly be manufactured in spite of Mom's or Granddad's best wishes. Being genuinely, sometimes brutally, honest is one of the things Collins identified in his research on great companies. Leaders in those companies accepted the facts no matter how uncomfortable they were and took action based on reality rather than avoiding challenging issues in a misguided attempt to preserve an atmosphere of harmony (while we're at it, let's challenge the precept that most family companies exist in a state of harmony. What they really have is a state of détente).

Avoiding open, frank discussion and postponing decisions simply to maintain a cease fire is limiting over the long run. Covey writes about a successful entrepreneur who was asked the reason for his success. His response: "Good decisions." The second question was: "Well, how do you make good decisions?" The response: "Experience." And then the final question: "How do you get experience?" And the response: "Bad decisions."

More Covey: "We learn by our experience. We learn by our mistakes. We learn by attempting something. Sometimes it works and sometimes it doesn't, but we find the better way. Do whatever it takes to get the fear of failure out of your system. Failure is a marvelous, magnificent blessing that teaches us how to grow. By over-emphasizing the unattainable goal of perfect family harmony, family companies present a happy face to the outside world, but in the absence of brutal honesty and strategic decision making they don't learn much either."

Resolving and Reducing Conflict in the Closely Held Business

Conflict is a fact in family business life. How common is conflict in family and closely held businesses? According to the Family Firm Institute, 20% of family businesses report weekly conflict, another 20% report monthly conflict, and 42% report conflict 3 to 4 times per year. You can draw your own conclusions about the 18% who report no conflict at all! It's worth noting that not all disagreements rise to the level of conflict. Disagreement is a difference of facts, perceptions, beliefs, or expectations. Conflict is a higher level of disagreement; it's the belief of 2 or more people that their positions are mutually exclusive. A fascinating conflict fact is that the person with the least vested interest in the outcome has the most power in the conflict relationship. The person with the highest vested interest in the outcome has the weaker bargaining position. Here's an example:

> 6 brothers in business together are looking at strategy and planning for the future. The oldest brother is just 18 months away from a well earned retirement and being able to cash in his shares so he'll have – for the first time in his working life – some serious "walking around money." The youngest brother, however, is much more concerned with the company's capital and IT needs over the next 6 months and has about 15 years before his retirement. The oldest brother has the higher vested interest, and his youngest sibling the lowest. Even though the clear consensus was they needed to begin planning now, the youngest brother prevailed on the group to delay the project for at least 6 months, and that's the choice they made. Lowest vested interest carried the day (again).

There are 3 common myths in closely held businesses about conflict. The first says, "If we really loved each other, we wouldn't have conflict." The opposite is reality; if you didn't care, it wouldn't matter! Another is: since Mom (or Dad or Brother) won't change, there's nothing I can do about the situation." This is simply not true, and it surrenders control of your life or your business to forces beyond yourself. One can always work on herself; she can always adopt and model the positive behavior or changes she'd like to see. As Goldsmith writes, "Change is not a one way street. It involves 2 parties: the person who's changing and the people who notice it." The third myth has to do with assumptions. A frustrated son-in-law says, "I raised the issue with my father-in-law 3 years ago, but he wasn't interested and wouldn't talk about making any changes." Failing to raise the issue with the father-in-law based on something he said 3 years ago is capitulation. Yesterday's decisions are not permanent, and yesterday's people are different today.

For example, a son in a gasoline distribution company desperately wanted his dad to complete his estate and stock transfer planning. The son was in his early 50s and the dad was in his mid-80s. Dad would get to the point of making important decisions, and then stop. The son, an enterprising leader who had expanded the company significantly on his watch, was becoming increasingly frustrated. At one meeting – a final, desperate attempt to get Dad to pull the trigger on all the planning the advisors had prepared – he readily agreed to sign off on the documents and displayed an enthusiasm he simply hadn't in previous sessions. What in the world had happened to change dad's attitude 180 degrees? The night before, his next door neighbor and golfing companion had suffered a massive heart attack. Dad was awakened in the middle of the night by an emergency services helicopter landing in his backyard in order to ferry his neighbor to a hospital in a city about 45 minutes away. Hearing and watching that helicopter and the technicians who had his friend swaddled in tubes and machinery changed Dad's mind completely about the necessity of finalizing his ownership transfer plans.

Family and closely held companies can be tense places ripe for conflict escalation. There can be tension within the founder of the company who's concerned about the future success of his business and family. He's also frustrated with his need to confront his age related reductions in capacity. There's a destructive generation gap or Oedipal competition between fathers and children as they struggle with who has primacy in the company. The struggle can often create animosity and factions among family members and employees. Another tension is that of sibling rivalry or rivalry among cousins – the lack of a common vision among them is a contributor – as well as competition over who eventually will have what responsibilities. Finally, there's tension outside the family among long term employees and customers who don't welcome the loss of relationships with senior generation or departing family members. Each of these tensions in its own way can contribute to an atmosphere of conflict ready to ignite.

174

There are 4 primary sources of conflict in closely held companies. There is the violation of people's sense of fairness. There may be the perception, especially in family businesses, of favoritism, unequal or unfair compensation issues, or even a lifestyle gap for family members who have elected employment elsewhere and who may not enjoy the financial windfall of being employed by the family enterprise. A second source of conflict is feeling unacknowledged by others in the business. Junior generation members feel unacknowledged by their parents for their current contributions while senior generation individuals feel unacknowledged by the junior generation for their past sacrifices, hard work, and achievements. A third source stems from feelings of powerlessness. Junior generation family members feel the fear of never being "their own man" or for never having true decision making authority and responsibility in the business. They can become afraid that their peers in the business community will see through their titles and salaries and realize that they have no power. Fourth, unclear roles and responsibilities in the business and in the family can easily lead to overlap and conflict.

The debilitating, pervasive lack of time (as discussed in Chapter Three) is a conflict contributor. If closely held business leaders had highly developed self management and time management skills, they might have the time and resources available to communicate more effectively and to engage in proactive, forthright discussions which would lead to a reduction in conflict. However, as we've seen before, the lack of time is the number one complaint of family and closely held business executives.

There is a fair amount of confusion between *suppression* of conflict and its *resolution*. When parents have small children, they can use their physical size and moral authority to stop conflict in its tracks. It's easy to separate battling siblings by simply saying "don't hit your sister" and sending the children to their rooms. That technique, because it's pretty successful, gets repeated in families. Unfortunately, it's not nearly as effective when your children are 40 as when they were 4. The overwrought desire for harmony and falling back on the separation techniques of the past mean that conflict is more frequently suppressed or avoided than genuinely resolved.

Poor decision making techniques in most closely held companies also contribute to a conflict environment. Unless there is an autocratic, clearly defined leader (almost always the founding owner of the business during his lifetime), decision making in family companies gets awfully muddled. No one is really sure what decisions can be made unilaterally or what decisions require consultation. If a decision does require consultation, with whom? Who (if anyone) has veto power? When do they have veto power? By what virtue? Does *everyone* have veto power? What decisions actually require a shareholder's vote? Are there certain decisions that require a super majority or unanimous consent? If so, what are they? When do we need to take a vote, what's our voting procedure? Is it one person one vote, or do some votes have unequal weight? These kinds of questions rarely come up in closely held companies until it's too late, and that leads to the decision not to decide. Closely held business leaders fail to recognize that not making a decision *is a decision* and is almost always suboptimal!

Most family and closely held business leaders haven't fully calculated or don't fully appreciate the costs of ongoing conflict. They say, "It's the norm around here; we've learned to deal with it so it doesn't affect our business or our family." They're wrong, and it's naïve to assume that pervasive conflict isn't constricting the growth and health of the business. Employees recognize conflicts among leaders and family members, and they can easily find themselves divided into factions. Key managers could leave the closely held company; the stories of talented but frustrated managers who've left companies because of conflict between family members are legion. Businesses with pervasive conflict have effectiveness and efficiency issues. People suffer from poor health. Morale is low, and there is a lack of enthusiasm for the work of the company. The opportunity costs of conflict are difficult to quantify, but refusing to admit that they exist is ridiculous.

Disagreement and conflict, in spite of what most family business members think, isn't necessarily bad. Healthy conflict – which is resolved effectively – is a great thing in business because it challenges people to think and to defend their positions in an atmosphere of collegial debate. Conflict can be bad, however. When it's continually suppressed and begins to fester, that's a danger sign. When there are consistently repeating patterns of conflict over time, that's an issue. When conflict leads to bitterness and retaliation, that requires intervention. When other people (spouses, in-laws, people outside the closely held business system) get sucked into the conflict, that's a red flag. When job performance suffers because of conflict, it's time for some relief.

Figure 8.3

Common Fears About Conflict vs. Reality	
FEARS	**REALITY**
We have so much conflict; it's just not normal!	Conflict is the RULE in closely held companies, not the exception
Our conflict is DANGEROUS to address	NOT addressing the conflict is what's most dangerous over time
That (*fill in name here*) is always after us about our conflicts; I wish he'd just go away	Shooting the messenger doesn't help resolve the issues. It just allows for a short term return to old, tension-filled status quo
That (*fill in name here*) is always after us about our conflicts; I wish he'd just go away	If you're not careful, he will
We have our blow ups at work, but after 5:00 we're all one big happy family	If your conflicts aren't resolved constructively, you're NOT one big happy family!
We battle almost every day, but I know in my heart our conflicts are resolvable	They may NOT be; sometimes you must prune the family tree

Since conflict is the rule and not the exception in closely held and family businesses, what can you do about it? The first thing is to engage in a broad process of communication and analysis. The old way of doing things in family companies was to have Mom and Dad and their advisors keep their own counsel and to make top down decisions which the senior generation believed would be in everyone's best interest. Later, some family business consultants came up with a novel idea; since subsequent generation leaders have responsibility for the family business in the future, these consultants developed a process for developing strategies based on what the junior generation wanted to have happen. Once that was clear, the junior generation and their advisors would present the desired outcomes to Mom and Dad, and all would be documented. As you might imagine, the moms and dads of the world didn't think this was a very good process at all! The modern iteration of closely held business planning says that all stakeholders' views are valuable and should be solicited. That means moms, dads, daughters, sons, in-laws, and key family business managers are all involved collectively in analysis and conflict resolution training.

A second key to resolving conflict is to set up simple ground rules. For example:

- Discussions of the past are irrelevant; we're here to address the present and future
- We won't use aggressive speech or body language with each other
- We will refrain from issuing ultimatums and drawing lines in the sand

Once the practitioners have agreed on the ground rules, they should be posted and placed in the room so that the meeting leader can refer everyone to them.

Another key is to be self aware. Socrates dispensed the following advice several thousand years ago: "Know thyself." We'd like to take that a step farther by saying that in addition to knowing yourself, you should know the others in the group too. There are many readily available psychometric testing and evaluation tools which family and closely held business leaders can use to know each other in new and different ways. Just because you spent the first 18 years of your life in the same household with someone, that doesn't mean that you truly know who they are today; it helps to become reacquainted and get in touch with others in the group all over again. It also helps in fleshing out a portrait of oneself. Let's face it; it's awfully hard to be objective about yourself.

Conflict resolution requires forethought and advance planning. It's helpful to plan for your own constructive behavior and how you'll act in the meeting. Ask yourself how you can satisfy the other people's interests. Find out if there's another way or source to get what it is that you want. Plan for delivering your message in a way that can help the other side empathize with you and your wishes. Develop alternative plans A, B, and C. Determine what's acceptable to you and what's not. Try to puzzle out what might be acceptable to the others. Find the win/win and the common ground, and you're well on the way to resolving conflict.

Don't be afraid to give in on some things; use your willingness to give as a negotiating tool: "If I give on this, will you give on that?" There's a caution here; don't give in in an area where you may be rewarding intimidation or aggressiveness. In some conflict resolution situations, it's okay to withdraw. The advantages of withdrawal are that you can do it unilaterally, and it may save time and even nerves. The negative of withdrawal is that it generally happens as a result of frustration over time, and there may not be win/win benefits. If withdrawal becomes a pattern, it would be easy to begin to resent the other party(s).

Conflict resolution sessions should be undertaken at quiet and private places. There should be a well defined beginning and ending time. You should agree that you will meet for one hour to 90 minutes at the maximum. If you can't resolve the conflict in the allotted time, agree on a date and time for continued discussion. If conflicts are serious and deep-seated, you may need a third party, objective outsider to run or mediate the session. Ultimately, you'll want to develop the conflict resolution plan *in writing* for all parties to sign.

As the sheer number of self help and family planning books attests, family management isn't easy, and adding the never-ending demands and pressures of a business only makes it harder. It's a good idea for families to create sacred time together and to utilize the family business consultant's best friend, the Family Council. People have meetings and undertake planning at work, at church, and at civic organizations. Yet they never seem to bring that same sort of structured thinking to their families. Family life is arranged informally which means we ultimately tend to wing it and become reactive to issues and problems as they arise. Running a family like a business could be oppressive for some and could drain some of the adventure out of family life. But there is a happy medium, and creating additional structure around the business of one's family is generally a great idea. Here are some excellent questions as you consider how to best manage your family:

- What makes us unique as a family?
- What is the *purpose* of our family?
- What are our family's top priorities as a group?
- How does our "familyness" affect our business positively? Negatively?
- Are our family members representing themselves to the outside world in a way consistent with the conclusions we've reached above? If not, what needs to change? How do we make the changes we need?
- Once we arrive at conclusions, how are we going to talk about and use the answers to these questions?

In the next chapter, we'll talk about the one unique process which combines all 8 of the building blocks to manufacture results consistently in virtually all family and closely held companies – and how to properly execute the process.

Building Block #7 – Family Management

Executive Summary

⇨ Family management in the closely held business is always a challenge, and putting the 6 building blocks previously discussed into place will dramatically reduce disharmony and friction

⇨ Harmony – at least perfect harmony – is an illusion or a myth in closely held companies. Some level of conflict *always* exists; therefore, instead of avoiding conflict, families need to build their conflict resolution abilities

⇨ Trust – belief in and reliance on the integrity, strength, or ability of a person or thing – is a vital sustainable ingredient for your business

⇨ Successful business families distinguish the responsibilities, rights, and rewards of *management* from those of *ownership*

Chapter Nine
Building Block #8 – Strategic Planning and Weekly Execution

A few years ago, I was at a meeting of about 60 family business consultants from 14 different countries around the world. As part of an exercise, we viewed a video family business case study and broke up into small groups to dissect the business family's problems and prescribe solutions that would help them find a better way. The advisors consisted of attorneys, psychologists, academics, financial services professionals, and family business consultants. There was consensus in the room – almost. Virtually every family business advisor thought the first order of business was to get this family into a Family Retreat as soon as possible in order to discuss the sorry state of their communication and how to better come together as a family.

I was the only holdout. My contention was that putting this family together in a retreat setting would be completely alien to them and was just as likely to produce fireworks as harmony. The family simply didn't speak the language of love and relationships; they spoke the language of business, tasks, and finance. Putting them together in a retreat was too risky and potentially dangerous; if it got out of control, the failure would be so painful to the family they'd likely never take the plunge again, and they could be left without hope for improvement. My heartfelt recommendation was that they should engage in a process of *strategic business planning*. There were several reasons for this:

- The level of unrest and poor communication was likely to hamper the family's ability to come to agreement, resolve long term issues, and produce a satisfying retreat
- They already spoke the language of business and were comfortable with it
- Talking about the future of the business was less threatening
- Focusing on coming together for the purpose of building the

business was far less emotionally risky for the family members
- During the process of business planning, they could be subtly coached on building communications and conflict resolution skills, and coaching would be useful for improving family relations later on
- Business planning would inevitably require them to focus on some if not all of their shortcomings which would have been spotlighted in the retreat AND they'd be working on business improvements to boot

My recommendations were roundly put down! It dawned on me that the gospel of the family retreat had become so ingrained in the family business consulting industry that most weren't willing to hear of an alternative approach!

Luckily, the Family Firm Institute published some research on the heels of that meeting which demonstrated beyond a shadow of a doubt that not only is strategic business planning a great tool, *it's the best tool known to exist for producing family harmony!* Why is this? There's truth in the statement we made in the last chapter about harmony being better on a winning team. In addition *(Figure 9.1),* the academic study documented that the use of planning, management tools, strategic planning, and governance practices increased the amount of communication, information, and knowledge sharing in closely held companies which strengthened their organization and culture and increased business opportunities – all of which served together to increase the level of family unity and harmony. If there's ever a magic bullet solution to pulling together fractious family and closely held business members, strategic planning is it! We maintain that undertaking strategic planning is the single best, most predictably successful practice for simultaneously improving business and family conditions.

If strategic planning works so well, why is it so infrequently adopted by family and closely held businesses? Over our almost 200 years of collective experience, we've probably heard every objection in the book as to why people won't adopt a strategic planning process. Some of the most common appear as myths versus reality in *Figure 9.2.*

Figure 9.1

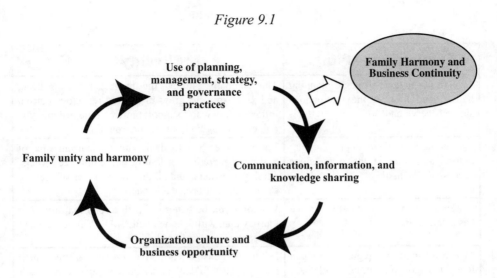

Source: Family Business Review

If you don't know anything else about strategic planning, understand this: companies that plan make more money than companies that don't! They're better situated for handling the demands of growth – or any other changing business conditions for that matter. Communication is better in companies that plan. Harmony is greater, and people can more easily understand and subscribe to the vision of where the company's headed.

Many closely held company leaders are avid sports fans. How would they react if the coach of their alma mater's football team had no game plan and rarely coached his players on their specific roles and responsibilities, assignments, and accountability? Furthermore, if the coach didn't have a Plan B and a Plan C as contingencies in a hard fought game, they'd be calling for his head! If strategic planning and all of the components associated with it work so well for college football teams, for big business, and in the military, why can't it be expected to work just as well in a closely held company? Covey says:

> "Planning is predetermining a course of events – working through what must happen if a desired result is to be brought to pass. Writing your plan is vital to actually seeing it happen. Until you produce a written plan, your profound thoughts too often will remain in the 'some day' stage of development. A written plan on the other hand seems to produce a power and commitment that jump starts the 'doing' part of the effort."

Figure 9.2

Objection (Myth)	Reality
"We've never done strategic planning before, and look at the tremendous success we've had!"	The company is now the biggest it's ever been, and you aspire to grow in the future. Your current infrastructure won't support more complexity, and you risk everything without an underpinning
"We've never done strategic planning before, and look at the tremendous success we've had!"	You've never had to deal with the current mix of multiple generations of family, non-employee owners, employee owners, and all the complexities of keeping stakeholders informed and happy
"The plan won't be accurate. No one has a crystal ball."	Wouldn't you be better off with a road map for your journey than without one ESPECIALLY if you have to make course corrections?
"We tried to do strategic planning a few years ago, and it didn't work."	Is it the first business initiative you've ever tried which proved unfruitful? What are the component reasons it didn't work as expected? Might it not pay off if it's properly executed over time?
"We don't have time to plan."	Then you've reached your maximum company size or – WORSE – you've begun to slide backwards already. How will you communicate your future direction to your managers and other stakeholders?
"We don't know how to plan."	Keep reading
"We don't have the right people to plan."	An ever more compelling reason to plan. How will you identify the present and future gaps you have in order to best fill them?
"We don't see the payoff of planning."	Planning will pay off in spades in a clearer vision for all, better teamwork, better needs anticipation, improved communication, etc. BE ADVISED: some of those outcomes take a long time to materialize and depend in part on how well you EXECUTE the plan and how accountable you hold people for finishing what they start

In studying projects that looked like winners but failed to produce bottom line results, McKinsey and Company identified some key elements. Their main finding was that undertaking planning will produce lasting results *only if senior executives invest their time and energy.* "Without strong leadership from top management, the psychological and political disruptions that accompany such radical change can sabotage the project. Inevitably, managers and employees may feel that their turf, jobs, and organizational equilibrium are under attack." They also found that only projects which were sufficiently broad and deep (practically the definition of comprehensive strategic planning) produced widespread and long lasting bottom line results. Finally – and this is vitally important – top executives spent between 20 and 60% of their time on the planning project. That means that a leader of a closely held or family business must be willing to take ownership of this project and devote *one to three days of his work week* to making sure the planning project goes as designed. Furthermore, successful companies assigned another senior manager to be on the project at least 50% of the time during the critical implementation stage. That incredible signal of commitment from the top of the organization sends a crystal clear message to everyone else – this is important to our successful, sustainable future! For more on this, please read *Planning... You Don't Need It, But Your Children (and Employees) Do* at www.familybusinessinstitute.com/8blocks/.

In a sense, founding generation business leaders have it easy. They can have management meetings between their ears. As the companies grow and prosper, however, the need for communication grows exponentially; brothers, sisters, cousins, non-family managers, non-employee owners, and other stakeholders have to be brought into the communication loop. Decisions must be made by groups of strong willed individuals instead of by one.

An easily understandable analogy for the importance of strategic planning is this: in the absence of weed control, you get weeds. Anyone who has tried to grow a beautiful lawn knows how challenging that can be. Preparing the soil, fertilizing at the right times of year, exercising weed control initiatives, planting grass, assuring proper levels of moisture, etc. is pretty complicated – and sometimes you still don't get the lawn you want. Think about how much more complicated it is to coordinate all of the minds and hearts of the people in your closely held company. That is the ultimate goal of strategic planning.

A lament about strategic planning is: "We did planning a couple of years ago, but the consultant left us with a big binder of information which just sat on the shelf and gathered dust." That begs the age-old question: whose responsibility was it to implement the plan: the consultant's or the closely held business leaders? Another reason strategic plans are so poorly implemented is because they set unrealistic time views for both planning and goal achievement. Leaders arrive at work every morning with a list of things they have to accomplish that day. Most managers also set long term goals for themselves and their companies. What they lack is a unit of time to bridge the gulf between daily, short term tasks and long term strategic initiatives. Covey recommends that the gap in planning be filled by a *weekly* check in and perspective. He believes it helps connect the urgency of daily tasks with the long term importance of strategic tasks. Weekly check in aligns daily tasks and activities with big picture direction. It's easy to imagine that an important task scheduled for a Monday might get put off until later in the week; a key manager or customer might be sick and may not be able to participate, or an important part or building component may not arrive on time. Setting daily goals is probably too ambitious in the sense that too many things could go wrong with goal achievement on any given day. Using a monthly time frame doesn't work very well either. If you have an important goal, and 30 days pass before you check in on goal achievement, that's too long – one-twelfth of the year has slipped by with no intervention from you! The week is a happy balance point between short term, daily tasks and long term goals. In the course of a normal work week, it should be possible to track goal progress and take corrective actions if necessary.

The goal of strategic planning and weekly execution is to allow entrepreneurial companies to adapt a more professional style of management. Does this mean that closely held companies should throw out entrepreneurial thinking and behavior? Absolutely not! It simply means that entrepreneurial, seat of the pants management is insufficient to fuel a company's growth and sustainability once it reaches a certain size. At that point, more professional management thinking and planning must be the rule of the day (*Figure 9.3*).

Figure 9.3

Entrepreneurial vs. Professional Management		
PROFIT	Profit seen as a by-product of sales	Profit orientation – Dollar targets precisely defined for all functional departments
PLANNING	Informal, erratic and sporadic planning Focused on problem solving and crisis management	Clearly defined, systematic forecasting and planning: Strategic Planning Operational Planning Contingency Planning
ORGANIZATION	Informal structure with overlapping and undefined responsibilities Grows and spreads informally to meet the needs of the entrepreneur(s)	Documented, clearly stated job descriptions that are mutually exclusive and exhaustive Grows by design to meet the needs of the customers and to self-perpetuate
CONTROL	Erratic, personalized control, seldom objective formal measurement	Clearly defined, planned system of organized control, including precise objectives, targets, measures, evaluation, and rewards
MANAGEMENT DEVELOPMENT	Sporadic development principally through on the job training and trial and error	Formal management training and development Identification of requirements Design of programs
BUDGETING	Standards not defined No follow up on variances	Management by formal standards and variances
INNOVATION	Ranges from major risk taking to risk aversion, based on lack of reliable information	Orientation to incremental innovations; willingness to take calculated risks
LEADERSHIP	Styles vary with personality, from very directive to noninterference	Consultative or participative styles
CULTURE	Loosely defined, extended "family"	Well-defined culture

If a company does undertake strategic planning, how long will it be before it sees positive results? There are 2 answers to that question. First, it will see immediate results as people on the team take ownership of the strategic planning process, participate in strategic planning project team (SPPT) meetings, and redevelop their enthusiasm and excitement for the company's mission and vision. However, to see long term, lasting results will take longer. Collins theorizes that it takes about 4 years for companies to get strategic planning right. He writes about the "flywheel concept":

> "Picture a huge, heavy flywheel – a massive metal disc mounted horizontally on an axle. Pushing with great effort, you get the flywheel to inch forward, moving almost imperceptibly at first. You keep pushing and, after 2 or 3 hours of persistent effort, you get the flywheel to complete one entire turn. You keep pushing, and the flywheel begins to move a bit faster, and with continued great effort, you move it around a second rotation. You keep pushing in a consistent direction... 3 turns...4...5...6...the flywheel builds up speed...7... 8...you keep pushing...9...10... it builds momentum...11...12...moving faster with each turn...20...30...50...100.
>
> Then, at some point – breakthrough! The momentum of the thing kicks in, in your favor, hurling the flywheel forward – turn after turn...whoosh! ...its own heavy weight working for you. You're pushing no harder than the first rotation, but the flywheel goes faster and faster."

The point of Collins' analogy is that it takes a tremendous amount of time, energy, and effort to get strategic planning or any other large initiative moving forward; then it takes more time to produce lasting results. However, once those results are beginning to manifest, it's easier to keep the flywheel moving with less and less effort. Collins also notes that there's never one big thing that causes the flywheel to sustain its own momentum: *it was everything!* "There was no single defining action, no grand program, no one killer innovation, no solitary lucky break, and no wrenching revolution. Good to great comes about by a cumulative process." So it is with strategic planning.

Once a company has decided to undertake planning, who should participate? In the old days, it was usually a senior generation making plans, hopefully in everyone's best interests, and more or less imposing those plans on everyone else. Strategic planning doesn't and shouldn't work that way. The top down methodology of that sort of management doesn't allow for buy-in from people or family members farther down the food chain. It's essential that key managers and family members get involved from the very outset with the strategic planning process in order to make it work properly; it should be bottom up, not top down. Strategic planning is not only about what the firm wants to achieve in terms of long term objectives, but it's also about how it's going to hit targets, who's going to do it, how much it's going to cost, and what the deadlines are. In order to communicate that throughout the organization, it's necessary to put the best minds in your organization to work for you. Furthermore, it has to be a company-wide initiative. It wouldn't make sense for one group or one department to be celebrating successes when the rest of the company is doing poorly. That would be the same as a star baseball player claiming success because he hit 40 home runs while his team lost 100 games that season. He enjoyed individual success, but his team suffered all the same.

Strategic Planning For Closely Held or Family Businesses

Over the years, we have seen some interesting definitions for the term "strategic planning." People have sent us everything from hand written, half page summaries to summary lists of goals to extensive, bound and printed documents all purporting to be strategic plans. Obviously the term has different meanings for different people. The working definition for purposes of this book is: *Strategic planning is a process of formal consideration of an organization's future course resulting in an actionable, written plan.*

A few caveats and tips about strategic planning. There's no right, wrong, or perfect way to do it. Developing strategic plans properly is a continuum; your effort in year one will be less elaborate than in year 3, year 3 will be less detailed and accurate than in year 5, etc. When it comes to doing strategic planning, doing something is infinitely preferable to doing nothing. Just as when you enter a dark room and feel disoriented, the least ray of light can help you find your way; even a poor strategic plan is better than none at all.

Research and analysis of the current landscape is an important prerequisite to strategic plan development. It's important to know where you are before you try to determine where you're going. In terms of research, the use of ownership group, employee, and customer surveys or interviews is a great idea. Using these diagnostic tools will help get all stakeholders involved and identify key issues and opportunities. Give yourself at least 90 days before your fiscal year end to assemble your SPPT and to begin the process. Especially if this is your first attempt, it will take you longer than you think to get it done, and there will be quite a few hiccups along the way. Don't try to set more than 3 to 5 overall company goals, although individuals and departments within your company can have their own goals which support the broader ones. More than 3 to 5 make it too complicated for people to focus on common, overarching goals. If your strategic planning process uncovers other projects which need to be rolled up into the larger effort, don't be discouraged. It might seem disheartening and might mean more work over the short run, but the process of strategic planning is *designed* to give you a brutally honest view of where your company is both good and not so good. You'll eventually want to tie your planning discoveries and results to your annual budget. Failing to tie the plan to budget numbers severely reduces the overall quality of the plan and will make it less effective and quantitative. The plan could vary in length from 10 to hundreds of pages. Ideally, you won't have more than about 50 pages in the overall written plan, and it's a great idea to get it down to a one page or even postcard summary that all employees can keep on their desks, bulletin boards, etc. No one's going to read and reread a 50 page plan once a month throughout the year; it is, however, important that they be reminded of how their actions fit into the overall plan. More on that later, especially as we talk about action plans, objectives, and holding people accountable.

The most important thing to know about strategic planning is the most valuable part isn't the hard copy version you produce, it's the *overall process itself* of bringing your team together, analyzing your company, and mutually charting a direction. That's where the real beauty and power are.

Planning starts with DISCOVERY. Always start with a clear understanding of the owner or ownership group's goals and desired outcomes for the company. If those desired outcomes aren't crystal clear, that's step one in the planning process; make them explicit. Next, it's important to use DIAGNOSTIC tools. Use research and analysis to uncover issues and drive insights; *do not assume* that you know your customers, employees, or family members. Utilize interviews, survey tools, electronic survey software, or anything else you and your advisors can think of to quantify wherever possible. It's important to have a clear PRESCRIPTION coming out of your discovery and diagnostic processes. The prescription will present fact-based findings and recommendations to achieve desired outcomes. IMPLEMENTATION or, as some refer to it, execution means that you will work closely with your strategic planning team, your advisors, and your employees to manage the strategic planning process – and most importantly – the specific action plans for how you will achieve your strategies for attaining your big picture goals.

The Family Business Institute way for doing strategic planning for closely held or family businesses appears as a schematic in *Figure 9.4.*

While it may look a little daunting, it comes together in a very neat, orderly fashion, and we'll go over each of the steps. What's most important is that strategic planning has proven to be the most important tool for improving a closely held business while simultaneously increasing the level of harmony

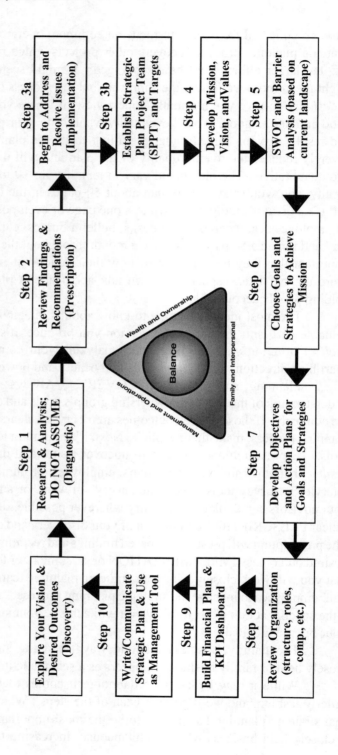

Figure 9.4

Balanced Solutions and Strategic Planning for the Closely Held or Family Business

and satisfaction among owners and family members. When something better comes along, we'll surely employ it; but for now, strategic planning is the magic bullet which produces the best, most predictable, and longest lasting positive outcomes.

Before undertaking strategic planning, it's important to examine your goals. If you're an owner, family member, or key executive in a closely held company, you should subscribe to Covey's Habit 2: BEGIN WITH THE END IN MIND. If you have a vision (both personal and business) for the future, great! You're ahead of the game. If you don't, you'll need to think through your vision to be able to establish your desired outcomes. Later in the chapter we'll have a step by step guide and definitions for mission, vision, values, goals, strategies, objectives, and action plans which you can utilize for undertaking your own strategic planning process.

Step 1: Research and Analysis

While it may have been a little cynical, I used to tell family business leaders about their estate plans that what they thought they had, they didn't, and the reality of what they had wasn't what they wanted! It was probably a little too "in your face" for some people, but it was (and probably still is) true. The assumptions they made about their businesses and families were just that – assumptions. They hadn't kept current on changes in employees, customers, business conditions, etc. By way of research and analysis, businesses should undertake regular "voice of the customer" surveys. If your customers are too few to do quantitative surveys, it's okay to do one-on-one interviews with key customers to provide qualitative data. Along with voice of the customer surveys, "voice of the employee" surveys or interviews are helpful. Benchmarking executives and "star performers" across the organization can help in the research and analysis process as well. In addition, it's a good idea periodically to engage in psychological profiling instruments or 360° evaluations. It would be maddening to attempt to employ all of these tools at once, so they're best utilized over periods of time with periodic updates in order to chart changes. The point of all this is that in the research and analysis phase of strategic planning, you're not flying by the seat of your pants or simply going with your gut. While you will always continue to utilize your hard earned business intuition, you'll supplement it with solid data and probably learn some new things about your customers or your company.

It's also important to do financial analysis. We spent a great deal of time earlier talking about benchmarking. Benchmarking your company's performance against the cream of the crop in your industry would certainly fall under the heading of research and analysis. If you haven't done so, you should also "deaverage" your sources of profitability. You need to understand your profitability by: customer, product and/or service offering, division, channel, geography, etc. You should review your current capital structure and whether or not it's adequate for present and future. Finally in the financial analysis phase, if you don't have key performance indicators (KPIs), you'll want to think them through.

Research involves analyzing the competition, too. What are their product and/or service offerings? What is their unique selling proposition? What's their market share or market position relative to yours? What are their strengths and weaknesses? Are there any best practices they employ that you could utilize in your own company? Still another part of research and analysis is to review your management succession plan, your ownership succession plan, and your contingency plans including your personal "drop dead plan." All of this research and analysis will probably take 30 to 60 days and is the foundation upon which you'll build many of the elements in your strategic plan.

Step 2: Findings and Recommendations

In the findings and recommendations phase, you'll now look back over all the data you've compiled and determine what you need to learn. It's not enough to simply have the data at your fingertips, you have to be able to infer what actions and planning the data dictate.

Step 3: Establish Strategic Planning Project Team and Targets

We talked before about the difference between top down, bottom up, and all-hands planning. Strategic planning is a process best done by the group of best thinkers in your company. Don't make the group too big; a client recently tried to impose a 16 person SPPT on us; that's too many. The ideal size of the group is 7 to 12; more than that becomes unwieldy. It's okay for people in the group to form committees utilizing other people in the organization, but they should push information back up to members of the SPPT for use in building the plan.

Ensure proper representation from people in your company. For example, it wouldn't make sense to exclude sales, operations, or production from having a voice in the strategic planning process. Make sure the SPPT has a leader. Provide the necessary administrative support to the SPPT; they'll need documentation of all the brainstorming they produce in order to be able to move their thinking forward from meeting to meeting. The team reviews, asks lots of questions, reflects, brainstorms, analyzes data, makes preliminary decisions, sketches out the plan, and ultimately has responsibility for producing the final plan and communicating it throughout the company. If the SPPT isn't already your leadership group, it soon will be. Senior generation family members have to be warned here: back off a little; don't dominate the meetings!

Once it's formed, the SPPT will schedule a series of meetings and also make sure they've blocked off time to do homework between meetings. The process will take longer than you think, so you should target at least 90 days from start to finish. The process requires 6 full day SPPT meetings (2 days per month). Obviously, perfect attendance for members of the SPPT is mandatory; if the candidates for your SPPT aren't willing to make this their top corporate priority, they shouldn't be on the team. That would send the wrong message to other people, and that message will ripple throughout the company. Finally, it's important to hold everyone on the SPPT accountable for results. The first accountability result is the production of the strategic plan itself. Later, they'll be responsible for individual action plans supporting the broader strategies in the plan.

Here are the goals for the team in their first formal 2 day SPPT meeting:

- Discuss current landscape details from Steps 1 and 2
- Review strategic planning process and ground rules
- Establish project time line
- Assign roles and responsibilities
- Select project tools (software, books, audio recordings, past planning tools, outside consultants, etc.)
- Set strategic plan time horizon (one year, 3 years, or 5 years)
- Develop high level targets with ownership input

Potential hard targets include: gross revenue, gross profit margin, net margin, ROI, units sold or produced, inventory turns, etc. Potential soft targets include: employee morale, customer satisfaction, market share, new product development, new markets, new technology, etc.

Step 4: Develop Mission, Vision, and Values

Developing (or reviewing and reevaluating) mission, vision, and values is the work of the second full day SPPT meeting. Many companies have already undertaken work to develop a mission statement, vision statement, and company values. In fact, this was all the rage in the early 1980s; there was a veritable industry of mission statement consultants which seemed to appear overnight and then disappeared just as quickly. If your mission is defined and is hanging in a frame in your lobby, yet no one can state it succinctly or it no longer fits the current iteration of the company, start over again and improve on it.

Your mission is a simple statement for why your organization exists – its purpose. Here's the definition for mission: *a statement of the overall purpose of an organization*. Your mission should apply both to your company today and for the life of your strategic plan; it should be all encompassing. A benefit of your mission statement is to help keep everyone focused. Choices you make in the corporation can be held up to the mission statement to determine alignment; either the actions you take are *on purpose*, that is, consistent with your mission statement, or they are *off purpose*, that is, inconsistent with your company's mission.

Vision is a little different. The definition of vision is: *a picture of the "preferred future" (not present) of your business*. Your vision statement describes how your company will look if it achieves its goals going forward. Your vision, as discussed in Chapter Two, is the most powerful motivator in an organization. The mission and vision will drive what are either implicitly or explicitly stated as your company's values. Values are defined as: *guidelines that set the foundation for how your organization will operate*. Your values reflect the core priorities of your organization's culture; that is, how you want to conduct yourself in business. Values are guiding principles that provide a vehicle for "operationalizing" a business' beliefs and traditions. The mission, vision and values must complement each other, fit together, and reinforce each other. It's important for management not just to talk about and write down the mission, vision, and values, but to *live them*.

Steps 5 and 6: SWOT, Barrier Analysis, Goals, and Strategies

The third full day SPPT meeting encompasses both Steps 5 and 6. The first part of the session is devoted to feedback or new thoughts on the company's mission, vision, and value statements and to determine if any changes or updates are required. Turning to new items, the group will review the current company and competitive landscape and what research has turned up so far. Next comes a discussion and review of the recent past and what lessons the SPPT members have learned during this period (typically the most recent fiscal year). Next, the group will brainstorm (everyone at one time or another has understood the meaning of brainstorming, but it's worthwhile to go back and refresh your memory on how brainstorming works so you don't kill ideas and thinking before they get off the ground). The group should allot about 15 minutes of time to brainstorm Strengths, Weaknesses, Opportunities, Threats, and Barriers. Total time for this shouldn't be more than one or 2 hours. This is actually among the most fun elements of strategic planning and one of the most often utilized even in abbreviated planning processes. The SWOT analysis should look at the company as a whole and then should drill down by department. For example, the company may have a strong marketing presence, but the marketing department representative on the SPPT may feel that the actual marketing collateral isn't as good as it could be and needs additional work. Drilling down by company function is an essential part of SWOT analysis.

A new wrinkle in SWOT analysis is to analyze barriers. SWOT has always turned up opportunities and threats, but it wouldn't make sense to try to develop plans around those without some analysis of the barriers that might prevent the company from achieving them. For example, there may be an opportunity to expand geographically into a new territory where there's little competition. Barriers to that strategy, however, might include limited capital or limited human resources. An opportunity isn't really an opportunity if the barrier is big or scary enough so it can't be overcome. Being realistic, but not pessimistic, about barriers will shape the thinking of the SPPT.

In terms of reviewing the recent past and lessons learned, questions include:

- What succeeded and why?
- What did you learn?
- What failed and why?
- What did you learn?
- What are your frustrations?
- Are they actionable?
- Of what do you have too much?
- Of what do you have too little?

The SPPT will brainstorm a wide variety of overall company goals (20 to 30 in total). Since that's way too many to provide any focused guidance, the team should work to aggregate and consolidate them. Ultimately they'll want to get down to 3 to 5 key company-wide goals. This process of brainstorming, consolidating, and setting goals is as old as planning itself. A key step that many closely held business leaders fail to undertake next is the key component of developing a STRATEGY for how to achieve each of the goals. See *Figure 9.5* for how the mission, vision, and values can be distilled all the way down to action plans and target objectives.

Goals are general statements of what you want to achieve over the next one or 3 years; the strategies which support the goals are general statements of how you are going to achieve individual targets. Goals of companies tend to endure, while strategies come and go due to trial, error, and changing business or market conditions.

Figure 9.5

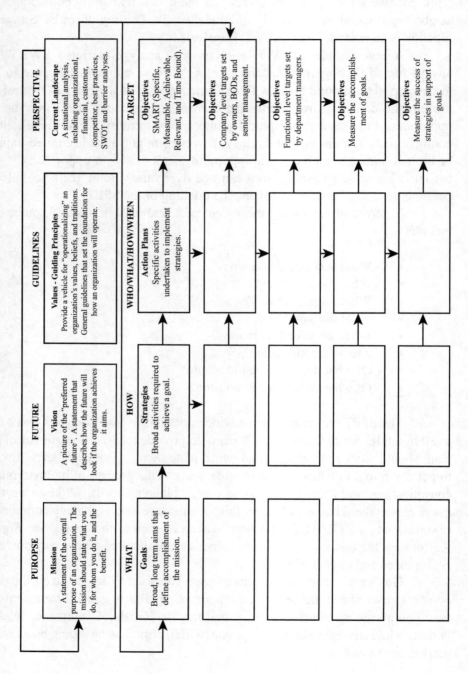

Step 7: Develop Objectives and Action Plans

In full day SPPT meeting 4, the group will review the goals and strategies discussed and settled upon in the previous meeting and move on to developing SMART objectives utilizing key performance indicators (KPIs). Ultimately, they'll develop detailed action plans supporting each strategy (again see *Figure 9.5* for how all this fits together).

Objectives are milestones for measuring the progress of accomplishing an organization's goals and the success of its strategies. Objectives must be SMART; that is they have to be:

- Specific – what is to be achieved?
- Measurable – can it be measured?
- Achievable
- Relevant
- Time bound – are there deadlines for the objectives?

Key performance indicators (KPIs) are financial and/or nonfinancial measurements which help to define and discern progress and milestones. Action plans are detailed initiatives spelling out specific activities necessary for achieving strategies, who is responsible, what the specific deliverables are, due dates, and budgetary costs associated with the action plans. It's helpful to pull out the employee job descriptions you developed to see if employee descriptions, priorities, and objectives are in sync with the newly developed action plans. *Figure 9.6* is an example of an action plan template assigned to a third party consultant by the SPPT in support of the strategy of developing and communicating the company's management succession plan to the family, key managers, and employees as a group (for a sample action plan, please visit our website at www.familybusinessinstitute.com/8blocks/).

Action planning templates can and should be utilized to hold people accountable. They're useful even outside the context of a strategic plan; why wouldn't it be helpful to develop a short action plan for assigning the purchase or lease of a new copy machine to your administrative assistant? Action plans are wonderfully useful for holding people accountable and keeping them on the same page when tackling short term initiatives such as:

- Relocating company offices
- Hiring managers and other employees
- Producing marketing materials
- Tracking sales activities and key account development
- Purchasing or selling company equipment

Figure 9.6

XYZ Construction – 2009 Strategic Plan – Action Plan Template

Goal:	Recruit and retain top quality employees						
Strategy:	Develop and communicate management succession plan						
Action Plan:	Task	Start Date	✓	End Date	✓	Person Responsible	Other Key Participants	Incremental Cost
	Interview each member of Senior Leadership Team (Barry, Pete, Leigh, Elton, James, Bob)	8/13/08		8/13/08		Wayne Rivers	Senior Leadership Team	$0
	Conduct research and analysis	8/1/08		9/30/08		Wayne Rivers	Senior Leadership Team	$0
	Develop succession goals and strategies	10/3/08		10/4/08		Wayne Rivers	Senior Leadership Team	$0
	Follow up discussions with Senior Leadership Team members concerning current and future roles and responsibilities	11/5/08		11/7/08		Wayne Rivers	Senior Leadership Team	$0
	Map out transition of roles and responsibilities for each Senior Leadership Team member over next 1, 5 and 10 years	12/1/08		12/31/08		Wayne Rivers	Senior Leadership Team	$0
	Determine training and other developmental activities to ensure a succession transition to future leaders	12/1/08		12/31/08		Wayne Rivers	Senior Leadership Team	$0
	Document management succession plan	1/1/09		1/31/09		Wayne Rivers	Senior Leadership Team	$0
	Communicate Management succession plan	1/1/09		1/31/09		Wayne Rivers	Senior Leadership Team	$0
Objective(s):	By 1/31/09 have a management succession plan in place that meets the current and future needs of the Company and the individual Senior Leadership Team Members By 1/31/09 communicate key elements of the plan to XYZ employees (methods TBD)						

The danger is that you'll be inundated with 50 or 100 tiny action plans floating around. Try to keep the number of balls you personally have in the air down to a manageable few, and this shouldn't become a problem. If it does, it's a red flag that you probably are stretched too thin in the organization, and you either need administrative or other types of help.

Steps 8 and 9: Review the Organization and Build the Financial Plan

In SPPT meeting number 5, the group will review the goals, strategies, objectives, and action plans from previous meetings and drive forward. The key objective here is to assess the organization's ability to deliver desired results. Does the organization have the manpower and firepower to achieve the action plans? Are there management or ownership succession issues which need to be addressed? Are the roles and responsibilities within the company clearly defined in support of goal achievement? Are the performance appraisal and compensation systems in sync with the company's goals and objectives? To the degree that the group can't readily answer these questions, or if it's obvious there are gaps in the organization, the group must develop strategies supported by action plans for how to close the gaps.

Coming out of meeting number 5, someone in the group will be charged with developing the company's financial plan and KPI dashboard. Often this will be the company's CFO, but if your company is smaller and you don't have an internal financial professional, you may have to rely on an outsider to assist. The financial plan and KPI dashboards start with historical and current year financials and incorporate high level targets. The financial planning task is to create annual revenue and expense projections over the time frame of the strategic plan (one to 5 years). It's important to use the financials to tie the strategic plan to the budget for the coming periods and to plan for monthly budget variance review meetings. The dashboard helps managers run the company by creating a "heads-up display" of certain high level targets (sales growth, ROI, etc.). The dashboard will allow executives to track actual performance versus company objectives on a consistent, regular basis. They serve as "early warning indicators" so that management will be well informed in order to take corrective actions when necessary. They're also handy to identify excellent performance and to offer opportunities for reinforcement and feedback, either positive or negative.

Step 10: Write and Communicate the Plan and Use as a Management Tool

Coming out of SPPT meeting number 5, someone will be tasked with drafting the strategic plan; in fact, more than one team member may be charged with drafting certain components. Using the data captured in the meetings, begin an outline and develop the narrative. It doesn't have to be *War and Peace*; target the plan to the intended audience. If one of the primary goals of the plan is to help the company extend its working line of credit from $500,000 to $2 million, it should be targeted to financial professionals and be supported by plenty of data. If the plan is for internal use only, it need not be quite so elaborate. Once the plan is written (and it really helps to use business planning software to get all this done), the draft should be circulated to other SPPT members for comments, additions, and deletions. The final draft of the strategic plan will be presented to the SPPT at meeting number 6. For your use in developing your strategic plan, some of the component parts of a typical strategic plan are listed in *Figure 9.7*.

Figure 9.7

Administrative
  Executive Summary
  Mission, Vision, Values
  Goals, Strategies
  Objectives, Action Plans
  Executive Bios
  Company History, Location
  Organization Chart (Functional)
  People or HR Plan

Marketing
  People
  Voice of Customer research results
  including customer satisfaction data
  Define Target Market(s)
  Unique Selling Proposition
  Competitive Analysis
  Marketing Plan (including Website)

Sales
  People
  Unique Selling Proposition
  Sales Funnel with Historical Ratios
  Gap Analysis
  Customer Acquisition Costs
  Sales Plan

Operations
  People
  Industry Specific Data, Metrics, and
  Terminology
  Proprietary Processes
  Production Volume, Capacity, Quality,
  Backlog, etc.

Financial
  Company Financial History (last 3
  years)
  Benchmarking Analysis
  Profit and Loss Projections (next 3-5
  years)
  Balance Sheet & Cash Flow Projec-
  tions (next 3-5 years)
  Key Performance Indicators (next 3-5
  years)
  Budget for Next Year (monthly P&L,
  Balance Sheet, and Cash Flow projec-
  tions)

The sixth and final full day meeting of the SPPT will allow the team to review the final draft of the financial plan and the KPI dashboard, as well as the "dress rehearsal" draft of the strategic plan. They should allow plenty of time for discussion and editing of both. Next, they'll need to determine the communication strategy for rolling out the plan to the managers and ultimately everyone in the company. The idea of rolling out the plan is to orient everyone toward the company's mission, vision, values, and key initiatives. While it's not possible to get 100% of the people in your organization on board, think of the power you'd find in your company if you could take your number of dedicated, enthusiastic, productive employees from, say, 20% to 35%! That's a 75% increase in the number of people pulling in the same direction as you! The strategic plan isn't a document which sits on your bookshelf in a nice binder and gathers dust; it's a communications and management tool that you can use to motivate as many people as possible in your organization.

Now that you've got the plan, there are some other things you should do with it. You should use your KPI dashboards as weekly tracking scorecards and take action as necessary where you are either overachieving or underachieving targets. You should schedule monthly meetings with key managers to review the progress of strategies and action plans; use the action plans to hold your people accountable. Review your financial results versus your budget, and take swift action on items in variance. If you find you're off target in any part of the plan, schedule additional meetings or initiatives to determine how to get back on target.

Remember, the most valuable part of developing a strategic plan is the process of doing so. Follow the 10 steps; don't skip or shortchange any of them. Utilize a team approach, tie the goals and narrative to your budget, and use the plan as an evolving, dynamic management tool. By doing so, you'll have the best cutting edge tool available for turning your closely held company into a sustainable business while simultaneously improving family and team morale.

Building Block #8 – Strategic Planning and Weekly Execution

Executive Summary

⇨ To become SUSTAINABLE, closely held companies must make the transition from an entrepreneurial to a professional management style

⇨ Strategic planning – done properly – is the one tool demonstrated and validated to simultaneously improve both family harmony *and* business performance

⇨ To realize the greatest benefits from strategic planning, a company must use a team approach and a thorough, sound, deliberate process of planning

⇨ The primary benefit of strategic planning is not the document the process produces – it's the very process itself!

Chapter Ten
Applying the Building Blocks

"You can map out a fight plan or life plan. But when the action starts, you're down to your reflexes. That's where your roadwork shows. If you cheated on that in the dark of the morning, you're getting found out now under the bright lights."
– Former Heavyweight Champ Joe Frazier

What Does This Book NOT Cover?

This book, like any book, has limitations. There were many areas of family or business life we didn't discuss. Here are a few:

- Estate and other financial plans
- Compensation or incentive pay guidelines
- Family retreats or family councils
- Ownership succession methodologies
- Management succession methodologies
- Buy-sell agreements
- Technological innovation
- Budgeting
- Consensus decision making
- Change management
- Mergers and acquisitions
- Entitlement attitudes
- Gaining access to working capital
- Entry rules
- Family business advisory boards
- Family governance

For the data hungry consumer, information on all these topics and more is available on our website or at the local library. The purpose of this book is not to be the be all, end all bible for families in business together. The purpose of this book is to help people get a handle on their family or closely held businesses in order to achieve BALANCE *(Figure 10.1)* in their lives.

Figure 10.1

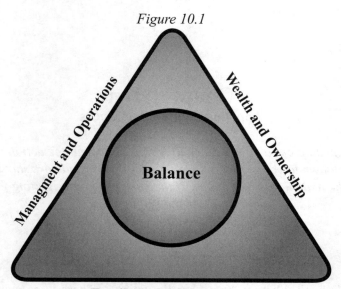

Family and Interpersonal

It's impossible to have balance in life if your business is slowly but surely sucking the life out of you, and that's the case for most family business owners today. Only by getting the business component of their lives under control can today's closely held business leaders hope to get closer to the peace, health, and personal satisfaction for which they so long.

Why are so many closely held business executives today – in spite of their outward appearance of success – unhappy? They've built companies which gainfully employ people, created opportunities for themselves and their families, and served their customers and communities well. Why then do they persist in working back breaking 80 hour weeks, neglecting their physical, emotional, and mental health, and failing to find the brass ring of personal success? Part of the reason is because so many business leaders live in what Dan Sullivan refers to as The Gap™. He describes The Gap™ as the permanent difference that exists between our actual results of today and our ideals. The ideal is a mental construct that enables us to come to grips with the future, a picture of desirable mileposts and situations that enables us to move forward in time. The ideal *doesn't actually exist* outside of our minds, nor is it achievable. It compels us to establish goals, motivate ourselves, and withstand hardships and difficulties. What most business leaders don't learn is that there will always be a permanent gap between their actual achievements and their ideals. If they don't have an attitude or plan to deal with this reality, they will probably lead chronically unhappy lives. There is a value in holding out the ideal as a mental construct; business leaders are wary of hitting a mark and then resting on their laurels. By never being satisfied with their actual results, they stay hungry and focused on doing and being more. That focus on the next thing – and the next and the next and the next – is what causes them to be unhappy. They don't take satisfaction in the daily and weekly achievements in their lives; they're focused only on what they have yet to do or the goals they failed to hit. Focusing only on negative outcomes or unfulfilled dreams – living in The Gap™ – is a recipe for mental misery.

Business Focused Families v. Family Focused Families

Dr. Russ Alan Prince studied 242 ultra-high net worth family businesses and their owners. In terms of psychographics, he found that 60% of survey respondents were "family focused." About 40% were "business focused." For business focused families, business decisions were made solely in the best interest of the business. Management was either composed of non-family, professional managers or operated as if it was. Decisions were made in the interest of furthering the goals of the company; the wishes of family were not influential in day-to-day management. Family influence was generally delivered at the highest level, that is, the Board of Directors. The owners directed the board which directed senior management. Business focused families clearly drew lines of demarcation between the needs of the business and the wishes of the family.

Family focused families were different. Many of their decisions were based on the needs of the family first with the business coming second. By way of definition, perhaps examples work best. A family focused family may elect to employ one or dozens of family members who are not particularly productive or accountable to others in the business. In other words, they see bloodline meaning that employment for family members is virtually guaranteed. Productivity and morale issues associated with employing underperforming family members are rarely taken into consideration. Another example has to do with perks doled out to the ownership family. Family centered businesses may elect to pass through certain family expenses to the business. They may expense to the company their family vacations, automobiles, boats, and aircraft which are really assets of the family and tools the family uses only for its convenience and pleasure. Family focused families frequently utilize their companies as a fringe benefit or tax advantaged vehicle for the family's lifestyle purposes.

205

What are the primary differences between business focused families and family focused families? Business focused families *have far fewer family problems!* While the research isn't entirely clear on this, we theorize that a business focused family has much clearer boundaries and definitions for things like family employment, the distribution of business wealth, accountability for family employees inside the company, active boards, etc.

Which type – business focused families or family focused families – has the most concern about protecting the family fortune? Your answer is probably wrong. Business focused families had a significantly higher concern about protecting the family fortune. Why is this? Since their focus is the preservation and maximization of business opportunities, that has the effect of *increasing* family fortunes over time. Having underperforming family members on the payroll and having expensive perks for the family as an expense to the business are drains on the company, and, while they may have indirect lifestyle or fortune building attributes, that methodology simply doesn't stack up to the alternative.

Which group – business centered families or family centered families – has the highest incidence of succession planning? Again, your answer is probably wrong. There are 3 business focused succession plans for every 2 family focused succession plans. Since the goal of the business focused families is to maximize operations and return on investment over time, they recognize that having a management succession plan (not an ownership succession plan which is done at the individual or family level) is vital to long term sustainability of the business.

Which group – the business focused families or the family focused families – actually implement their succession plans at a higher rate? The business focused families implement their succession plans at a rate more than 2 times that of the family focused families. The family focused families simply are poor at implementing succession plans. That is easily explained because the family lets the development and implementation of a succession plan become influenced and even stalled by issues and fears (most imagined) surrounding the family.

Finally, in terms of psychographic characteristics, Prince has done some groundbreaking research. One of the characteristics of the most successful family business individuals is that they are "centered." What is the definition of centered? These people are:

- In touch with themselves and their responsibilities
- Clear about their unique skills and talents and how to best leverage them to a specific set of goals
- Able to focus on the key challenges and obligations in front of them

• Armed with resolve, confidence, and determination

It may be said that people who are more centered are more self-actualized. That is, they understand themselves, their motivations, their strengths, and, perhaps most importantly, their weaknesses. In terms of the business, they have defined for themselves their highest and best uses. They seek to maximize the things at which they are really good, and they delegate things at which they're not.

Business focused individuals were more highly centered than family focused individuals by a significant amount. Why is this measure of good psychological health important? For every dollar of net worth the less centered people exhibited, the highly centered people had $6.2 of net worth. Extrapolating this data, it is possible using good psychological health and excellent business practices to transform a $10 million family business into a $60 million family enterprise over time. Being centered correlates directly to net worth! In Prince's own words, "more delegation equals higher net worth."

What Prince has documented is that the best practices of successful businesses including strategic planning, having the right people in the right roles, delegation with accountability, open communication, and business transparency have a direct impact on long term family business success and – just as importantly – long term family harmony and wealth.

Where Do We Go From Here?

My son is an enthusiastic baseball player, and last season he was struggling at the plate. We arranged for him to get some hitting lessons. The coach observed Hart's approach at the plate and began to make a few suggestions. Each time Hart made a modification suggested by the coach, his performance improved. At one point, however, the coach had made one too many adjustments, and Hart exclaimed, "I'm just not comfortable doing that!" My first reaction was, "Does my son realize how absurd it is for a 13 year old who is struggling against middle school pitching to be telling a man who batted .350 in the major leagues he's not going to accept his recommendation?" Upon reflection, however, I realized Hart's reaction was perfectly normal, and it's the same reaction most family business executives have on reading a self-help book like this. They're just not comfortable!

Doing the things we prescribe in this book will force you to get outside your comfort zones, and most people struggle mightily with that – especially if they have a 20 year track record of success. The point of this book is to challenge your conception of what success really means to you and to try and break through the artificial ceiling you impose on yourself and your company by improving your leadership, focusing on your time management and CEO duties, and undertaking strategic planning.

Covey writes:

> "We settle for the illusion society sells us that meaning is in self focus – self-esteem, self-development, self-improvement – it's "what I want," "let me do my own thing," "I did it my way." But the wisdom literature of thousands of years of history repeatedly validates the reality that the greatest fulfillment in improving ourselves comes in our empowerment to more effectively reach out and help others. Quality of life is inside out. Meaning is in contribution, in living for something higher than self."

Family and closely held business owners have a wonderful opportunity to leave a legacy. But the statistics which tell us that so many family businesses fail and so many more fail to reach their potential mean that the quest for legacy goes unfulfilled. Maxwell says: "Success comes when he empowers followers to do great things *with* him. Significance comes when he develops leaders to do great things *for* him. But a legacy is created only when a person puts his organization into position to do great things *without* him." The only way to create a sustainable organization which doesn't depend on you or a tiny handful of your most motivated followers is to **PLAN**.

We are often asked; when is the right time to begin planning? Is it in boom times or in recession? When I'm 45? When I'm 65? When my children reach age 35? When they are 55? When I'm ready to sell the business? When I'm ready to retire? The answer is that the best time to plan is *right now*! There is never a time – and there probably will never be – where you have 10 or 20 free hours a week to devote to planning. There is never a perfect moment when the stars and planets align, cymbals clash, and a whistle blows to let you know you've reached your moment. There is never a right stage, there is never a right size, and there is never a right time to undertake planning. In short, if you are serious about creating a sustainable closely held company, the time to start is now.

Family business owners have more opportunity – with the possible exceptions of ministers and doctors – than anyone else in society to influence other people positively. Think about all the people that a family business leader comes in contact with during the course of a working lifetime: family members, employees, customers, vendors, community leaders, etc. Family and closely held business leaders – the salt of the earth and the backbone of the American economy – are heroes and pioneers. Their potential for doing well is limitless, and the way to maximize that potential is to put the 8 building blocks to work so their companies can be more than just successful, they can be sustainable.

208

APPENDIX

Suggested Reading List:

The 5 Dysfunctions Of a Team – Patrick Lencioni – Jossey-Bass

The 7 Habits Of Highly Effective People – Steven Covey – Fireside

The 7 Habits Of Highly Effective Families – Steven Covey – St. Martin's Griffin

The 9 Natural Laws Of Leadership – Warren Blank – Amacom

The 10 Day MBA – Steven Silbiger – Quill Books

The 21 Irrefutable Laws Of Leadership – John C. Maxwell – Nelson

The Art And Science Of Leadership – Afsaneh Nahavandi – Prentice-Hall

Churchill On Leadership – Steven F. Hayward – Forum

The Dynamics Of Family Business – Kenneth Kaye – Amacon

The E-myth Revisited – Michael Gerber – Harper Business

First Things First – Steven Covey – Simon & Schuster

Good To Great – Jim Collins – Harper Business

Jesus, CEO – Laurie Beth Jones – Hyperion Publishing

The Knowledge Based Organization – Dr. Michael C. Lyons – Erwin

Learning To Avoid The Gap – Dan Sullivan – The Strategic Coach

Managing The Professional Service Firm – David H. Maister – Free Press

Mastering The Rockefeller Habits – Vern Harnish – Select Books, Inc.

No Man's Land – Doug Tatum – Portfolio

Now, Discover Your Strengths – Marcus Buckingham and Donald O. Clifton – Free Press

The One Thing You Need To Know About Great Managing, Great Leading, and Sustained Individual Success – Marcus Buckingham – Free Press

The Path – Creating Your Mission Statement For Work And For Life – Laurie Beth Jones – Hyperion Publishing

Prescriptions For A Healthy Family Business – Wayne Rivers – The Family Business Institute, Inc.

Unique Ability – Creating The Life You Want – Catherine Nomura and Julia Waller – The Strategic Coach

What Got You Here Won't Get You There – Marshall Goldsmith – Hyperion Publishing

What Matters Most – The Power Of Living Your Values – Hyrum W. Smith – Fireside

Workplace Wars and How To End Them – Kenneth Kaye – Amacom

**For More Information,
Contact The Family Business Institute, Inc.**

info@familybusinessinstitute.com

Toll Free: 877-326-2493   *Fax: 919-783-1892*

Name _____

Company _____

Title _____

*Address*_____

Telephone _____

Fax _____

Email _____

I'm interested in:
☐   *family business consulting*
☐   *Performance Roundtable Groups*
☐   *speaker opportunity*
☐   *knowledge products*
☐   *other (specify)* _____

_____

_____

THANK YOU!